C000101857

Introduction

This is the fourth edition of *Babies & Kids in the City* – a fact we're very proud of. We started back in 2008. The three of us were on maternity leave and met through a toddler group. Over countless coffees and custard-creams, we hit on the idea of pulling together a guide-book that recommended all the best places to go in the local area for families. It was a simple premise – we'd road test everywhere that we went to with the children, take some photos and write up our thoughts.

Six years on, we've visited over 500 venues of one description or another and have had the best time compiling *Babies & Kids in the City*. We love what we do and we hope that our reviews give you some fun, new ideas of things to do with your kids.

Jo, Louise and Vanessa x

PS - Please take a look at our website for monthly events, new openings and other interesting stuff!

www.babiesinthecity.co.uk

Published by Babies in the City Ltd
37 Old Lansdowne Road
Didsbury, Manchester M20 2PA
Tel +44 (0)161 438 2086
Email info@babiesinthecity.co.uk
Website babiesinthecity.co.uk
Website babiesandkidsinthecity.co.uk

Publisher Jo Maxwell
Editor Louise Taylor
Illustrator Vanessa Redmond
Authors Jo Maxwell, Louise Taylor and
Vanessa Redmond
Sub-Editor Sharon Brown
Contributors Jennie Bateson, Sharon Brown,
Nicola Lynn and Kathy Whitaker

This edition is first published in Great Britain in 2014
by Babies in the City Ltd
ISBN: 978-0-9561215-3-0
A CIP Catalogue record for this book is
available from the British Library
Printing by Polestar Wheatons, Devon.

© Babies in the City Limited

p154-155 City Centre Map courtesy of Marketing
Manchester
p156-157: Contains Ordnance Survey data © Crown
copyright and database right 2011

Prices correct at the time of going to press. Where
in operation, prices include a voluntary 10% gift aid
donation. Many places listed are closed on Christmas
Day and New Years Day. Opening times may be
different on Bank Holidays. Last admissions are
generally one hour before closing.

35

Contents

95

67

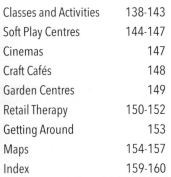

19

86

39

71

6

35

Museums and Art

There is a diverse range of museums and galleries to visit and enjoy in the region, with important and varied collections ranging from priceless Lowrys to Maradona's football shirt! Most are free and in the holidays offer terrific family activities.

MUSEUMS AND ART IN THE CITY CENTRE

Imperial War Museum North

From the stunning, aluminium-clad building sporting splendid views over The Quays, to the Big Picture Show, a bold 360-degree light and sound display – a trip to the Libeskind-designed Imperial War Museum North (IWMN) may bring on a sensory overload!

Outside the museum sits a Russian tank captured from Iraqi forces in 2003. Once through the doors, there's a wealth of historical objects to study. Of most interest to me was the field gun that fired the British Army's first shell of World War I near Binche in Belgium and the enormous, seven-metre twisted section of steel, wreckage of the World Trade Centre from 9/11. It is truly sobering.

IWMN is a social history museum showing how war has shaped people's lives. As well as large exhibits on display, don't forget to look through the small, personal items as they're equally fascinating.

For older children, various Action Stations inspire a more in-depth look at history. These encourage families to dress up – maybe you're in camouflage or perhaps you're getting ready for evacuation. Also, there are Time Stack sessions running for 20 minutes at 12.30pm most days where you can handle artefacts and learn the individual stories behind them. There's plenty of activities and space for little ones to run around plus there's often story-telling under the Harrier Jet.

We enjoyed lunch at the WaterShard Café, where despite the views my boys were more interested in the football table. At least it kept them amused long enough for us to have a coffee after lunch!

The IWMN always holds lots of fantastic events

Ted finds the Matchstick Man he's after at The Lowry.

4

and temporary exhibitions throughout the year so do check the website for the latest information. Every weekday (11am) and weekends plus school holidays (11am & 2pm) The Big Picture Show screens *Rotten Rationing*, specially created by the Horrible Histories team, a must-see for HH fans! If you've got time and you're not scared of heights then before you leave, take a run up the 180 steps to the 55m-high Air Shard complete with viewing platform.

Daily 10am-5pm. Admission free.
Car Park 0-3hrs £4. Air Shard: Adults £1.20, Child 60p.
IWM North, The Quays, Trafford Wharf Road, Manchester M17 1TZ
Tel: 0161 836 4000 iwm.org.uk

The Lowry

One rainy Saturday afternoon, my eldest boys were playing footie and I had a few hours to spare with my youngest, Ted. A great opportunity for a little bonding time, I thought; and perfect timing to indulge in a museum together, without the big ones moaning!

The Michael Wilford designed building is beautiful – housing a theatre, drama workshops and several galleries, as well as a restaurant and coffee shop. We were here though, for the art (and possibly a quick shop in the Lowry Outlet afterwards!) Every time I come here I'm blown away by the gallery's permanent exhibition, Lowry Favourites, an incredible selection of over 400 L.S. Lowry paintings and drawings. The artwork is set off dramatically on blood red walls. As we went in, Ted was given a laminated sheet of eight clues which we

had to find in the original artworks; it really makes you look at the paintings properly. Blank postcards and pencils are dotted around so you can show off your own artistic skills: Lowry's paintings are ideal to try and copy, with plenty of animals, trains and stick people to capture children's interest. Ted drew a pretty impressive dog and proudly displayed it on the gallery walls.

Temporary exhibitions by contemporary artists regularly change, and are well worth checking out. Across from the gallery entrance is a brand new children's space called The Lookout. Inspired by the fantastic views of the Quays, you can sit and draw, or play games and there's a dedicated area for tots with plenty of toys.

Every Friday they run sessions specifically for the under fives, exploring music and dance; with a doodle workshop for budding artists. And for older age groups, drop into The Lookout on a Saturday for a free art session. There are also plenty of regular workshops which link in with the current theatre production.

The Lowry is magnificent! Hugely creative and family friendly, we are so lucky to have it on our doorstep.

Sun-Fri 11am-5pm, Sat 10am-5pm. Admission free.
The Lowry, Pier 8, Salford Quays, Manchester M50 3AZ
Tel: 0843 208 6000 thelowry.com

5

Manchester Art Gallery

Serious art lovers head to Manchester Art Gallery to view its renowned collection of Pre-Raphaelite paintings, and works by artists including Lowry and Bacon. But don't overlook it when planning a family day out, it's an excellent place to go with kids.

The last time I visited, heavily pregnant and with a small toddler in tow, we had a wonderful time exploring the Clore Interactive Gallery; so I was disappointed to hear that it had closed. However, it has been replaced by the Clore Art Studio, a constantly-changing space which reflects the Gallery's main exhibitions. The mirrors and dressing-up clothes are gone, but a still-life drawing station remains and children are encouraged to engage with real works of art. My one-year-old loved playing with the colourful objects on display in the Grayson Perry-inspired installation.

Now, with two children, mooching around a gallery at leisure is an impossibility. So, to keep everyone happy, I plan what I want to see and find a way to involve them. The information desk helps with this task. There are free 'tool kits' to borrow, so youngsters can explore the exhibits with hard hats and magnifying glasses; and story bags complete with a rug to sit on, a book and fun suggestions of what to do in the gallery. The bags come in four themes: line, shape, colour and texture. We took 'texture', which had great activity ideas, including

The new Clore Studio at Manchester Art Gallery.

looking for rough or spiky objects in the Gallery.

The lovely café is a popular place to eat, and the staff helped us to a table with our food – crucial, as I struggled with a toddler, a baby, and a buggy to manoeuvre. There was a delicious selection of cakes and savouries. The kids' lunch box (sandwich and selection of snacks) was £3.95, or a hot meal (Bangers'n'mash on our visit) was around £5.

Check the website for details of family events like the monthly Baby art and Mini art clubs. And here's a tip to keep your older children entertained – who can find the Banksy?

Daily 10am-5pm (Thurs night until 9pm). Admission free.
Manchester Art Gallery, Mosley Street,
Manchester M2 3JL
Tel: 0161 235 8888 manchestergalleries.org

Manchester Museum

This super museum is full, of absolutely everything! From skeletons, fossils, rocks, lizards (alive!) and tigers (not alive!); pottery, wood carvings, metal work and tribal costumes; to Greek helmets, Mongolian bows, Japanese arrows, sea urchins and even a Tyrannosaurus Rex!

Displaying works of archaeology, anthropology and natural history, this diverse museum, owned by Manchester University, is a superb resource for families with children of all ages.

The museum is renowned for housing one of the UK's largest and most important collections of Ancient Egyptian artefacts, and our boys' favourite find was the huge Egyptian Tomb, complete with mummy! My little girl was less impressed with this discovery but soon settled down when we found the play zone where she could colour in and play with some toys! The Discovering Archaeology section is a highlight of the revamped Ancient Worlds galleries, exploring how historians use objects to help understand our past. The exhibits on facial reconstruction were amazing.

Nature's Library is the complete refurbishment of one of the museum's Grade II* listed Gothic galleries. This was originally designed by the renowned Victorian architect Alfred Waterhouse, who also designed Manchester's Town Hall and the Natural History Museum in London. It showcases an outstanding collection of four million preserved animals, plants and fossils, from around the world. Adjacent to the main entrance, you'll find the Allotment with wormery, bug house and a feast of vegetables and plants – the Living World in action!

Daily 10am-5pm. Admission free.
Café on site serving children's meals.
Manchester Museum, The University of Manchester,
Oxford Road, Manchester M13 9PL
Tel: 0161 275 2648 manchester.ac.uk

What big teeth you've got! The Manchester Museum is full of all sorts of creatures – dead and alive!

Museum of Science & Industry

City Babies LOVE & Kids in...

The Museum of Science & Industry has emerged from a major overhaul as an even better museum than it already was, an incredible achievement. Due to its sheer size it is still a place you will have to visit a number of times to do it justice.

Renovations in The Great Western Warehouse, the main entrance, mean you are now greeted by a towering digital, tree-like sculpture which forms the centrepiece. It's tremendous. Your picture is taken at one of the many pods below the sculpture and your photo will zap up the tree to ping onto one of its multi screens. The kids loved it, although I must admit to having a couple of goes before I got a picture I didn't mind everyone in the museum seeing – me vain? Hah!

The Revolution Manchester Gallery is in six sections and designed to give you a taste of the city. From textile factories to Factory Records, the interactive gallery celebrates Manchester's indus-trial, technological and cultural heritage, as well as looking to the city's future. The most impressive exhibit for me is 'Baby', a replica of the world's first computer. At 5.2 metres long it has less computing power than a calculator; I find it hard to relate this monster machine to my iPad!

Upstairs is the updated Experiment! gallery,

a fabulous hands-on children's science space, featuring a recycling waste section, a new and improved toddler area, plus all the old favourites such as 'Lift the Mini', the tornado zone and cycling skeleton. Once a month on a Friday morning MOSI runs an **Experitots** session (see page 143), exclusively for under-fives.

Also on this level is the larger of MOSI's two cafés. Main meals start from £5.95 and for children, a lunchbox is £3.95. There are picnic areas if you want to bring your own food.

Four other major buildings make up MOSI – the 1830 Warehouse, Station Building, Power Hall, and

Not exactly an iPad, the replica 'Baby' at MOSI.

SHOT STOPPER

Will and Dad practising their goalie skills at The National Football Museum.

The National Football Museum

City Babies & Kids in the LOVE &

Whenever we head into Manchester my boys ask if we can go here – they just can't get enough of the place! Housing a Hall of Fame and the world's greatest collection of memorabilia (including Maradona's 'Hand of God' shirt) – the National Football Museum also gives your budding Aguero or Rooney the chance to test their skills at everything from shooting at goal to commentating.

There are plenty of interactive exhibits on the first floor, together with stacks of interesting stuff to read. My boys were particularly fond of the matching flags to their countries game, a hologram film of Gary Lineker, FA cup jigsaws, and a booth in which they giggled at funny footie television clips. There's also a small cinema where we watched a lovely short film, 'Our Beautiful Game', a day in the life of football, from grass roots through to Wembley Stadium.

There's so much to do here that we decided to take a half-time break: coffee and juice in the café (open 8am-6pm, breakfast, lunch and afternoon tea is served here) before heading to the second floor for Football Plus+. There are seven activities to try out, from testing your

reactions with Shot-Stopper, to trying your hand at being a pundit on Match of the Day Commentary Challenge. You buy credits for these activities downstairs, and get your own user ID so you can watch yourself online afterwards when you get home. A huge hit with my boys! There's also a Discovery Zone for under-fives with a soft play area, dressing up and activities. Felix had a quick bounce around in here, but was soon distracted by his brother's shouting – he'd discovered a virtual game of football. After dragging them away from diving and skidding around, we spent several calm minutes looking at a display of football toys before embarking on a raucous family game of 'You are the Ref!'

There are regularly-changing exhibitions on the third floor, which don't always have football as their theme, and a wide range of family activities during schools holidays. We all had a brilliant time here, and headed home with huge smiles on our faces to watch our commentaries and skills. This museum is an absolute must for football fans of all ages.

Mon-Sat 10am-5pm, Sun 11am-5pm.
Admission free. Football Plus: 1 credit £2.50.
National Football Museum, Urbis Building, Cathedral Gardens, Manchester M4 3BG
Tel: 0161 605 8200
nationalfootballmuseum.com

Air and Space Hall. The Power Hall has a superb range of trains on show as well as one of the largest collections of working steam mill engines in the world. It's a large area, so a great place for little ones to let off a little steam themselves! MOSI also has a ride-on train – a replica of Stephenson's Planet steam locomotive, which operates during holidays and weekends. The train puffs majestically past the oldest surviving passenger railway station in the world and back again. The trip only lasts about 10 minutes (adults £2, children £1) but it is definitely worth it.

Located in the building across the road is The Air and Space Hall. It's full of planes, cars and motorbikes, as well as the fun motion simulator Morphis (charges apply and height restriction of 110cm). The Station Building is where you'll find the Victorian Sewers, a must for those children who find poo hilarious.

MOSI has loads to offer children of all ages. From Saturday Science to 4D theatre, you're sure to find something your children will love.

Daily 10am-5pm. Restaurant 11am-4pm. Admission free.
Car parking £7 before 9am, £5 after 9am and £3 after 3pm.
The car park entrance has moved to Water Street.
MOSI, Liverpool Road, Castlefield,
Manchester M3 4FP
Tel: 0161 832 2244 mosi.org.uk

Testing Tom's brain cells in the Experiment gallery at MOSI.

Hard at work in the kitchens at Ordsall Hall.

Ordsall Hall

This wonderful hidden gem, nestling incongruously in a Salford housing estate, is a must. The Grade I listed Tudor Manor with origins dating back to 1210, has had a chequered, often threatened, history. However, a recent cash injection from lottery funds has galvanised a wonderful restoration project, safeguarding Ordsall Hall's future for all to enjoy.

A friend and I visited on a beautiful sunny day with our children, both three years old. Firstly we headed to the garden; the children ran around happily, very taken with the wood sculptures of a swan family "swimming" on the grass. Once inside the Hall, there are many beautiful period features for adults to admire – the Great Hall being the most impressive. The enormous trestle table was laid out for 'dinner'. The kids were in their element as Lord and Lady of the manor, toasting each other with silver chalices. The kitchen captured their imagination too, the Hall gives a very real sense of what it was like to live in days gone by. If you like a good ghost story, you might be interested to know that Ordsall is reputed to be haunted by the White Lady – check out the live ghost cams on their website. We avoided mentioning the ghost to our tots, but older children might be intrigued by the idea!

Further on through, the children were able to dress up in chain mail, solve some puzzles, bang

about with musical instruments and be captains of a little sit-in boat.

On the top floor there's also a small, colourful children's zone with cute costumes to try on and various items to play with. Another highlight back downstairs was the solid glass floor over the well on which you can stand and peer down – if you dare!

On the first Sunday of each month it's family-friendly Tudor Live day. Plenty of activities are laid on for children and the volunteer staff wear historical costumes.

Mon-Thurs 10am-4pm, Fri-Sat closed, Sun 1-4pm. Admission free. Car Park 0-3 hours £2. Small café sells sandwiches and cakes (no specific children's menu)
Ordsall Hall, 322 Ordsall Lane, Ordsall, Salford M5 3AN
Tel: 0161 872 0251 salfordcommunityleisure.co.uk

People's History Museum

This museum might initially seem an unusual choice for the parents of a six-year-old and two-year-old to choose to go to, but we did and I urge you to do the same. The PHM houses an enormous collection of material that chronicles the lives of working people in Britain, with a particular focus on Manchester.

It is bursting at the seams with exhibits and displays – too much in my opinion for just one visit so best to approach it with a bite-sized chunk attitude, far less daunting! Adults get the chance to brush up on their knowledge of social history (and in my case learn about The Peterloo Massacre), whilst simultaneously our children were entertained satisfactorily by certain exhibits such as the factory clocking-in machine and the giant floor banner that allowed them to interact somewhat. With our six-year-old we were able to attempt some very basic history lessons, which held his attention well enough and thus was pretty rewarding.

There was a limited menu on the Sunday in the café, so we opted out, choosing nearby Spinning-fields instead.

Daily 10am-5pm. Admission free.
Left Bank café bar Mon-Sat 8am-5pm, Sun 10am-5pm.
The People's History Museum, Left Bank,
Spinningfields, Manchester M3 3ER
Tel: 0161 838 9190 phm.org.uk

Police Museum

Tucked away in the Northern Quarter of Manchester city centre is the Greater Manchester Police Museum. There are loads of dressing up clothes and handling items such as police helmets. You can see the original charge office and the Victorian cells with wooden pillows, which provide a graphic taste of prison life. Upstairs is a beautiful wood-panelled Magistrates Court dating from 1895; now it is often used to train new officers and staff in court procedures and giving evidence. There are lots of interesting pieces to look at and read about, the weapons confiscated from football games in the 1980s are horrifying! For toddlers I don't think it is worth a special trip and it's not great for prams, but if you're in the area and have an hour to spare, this is a lovely museum to pop into. There is a lift and toilets but no baby changing facilities. No refreshments are available, but you're not far away from **city centre cafés** (see page 108).

Meter parking is outside.
Tues 10.30am-3.30pm & Thursday in the holidays.
Admission free.
GMP Museum and Archives, 57a Newton Street,
Northern Quarter, Manchester M1 1ET
Tel: 0161 856 3287 gmpmuseum.com

Salford Museum and Art Gallery

Now sporting a new reception, shop and beautiful café following building works in late 2012, Salford Museum and Art Gallery is a really enjoyable place to visit. We started our visit with the ground floor, which is more the museum bit. The main feature is Lark Hill Place, a recreation of a typical Salford street during Victorian times. On the way in there are a couple of clothes rails and a mirror, so plenty of fun can be had trying on flat caps and waistcoats! Once inside it is a fantastically dark, atmospheric

experience crammed full of detail – toy shop windows, a cobblers, a Penny Farthing and lots more. Oliver felt like he'd just walked into Diagon Alley!

The art galleries are upstairs and offer changing exhibits which have plenty of activities to keep all ages amused whilst you take in some art.

The gallery also has an area dedicated to the craftwork and paintings of local artists which are all on sale so there is an opportunity for mums to fit in a bit of retail therapy too.

Don't overlook Salford Museum – it makes for a lovely morning out.

Baby changing in disabled toilet on the ground floor.
Pay and display parking £2 for 3 hours.
Tues-Fri 10am-4.45pm, Sat-Sun 1-5pm.
Admission free.
Salford Museum and Art Gallery, Peel Park,
The Crescent, Salford M5 4WU
Tel: 0161 778 0800 salfordcommunityleisure.co.uk

Whitworth Art Gallery

Currently closed due to a major building refurbishment. With a brand new huge glass extension, The Whitworth will double its size when it reopens in Autumn 2014. Can't wait to see it!

Art Baby classes continue at The Bridgewater Hall (see page 138 for more details).
The Whitworth Art Gallery, Oxford Road,
Manchester M15 6ER
Tel: 0161 275 7450 whitworth.manchester.ac.uk

Who let the dogs out at Salford Museum and Art Gallery.

Air Raid Shelters

With my nine-year-old studying World War II at school, we had a very good reason to visit the Stockport Air Raid Shelters. Carved out of red sandstone and about a mile long, they were the largest purpose-built civilian air raid shelters in the country. Opened in 1939, they could provide shelter for up to 6,500 people!

At the start a short film, with news footage from the war, is projected onto the walls and ceilings. Throughout the tunnels there are boards displaying wartime stories and information. Audio guides are available too, which play interesting talks and radio broadcasts.

A replica first aid post and sick bay are set up in the tunnels, with dressing up clothes and wartime props for the children, including gas masks. The 16-seater toilets were a sight to behold, with newspaper for loo roll! And they were ahead of their time in providing a breastfeeding room for new mums. During the war, the shelters were nicknamed The Chestergate Hotel because of their luxurious standard of accommodation!

A particular favourite with the boys was the recreation of an Anderson Shelter. They had been making models of these in school and enjoyed seeing the full scale version, and getting a sense of what things must have been like during the war.

We spent a very interesting hour here, and if you listened to all the audio you could easily spend longer. The Family Tours are worth joining and run weekends from 2pm. They also run Children's Explorer Tours during the school holidays (call to check times and book ahead). The Air Raid Shelters are easily accessible with a pushchair, and are very child-friendly. There is a toilet and a new gift shop but no café.

Tues-Fri 1-4pm, Sat 10am-4pm, Sun 11am-4pm
Adult £4.45, Child £3.25, under 5s free
Air Raid Shelters, 61 Chestergate, Stockport SK1 1NE
Tel: 0161 474 1940 stockport.gov.uk

Bolton Museum, Art Gallery & Aquarium

Housed in the beautiful neoclassical Le Mans Crescent, this museum and aquarium has a diverse, well put together collection, and is a great place to spend an afternoon with children for free. Armed with clipboards and activity sheets, and after posing for photos by the dinosaur skeleton in the foyer, we set off on our tour, beginning with the Egyptology Room. The sheets kept my two boys of five and eight absorbed as they hunted for patterns on vases and scarab beetles on mummies.

Throughout the museum we found different play areas – a dressing up station in the art gallery, a traditional game of Egyptian snake and a wooden industrial town to construct. 'Bolton Lives' gallery relates the story of the town and its global impact. The balcony above features a children's area plus lots of stuffed animals, which they seemed to love!

A basement aquarium included piranhas, pinstripe damba (now extinct in the wild) and catfish from the Amazon – as well as the very informative aquarium team.

There is a gift shop but no café, although you'll find one in the Octagon Theatre opposite.

Mon-Sat 9am-5pm (Wed 9.30am-5pm), Sun 10am-4pm.
Admission free.
Bolton Museum, Le Mans Crescent, Bolton BL1 1SE
Tel: 01204 332211 boltonmuseums.org.uk

Bury Art Museum

This art gallery was built to house more than 200 oil paintings, watercolours and ceramics collected by local paper manufacturer Thomas Wrigley. It displays world-famous paintings such as Turner's *Calais Sands* and Constable's *Hampstead Heath*, along with changing exhibitions. In the basement is the museum which, if you are visiting with a pram, is the first port of call as it has ramp access, avoiding the grand stone steps up to the main entrance. Here, visitors can view a variety of themed displays and exhibitions of Bury's past.

Fun in the dunny at the Air Raid Shelters in Stockport.

Harry creates a fab little lava lamp at Catalyst.

The art gallery is our favourite, as it is something of a work of art in itself, with fine mosaic floors and stained glass windows. Picture bags can be borrowed that are bursting with activities and drawing materials. On our visit during the school holidays, plenty of colourful paper, glue and pens were set out to inspire visitors to design feathers for a large bird mural. We followed this with a bit of dressing up. Brilliantly, costumes similar to those in the paintings are put on a rail, so children can dress up and then find themselves in the pictures. There

Refreshments on the go! In the café at Bury Art Museum.

is also a good game involving laminated sheets that show eyes which you have to spot in the paintings. New at the museum is Barney's Art Café selling steaming coffees, cakes and juices.

So if you're in Bury and fancy a bit of culture or a coffee, it's definitely worth stopping by. You could always combine it with a trip to **The Fusilier Museum** across the road (see page 15).
Tues-Fri 10am-5pm, Sat 10am-4.30pm. Admission free.
Bury Art Museum, Moss Street, Bury,
Lancashire BL9 0DR
Tel: 0161 253 5878 bury.gov.uk/arts

Catalyst Science Discovery Centre

A seasoned museum-goer, I expect everything to be highly visual and immediately accessible. The Catalyst Science Discovery Centre isn't like that and my first impression was that it was a bit dated. The reality is that the exhibits are actually pretty good and well worth taking a proper look at.

From UV lights, to body heat experiments, solar panels to water valves, if you take the time, you will definitely get a lot out of it. Catalyst is largely aimed at older children but there are free backpacks for younger visitors. You will need to ask for these from reception. There are also various themed trails for five to twelve-year-olds, but again you need to ask.

13

The ins and outs of how your tummy works at Eureka!

Eureka!

Eureka! is the National Children's Museum, full of interactive exhibits, designed quite simply with the ethos that children should learn through play. I often think that if this museum was in London, the tourists would be queuing for miles to get into it. Luckily for us, it's just over the Yorkshire border in Halifax.

City Babies & Kids in the LOVE

Laid out over two levels, we always start in the 'Living & Working Together' area on the ground floor. There is a garage where you can fill up with petrol and maybe change some car wheels, a Post Office where you can dress up and sort the parcels, a house with a kitchen ready for the little ones to prepare lunch, and a scaled-down M&S perfect for doing the weekly shop, and playing shopkeeper of course. Our eight-year-old boys loved the bank in particular where they were very enthusiastic about sending money up and down suction tubes, getting cash out of the ATM, and solving the combination codes to open up the safety deposit boxes in the vault.

Next we headed upstairs to the brand new 'All About Me' gallery. This whole section is really super – spacious and bright. As soon as we went in, our kids ran around trying everything out, disappearing up giant nostrils and climbing into a huge set of gleaming white gnashers. Focusing on the human body, they witnessed the gurgling journey of food from mouth to bottom, saw how taste buds

Zoom – the interactive robot!

on your tongue work, looked inside a body using a scanning machine, and watched on a computer how a baby grows in the womb, finally feeling a baby's heartbeat on a mummy dummy! Without doubt though, their highlight was meeting Zoom the Robot who asks you questions and 'properly' talks back to you. Absolutely brilliant!

Other galleries to explore include 'Our Global Garden', displaying gardens from around the world, ranging from jungle to arctic. The SoundSpace gallery is a futuristic theatre encouraging children to discover the science of sound and music, ours loved the Control Deck. Two areas are specifically designed for the under fives, SoundGarden and Desert Discovery, both full of visuals, textures and padded bits to crawl around in – perfect for a break if the rest of the museum starts to get a bit busy.

The café is good, but inevitably busy at peak times. We'd brought along our own food and grabbed a table in one of the picnic areas ahead of the rush.

There are over 450 brilliantly-maintained exhibits at Eureka! And a trip here is guaranteed to keep my children fully entertained all day.

Term time: Tues-Fri 10am-4pm, Sat & Sun 10am-5pm, Mon Closed. Holidays: Daily 10am-5pm Adults and children £10.95, 1-2 years £3.75, under 1s free. Pay and display car park.

Your ticket price includes an Annual Pass, so you can come back for free as many times as you'd like within the year.

Eureka! The National Children's Museum, Discovery Road, Halifax HX1 2NE Tel: 01422 330069 eureka.org.uk

Felix steps into character in the 'Salford Pals' exhibition at The Fusilier Museum.

The Upstairs Observatory has games, microscopes and panoramic views of both the Welsh Hills and the Pennines. On the way up you'll find The Puzzle Room with plenty of hands-on activities which my boys all enjoyed. The only disappointing part of our trip was the 3D theatre so we left before the end – heading off to the main attraction of our visit, a workshop making lava lamps! Set in a modern, bright, discovery lab, this was fab! The staff were great with the little ones, but the workshops are particularly good for older children. After a couple of water experiments, we got down to the lava business! The boys loved it and were desperate to recreate them the moment they got home.

Outside there's a new, large wooden play structure and a zip wire alongside the original small play area for the younger ones. We took a picnic which we ate outside, but there is also a reasonably-priced café on site, serving hot and cold meals.

Catalyst is an educational centre, with plenty of fun activities and workshops available; from rockets and the universe, to blood and slime! Check the website to plan your trip before you set off and you won't be disappointed.

Term time: Tues-Fri 10am-4pm and Bank Holidays. Sat & Sun 10am-5pm. School Holidays: Mon-Sun 10am-5pm. Adult £4.95, Child £3.95, under 4s free, Family (4) £15.95, Family (5) £17.95.

Catalyst Discovery Centre, Mersey Road, Widnes, Cheshire WA8 0DF
Tel: 0151 420 1121 catalyst.org.uk

The Fusilier Museum

The award-winning Fusilier Museum is home to the collections of the XX Lancashire Fusiliers and the Royal Regiment of Fusiliers, commemorating over 300 years of history and heritage.

The curators have done a fantastic job of making the museum child-friendly, whilst still respecting the subject matter. Throughout the museum there are flaps to lift, puzzles to solve and plenty to learn about at the interactive computer stations, as well as a children's area where they can dress as soldiers or hide in a camouflaged tent. In the trench, the boys howled with laughter as they dared each other to sniff the revolting smells of carbolic soap, trench sweat and 'poisonous gas' lurking in holes in the wall.

One place where we reined our little ones in was the medal room, where six Victoria Crosses awarded to The Lancashire Fusiliers are displayed. We created a game, searching through the medals to find one which had been awarded to a soldier with the same surname as ours, and managed to find one in the last display drawer!

Continuing investment and changing exhibits help to keep The Fusilier Museum fresh and worth a return trip. The 'Salford Pals' exhibition tells the story of three local soldiers and includes a life-sized model of the terraced houses the men lived in. Our children loved opening the doors to discover stories and dressing-up fun behind them. Then 'Strike up the Band', new in summer 2013, is all about military bands, with colourful outfits and instruments galore.

This brilliant museum has successfully secured a £1.4 million grant from Heritage Lottery Funding which will result in a fantastic development of the first floor in 2014.

Mon-Sat (occasional Sundays) 10am-5pm. Adult £3.95, Child £2.95, Family £10.95. Buy one ticket and visit free for a year. Meter parking directly outside (2hrs max). Café on site.
The Fusilier Museum, Moss Street, Bury BL9 0DF
Tel: 0161 763 8950 fusiliermuseum.com

Gallery Oldham

Set in the town centre, Gallery Oldham is a well-used and modern facility. The striking glass-fronted building offers interesting views of the city and the peaks beyond. As well as regularly-changing exhibitions and galleries it also houses a huge library and the Naked Bean Café.

We came for a quick hour and spent longer. The series of light and airy galleries is home to a variety of objects from Oldham's past and present, including: paintings by local artists; displays featuring local comic actor Eric Sykes; and information about the first chip shop in the UK – Oldham is the birthplace of fish and chips!

The kids' favourite was the Oldham Stories gallery where activities include an owl trail with a bag of activities for little ones, an Edwardian chemist shop where you can identify various smells, and a badge-making area (no obvious connection to Oldham, but my boys liked it!)

The Naked Bean Café serves light meals and snacks at reasonable prices. On a warm day, you can head outside to sit in their lovely patio garden. We went during October half-term and there were free craft activities available for the kids.

Mon-Sat 10am-5pm Admission free.
Naked Bean Café Mon-Fri 7.45am-4.30pm, Sat 8.15am-4pm
Gallery Oldham, Oldham Cultural Quarter, Greaves Street, Oldham OL1 1AL
Tel: 0161 770 4653 galleryoldham.org.uk

Harry and Ted enjoy the art at Gallery Oldham.

Americana at Hat Works.

Hat Works

I'm rather fond of Hat Works. The museum – the only one of its kind in the UK – is home to a recreated hat factory with restored machinery, and a collection of over 400 hats from around the world. Because Hat Works is not on the usual tourist trail, it's often possible to catch it relatively quiet so I like to visit with a few mum friends and our little ones on a rainy day.

The children love trying on the hats and enjoy guessing what the different styles on display are used for. There's a family fun zone off the first floor which has several toys, dressing up stuff and chairs for parents! On the ground level, you'll find the machinery gallery with an array of working Victorian hatting machines along with a typical hatter's cottage and office.

The museum is free but if you require a more in-depth tour with a guide then this can be arranged for a small charge.

The main entrance to the museum is on the A6 – we parked on meters just to the side on Wood Street.
Tues-Sat 10am-5pm, Sun & Bank Holidays 11am-5pm.
Admission free. No longer a café on site.
Hat Works, Wellington Mill, Wellington Road South, Stockport SK3 0EU
Tel: 0161 474 2400 stockport.gov.uk

Jodrell Bank

Amidst bucolic Cheshire countryside, a massive piece of pure 1950s sci-fi punctuates the skyline: the colossal, gorgeous and iconic Lovell Telescope at Jodrell Bank. It's impossible not to be awestruck. If you think Space is boring then pop along and have your mind firmly changed. Jodrell Bank has seen quite a transformation, becoming a brilliantly hands-on and exciting attraction for all ages.

The main exhibition building, the Space Pavilion, allows visitors to find answers to the wonders of the Universe, listen to the sounds of the Big Bang and explore the invisible Universe using a range of activities you can touch. The kids had a lot of fun in here – the Black Hole which you roll balls into had them practically fighting over it!

We went in the school holidays, a time when the centre runs plenty of events (advisable to book ahead). Our entertainment of choice was 'Rocket week'. The day included a fun science show packed with audience-appreciated explosions. Outside the theme continued with children allowed to make their own simple rockets using old film cases and Vitamin C tablets. They loved it!

A million orange Vitamin C explosions later, we took the kids for a walk around the base of the giant telescope, trying to spot if it was moving... turning to look for life on other planets perhaps?

Jodrell Bank has introduced Planet Path backpacks that you can borrow, with maps and little experiments for children. It's a perfect activity to

The sheer spectacle that is Jodrell Bank.

do in good weather as it follows a trail around the site. Also, there is the arboretum with a new Galaxy Garden inspired by space and astronomy, plus a play area.

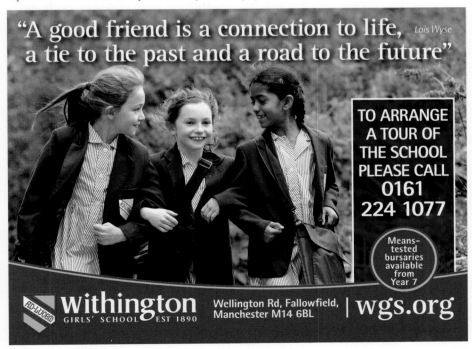

Through the Looking Glass at the Lewis Carroll Centre.

You'll find plenty of picnic tables if you bring your own lunch and in summer The Potting Shed, a pop-up café, serves a small selection from the main café. The Planet Pavilion Café is a destination in its own right, serving wonderful homemade food.
Daily 10am-5pm. Adult £7.50, Child £5.50, Family £22.
Jodrell Bank Discovery Centre, Macclesfield, Cheshire SK11 9DL
Tel: 01477 571766 jodrellbank.net

Lewis Carroll Centre

My 13-year-old niece was visiting from France. So, after the delights of Manchester's Afflecks Palace, I thought it was time to show her something a little more educational, a little piece of English history. Daresbury beckoned, the birthplace of Lewis Carroll, author of Alice in Wonderland and Through the Looking Glass.

The tiny Lewis Carroll Centre is joined to the beautiful 16th Century Grade II listed All Saints church, where the author's father was a vicar and where the young Charlie Dodgson (Lewis Carroll) grew up. Storyboards and an informative timeline tell visitors about his life, along with stories recorded by Ken

Dodd and Dillie Keen. The memorial stained-glass window to celebrate the centenary of his birth in 1932 is beautiful, featuring scenes from Alice in Wonderland including the White Rabbit, the Dodo, and the Mad Hatter's Tea Party.

Within a mile and a half of the church is the birthplace of Lewis Carroll, and the Lewis Carroll Centenary Wood. It is barely marked, with just one National Trust brown sign. Parking is very limited, enough for two cars, and it's not mentioned on the website. Apart from a few displays and the footprint of the original house laid out in bricks, there isn't much here as the parsonage burnt down in 1884. But there's a lovely path, dotted with white rabbit signposts, and it's a very peaceful spot. I did feel a little sad that there wasn't more here to remember Lewis Carroll by but, as we sat on one of the benches under the tree, I'm sure I saw a glimmer of the Cheshire Cat's grin!

To complete our trip, we stopped off for a quintessentially English afternoon tea at **Davenport's Tea Room** nearby, see page 133.
Mon-Sat 10am till late, Sun from 2pm. Admission free.
Lewis Carroll Centre, All Saints Church, Daresbury Lane, Daresbury, Cheshire WA4 4AE
lewiscarrollcentre.org.uk

Manchester Regiment Museum

The Manchester Regiment Museum is within the beautiful Victorian Town Hall in the main square of Ashton-under-Lyne. The museum tells the story of generations of Manchester Regiment soldiers from 1756 to 1958.

There are lots of historical objects on display, including 1,800 medals of which five are Victoria Crosses. You'll also discover a few interactive exhibits and clothes from various eras to dress up in. In one section there's a reconstruction of a First World War trench, which is very interesting but a bit dark, and may be quite scary for little ones. Every Wednesday during the school holidays from 11am-3pm you can meet the character of Tommy Atkins, a First World War soldier, try on his uniform and handle the equipment.
Tues-Fri 10am-4pm, Sat 10am-1pm. Admission free. Pushchair entrance at the side of the building.
Manchester Regiment Museum, The Town Hall, Market Place, Ashton-under-Lyne OL6 6DL
Tel: 0161 343 2878 tameside.gov.uk

Lights, Camera, Action! At the National Media Museum.

National Media Museum

City Babies & Kids in the LOVE

Devoted to everything film, TV, radio, gaming and photographic, this fabulous museum makes for a great family day out.

First off, the 'Experience TV' Gallery, where Will and Ellie became news presenters in a replica TV studio; before moving to the mock living room set to operate the cameras whilst directing an 'actor' (dad) in and out of a door and on and off a leather sofa! The kids' favourite thing though was experimenting with chroma keying, the special effects technique used in TV for layering two images together. Here, you choose between footage of Bollywood Dancing, Dinosaurs on the Rampage or Hover-crafting between Skyscrapers, then perform in front of a blue screen, and watch yourself integrated within your chosen footage, transplanted into a new world. It is a brilliant laugh!

Dragging ourselves away from chroma keying was nearly impossible, but the Magic Factory beckoned. This is a large interactive space, offering the chance to experiment and have fun with light and sound: Camera Obscura, Periscopes and Funny Mirrors amongst lots of other things. Will loved Dot Dot Dash, where he learned some Morse Code and sent his message out of the museum window, and up into Space.

Models of the Wombles, Morph, Wallace and Gromit were on display in the Animation Gallery, where the children were able to have a go at some stop motion animation themselves. We also marvelled at the first camera that made film possible, were intrigued by Thaumatropes & Zoetropes, viewed clips of influential moments in TV history and took a trip down memory lane when the robots from the 1980's Smash adverts revealed themselves in one glass cabinet!

The Games Lounge is hilarious for the grown-ups and inevitably compulsive for the kids; looking back at arcade games from yesteryear, with the opportunity to have a go on many of the old favourites. Remember Donkey Kong? Space Invaders? Pac Man? That ridiculous 70's tennis game, Pong (!!) with the very annoying 'Bip' noise. All in here! Go armed with 20p's to play on some.

We concluded our day with a late lunch at the fantastic café. I had a delicious wood-fired pizza (it was huge, you could easily share it between two). The kids had sandwich lunch boxes and my partner had a salad he said was excellent. I really recommend you make the trip to this museum. Given more time, we could have scheduled in a visit to the on-site IMAX cinema, and there are plenty of special exhibitions on throughout the year too. Loads to get stuck into – I look forward to a return visit very soon.

Daily 10am-6pm. Cinema, bar and café open till late. Car parks nearby. Admission free but charges for cinema.
National Media Museum, Bradford BD1 1NQ
Tel: 0844 856 3797 nationalmediamuseum.org.uk

Fab views from the Museum of Liverpool with plenty of actvities for kids too.

Liverpool

Liverpool is a cultural hotspot with amazing architecture and an abundance of world class museums and galleries. A great day trip!

Museum of Liverpool

Conveniently located at The Albert Docks, this super new museum is a dazzling addition to that familiar Liverpool skyline. Inside, the design is equally dramatic, and the content impressive. The museum tells the story of Liverpool through transport, architecture and its people. There's simply loads to look at, and wandering about this beautiful building is a treat in itself. Highlights for our family were – the life-size replica of a Liver bird, the beautiful Lion locomotive with a wooden carriage that my little girl pretended she was a passenger in, and a partial mock-up of an old Liverpool house – complete with privy – marvellous sound effects that had our eldest in stitches!

For younger visitors, the sparkling Little Liverpool gallery is bound to be a surefire hit. There are lots of colourful interactive toys including the fishing rod hooking game and a water table mini-replica of the River Mersey, complete with plastic boats. In order to avoid over-crowding in this area there is a timed entry scheme in operation, so you need to book in as soon as you arrive at the museum. We ate at the café on site which was pleasant – it's not huge so I'd advise you time it in order to avoid the lunchtime rush.

Daily 10am-5pm. Admission free. liverpoolmuseums.org.uk

Spaceport

An attraction all about the galaxy and space travel – you walk through several themed galleries with lots of interactive exhibits and audio-visual displays. Wallace & Gromit's Moon Base Exploration Station was a high spot for us. You get to see the orange rocket from the film, there's stuff to play on, a small soft play area for little ones and a plasticine station to create some aliens. But the crowning moment was definitely the 360-degree space planetarium show. I strongly advise you don't miss this as our party adored it.

Mon-Fri 10am-3pm, Sat & Sun 10am-5pm. Check online for prices.
spaceport.org.uk

The Tate

Having an art gallery of this calibre close by is a privilege. The Tate at Albert Dock hosts some remarkable exhibitions. Sure, small children are not going to tolerate a gallery of this size and weight for long, but a fly-by is undoubtedly manageable. The Tate's family area on the first floor of the gallery, with beautiful views across the River Mersey, certainly helps. It's a perfect space for kids to take time out, relax, play and create. Workshops are held over the school holidays so check the website ahead of your visit. I like lunch at the Tate Café, with a selection of sandwiches, salads and hot meals available. There is a children's menu (only available during weekends and half-terms).

Daily 10am-5pm. Admission free except exhibitions.
tate.org.uk/liverpool

Other destinations to check out: **Underwater Street** – The Children's Discovery Centre, with multi-playzones for kids (underwaterstreet.com); **The Maritime Museum** – with nautical artefacts and Sea Urchins play area (liverpoolmuseums.org.uk) and; **The World Museum** – with Egyptian mummies and Bug House (liverpoolmuseums.org.uk).

Portland Basin Museum

This family-friendly museum, housed in a restored nineteenth century warehouse at the junction of three canals, is the perfect place to have fun whilst exploring local history. Tameside was once a centre for the cotton industry, coal mining and transport, as well as farming, and there isn't a better place to experience it all under one roof.

We took a group of children aged from four to ten and they all found something that engaged them. There are many interactive exhibits throughout the museum from butter churning to taking a look inside the 1920s canal boat. Our children loved getting dressed up in glamorous film star costumes and trying on all the different styles of hats. There were some interesting smells to try and identify too, most of which resulted in giggles and shrieking. For the under fives there is a 'Nuts and Bolts' educational play area, and there was a drop-in craft activity session on the day we went.

The highlight for our children was stepping back in time in the 1920s street; complete with church, schoolroom, doctor's surgery, shops and a pub. We couldn't drag them away from the schoolroom as they re-enacted a 1920s school day, all taking turns to be a very strict teacher!

Outside there are moorings for canal boats. If it's sunny, you could take a lovely walk along the canal, or even a boat trip. Keep a close eye on young children near the deep water though. We ate at the Bridgeview Café in the museum. It was good value and had a large selection of hot and cold meals for children and adults alike. The coffee was great too!

There is a big free car park directly outside. Sign-posting to the Portland Basin Museum isn't brilliant so, if you're not familiar with the area, work out your route before you set off. Definitely worth a visit!

Oct-June Tues-Sun 10am-4pm, July-Sept 10am-5pm, closed Mon except Bank Hols. Admission free.
Portland Basin Museum, Portland Place, Ashton-under-Lyne OL7 0QA
Tel: 0161 343 2878 tameside.gov.uk

Port Sunlight & Lady Lever Art Gallery

The late 19th century village of Port Sunlight was built by William Hesketh Lever to house his soap factory workers at Lever Brothers, which eventually turned into the global giant Unilever. Today its streets, gardens, tearoom, art gallery and museum are open to all.

We started off our visit at the Lady Lever Art Gallery. In the basement there's an interactive space where you can discover more about William Lever and Sunlight Soap, draw pictures and dress up. It is worth going down here first because you can collect a trail which will help children explore the more beautiful but rather dry remainder of the gallery.

Next we bought a 'village trail' from the nearby museum and gave the kids a chance to run off some energy by strolling through the streets and some of the 130 acres of parkland surrounding the

The children enjoy classroom role-play at Portland Basin Museum.

The eponymous 15th century tower at Turton Tower.

village. There are 900 Grade II listed houses to see (some totally chocolate box pretty!) incorporating 30 different architectural styles, together with a war memorial, garden centre, pub, and other public buildings.

Back at the museum we couldn't resist a scone in the eclectic tearoom, aptly named Tea, on the first floor. The museum itself tells the story of the village and life in Victorian and Edwardian times. A couple of exhibits which interested my children were the reconstructed Victorian parlour and a village model.

Port Sunlight isn't an attraction aimed at children but it has a little bit of something for all ages, making it a good choice for a family day out when you might have a mixed age group of grandparents, kids and teenagers.

Lady Lever Art Gallery: Daily 10am-5pm. Admission free.
Art Gallery Café: Daily 10am-4.30pm with hot food served 12-3.30pm. Highchairs and children's menu.
Lady Lever Art Gallery, Port Sunlight Village, Wirral CH62 5EQ
Tel: 0151 478 4136 liverpoolmuseums.org.uk
Museum: Daily 10am-5pm.
Adult £3.95, Child £2.75, under 5s free.
Port Sunlight Museum, 23 King George's Drive, Port Sunlight, Wirral CH62 5DX
Tel: 0151 644 6466 portsunlightvillage.com

Staircase House and The Stockport Story Museum

This is a museum where you are positively encouraged to touch, walk on, smell and experience the 15th century exhibit – the oldest house in Stockport.

There are 16 rooms in the beautifully restored townhouse. On arrival children are handed a cloth pack with individual mini-bags providing an activity to match most of the rooms. One per family is probably enough. They're aimed at older ones but it is worth getting one whatever the age of your kids, just for the two glove puppets that are included. In all areas, bar the dining room, children can inspect and play with the objects, allowing you to relax and have a good look round yourself. One of the favourites for the under fives is the counting room, where you can write with quill pens and literally get covered in ink. Another is the dressing up area – the only downside is that it's hard to drag them away!

The Stockport Story Museum is attached and offers a background to life in the town. Of interest to little ones is the market stall and medieval costumes to try on, found on Level 4, plus the Victorian dressing up boxes and toys dotted on each level.
Staircase House: Tues-Fri 1-5pm, Sat 10am-5pm, Sun 11am-5pm. Adult £4.45, Child £3.25, under 5s free.
The Stockport Story Museum: Tues-Sat 10am-5pm,

Sun 11am-5pm. Admission free. Both closed Mon except Bank Hols. Café on site.
Staircase House, 30-31 Market Place, Stockport SK1 1ES
Tel: 0161 218 1460 stockport.gov.uk/museums

Touchstones Rochdale

Based alongside the Tourist Information Centre in Rochdale, Touchstones is a modern, well laid out arts and heritage centre. It is ideal for under-fives as there is just enough to keep their interest and I stayed much longer than I'd planned. Although the museum is all in one room, the space is really well utilised; loads of interesting objects accompanied by manageable amounts of text. My three-year-old enjoyed crawling through the coal pit tunnel and there were lots of hands-on activities in drawers including a bucket which smelt disgusting when you took the lid off, plus a lovely area with dressing up clothes and a large mirror.

In the art gallery's permanent collection there is a series of under-fives activity boxes linked to different paintings on display. On this visit they were themed around horses, robins and frogs!

I left Touchstones with a real sense of times gone by in Rochdale. The staff were helpful and, all told, it was a thoroughly enjoyable visit.

Tues-Sat 10am-5pm. Admission free. Café on site.
Touchstones Rochdale, The Esplanade,
Rochdale OL16 1AQ
Tel: 01706 924492 link4life.org/touchstones

Turton Tower

A trip to my parents in Bolton took us via Turton Tower and we happily whiled away a couple of hours here. The house has evolved over five centuries and its most striking element is its earliest architectural feature, the stone tower itself.

The rooms in the house take you on a journey through the centuries, through the Tudor and Victorian pasts of the families that once lived there. The guides at the house could not have been friendlier and did their utmost to engage our children in the history. It was a great place to explore and, with a bit of effort, the kids kept with it too. Inevitably though, it wasn't long before they persuaded us outside.

We walked around the gardens, finishing up with time spent in the woodland play area. We saw several families cycling past us in the woods. As there seemed to be plenty of nature trails, and the location is a popular walking area of the West Pennine Moors, it might be a good idea to take bikes with you when you visit.

Open Mar-Oct, Weds-Sun and Bank Holidays 12-4.45pm
Adult £6, Children free. Tearoom 10am-4pm
Turton Tower, Chapeltown Road, Turton, Bolton BL7 0HG
Tel: 01204 852203 turtontower.co.uk

Planes, Trains and Automobiles

Life-sized toys hold kids' attention like no other: the smell of diesel, the roar of an engine and the thunder of a jet. There is definitely something for everyone here. What are you waiting for? Hop on board!

Abbotsfield Park Miniature Railway

Abbotsfield Park in Flixton looks at first sight like any other small park. It's a recreation ground the size of a couple of football pitches, with a small children's play area.

However, just as you're crossing the bridge to the entrance, you're drawn to a plume of steam coming towards you at some speed. This is the Abbotsfield Park Miniature Railway, and miniature is the word. It's the smallest locomotive you've ever seen outside of a domestic train set. Our son watched, rapt, as this tiny engine thundered past with half-a-dozen people in tow. He couldn't wait to get on and do a couple of circuits of the park himself.

Arriving at the station, we discovered it was the HQ of the Urmston and District Model Engineering Society. This little railway is an absolute labour of love. It's been staffed by club members bringing delight to children since the late 1940s and is a local treasure. One to warm your heart.

Weather permitting, trains run Sundays and Bank Holidays 10am-4pm. Rides are 30p per person.
Abbotsfield Park and Urmston & District Model Engineering Society, Chassen Road, Flixton M41 5DH udmes.co.uk

Allostock Junction Railway Station

This miniature train is excellent fun for little ones and adults alike. At £1 per ride (for over-threes) it's great value for a ten minute spin round the garden centre, past the engine sheds and through the tunnel. The train driver was brilliant and let my little boy and his friend toot the horn for a ridiculously long time.

The café at the garden centre that the railway is attached to has a children's menu priced at £4.75, ice cream included.

Open Sat & Sun, Bank Holidays (except Easter Sunday) and school holidays 11am-4.30pm, Sun 11am-4pm. £1 per ride.
All-In-One Garden Centre, London Road, Allostock, Knutsford WA16 9LU
Tel: 01565 722567 allinone.co.uk

Bolton Steam Museum

Hidden away beside rows of terraced houses, and within an old cotton store warehouse, lies a little gem steeped in history, the Bolton Steam Museum. Its 'In Steam' days are well worth a visit, especially on a Nana and Pops outing with two energetic grandchildren. When we arrived, two small steam-driven trains and carts were giving rides, puffing furiously round the car park, a magnet of course for Will and Eleanor. Great fun albeit a trifle sooty from the fire producing the steam!

Once inside, most of the engines, though static, were running. A cross-section of the types of power once used in the north-west cotton mills, the display is the largest in the country. Laid out over two floors, the upper level, reached by a number of steps, afforded a super view of the working machines below. In total there are 25 rebuilt engines, each with a full description. Though the museum is perhaps more appealing to slightly older children, our six-year-old and three-year-old really enjoyed it – agog with the noise and smell. It is clearly a labour of love for the volunteers that run it, and they were without exception very friendly and approachable. There was a small café serving drinks, biscuits and crisps, plus a selection of souvenirs. It was a fun morning and enjoyed by us all.

2014 In Steam days 10am-4pm 4-5 & 25-26 May, 24-25 Aug, 13-14 Sep & 28-29 Dec. Admission free. Toilets but no baby changing facilities.
Bolton Steam Museum, Mornington Road, off Chorley Old Road, Bolton BL1 4EU nmes.org

Brookside Miniature Railway

This miniature railway is one of our favourite short trips out. The five immaculate locomotives – three steam engines and two diesel – live at their very own station, Brookside Central; a replica West Country station with authentic buildings, sidings, turntable and original signage on the miniature

All aboard! At Allostock Railway Station.

In the maze with the spectacular Anderton Boat Lift behind.

The Anderton Boat Lift

I've wanted to go to The Anderton Boat Lift ever since reading Louise's review in our very first edition. But believing that this trip was better suited to older children, I decided to wait a couple of years. My boys are now nine and seven – perfect ages to get the most out of a trip here. The Anderton Boat Lift is an incredible feat of Victorian engineering, and was built to allow boats to journey between the River Weaver and the Trent and Mersey Canal high above.

First stop is a good visitor centre, café and gift shop – with enough attractions to keep kids happy while they wait for the boat trip. The river cruise trip had left but we were able to book the last lift trip of the day. Boat times do vary throughout the year so check times before you leave home.

Outside there is a lovely picnic area, a small playground, a maze built out of the original cast iron counterweights and of course incredible views of the 60-foot iron boat lift. (You can access the visitor centre and outside area for free without doing the river or lift trip.)

Regular boaters will be well aware that nothing is done at speed on a canal! After boarding, we slowly motored into the lower cradle or 'cassion'. We then had a fairly long wait, while they filled up the top cradle from the Trent and Mersey Canal with three pleasure boats that were on their way down to the River Weaver. The passionate and extremely knowledgable guide kept us entertained throughout, with stories of the river and the history of the boat lift.

Being glass-topped, the view from the boat of the surrounding iron structure is amazing. Despite the slow speed you seem to quickly pass the boats in the other cradle as the hydraulic weight pulls you up and the counter balance drops them down. The sight of the canal emerging before your eyes is lovely. It gives you a feel for how incredible it must have been for travellers 100 years ago raising 50ft between the two water levels.

The Anderton Boat Lift was right at the forefront of the Industrial Revolution, and is one of only two working boat lifts in the UK. It's a great alternative day out, and fantastic that a structure with this heritage has been restored so brilliantly.

Entrance to the visitor centre, gift shop and café is free. Pay and display car park. Check website for up-to-date information on seasonal dates and opening times.

Lift trip: Adult £7.75, Child £5.75, Family £21.25, under 5s free.

Combined lift & river trip: Adult £12, Child £9, Family £33, under 5s free.

Anderton Boat Lift, Lift Lane, Anderton, Northwich, Cheshire CW9 6FW Tel: 01606 786777 andertonboatlift.co.uk

The glass-topped passenger boat.

platform. Inside the waiting room (which doubles as a gift shop and museum) you purchase your ticket, then it's all aboard!

The half-mile circuit through tunnels, over streams and level crossings and around the perimeter of the centre lasts about eight minutes. You'll find that one go is never enough! Next to the station is a children's play area with a life-size engine that you can climb on; several ride-on machines; and a kiddie tramway where the children ride along a short track by themselves.

Also on site is a children's pottery studio where you can paint your own pots. During summer months and school holidays there's a small old-fashioned fun fair at one end of the garden centre. The fair has its own little station so you can hop off for a quick game of hook-a-duck before boarding the next train home!

Sat & Sun 11am-3.45pm, £1.50 per person, 10 ride ticket £12. Café on site.

Brookside Garden Centre, London Road North, Poynton, Stockport SK12 1BY
brooksideminiaturerailway.co.uk

The 'small' controller at Bury Transport Museum.

Bury Transport Museum

This is a fabulous transport museum and if you have bought a full line return trip on the **East Lancs Railway** (see opposite page) then entrance is free and it's worth looking in. Situated across the road from Bury Bolton Street Station, it has recently undergone a £3 million refurbishment. Along with a beautiful restoration to the building, it has been transformed into a modern family-friendly museum.

We went on Harry's birthday, taking along a school friend who turned out to be a real railway enthusiast. On the ground floor you will find vintage buses, a tram, a 1950s fire engine, a post office van and a steam locomotive amongst others. A quirky addition is the Yelloway Mobile Museum, popular with thousands of families who holidayed by the seaside in the 1950s.

Upstairs is a lovely gallery with a great dressing up selection. There were also a couple of old telephones once used between the station and the points, the kids didn't have a clue how to hold them!

We had a quick bite at the Castlecroft Café, located in a former carriage outside the museum. It was pretty basic but served hot and cold drinks and excellent bacon barmcakes!

Weds-Sun plus Bank Holiday Mondays 10am-4pm. Adult £3.40, Child £3, Family £9. Admission free for holders of an East Lancs Railway full line return ticket.

Bury Transport Museum, Castlecroft Goods Warehouse, Castlecroft Road, Bury BL9 0LN
Tel: 0161 763 7949 eastlancsrailway.org.uk

City Airport & Heliport

Jo and I just love this place! It is the UK's first purpose-built municipal airport, dating back to the 1930s, and operates now as one of the country's busiest general aviation airports. It's literally on our doorstep and the fact that it welcomes little visitors, as well as those with wings, makes City Airport a perfect place to touch down...!

The airfield is located just off the M60 not far from The Trafford Centre. The Airfield Lodge is the on-site bar and restaurant (which is open to the public) overlooking the take off and landing area. There are plenty of tables and a menu serving food all day including: full English, bacon rolls, and Sunday roasts, plus a children's

City Airport – A perfect place for a flying visit or longer!

menu with fish fingers and mini pizzas.

We took Ellie and Ted, who are both four years old, on a weekday morning and there was just one other family in, but I understand that the whole place is popular on summer weekends. At the front of the restaurant outside, with great views over the airfield, there's a securely fenced-off play area, with Little Tikes cars, swings and a brilliant climbing frame. On the day we visited there were plenty of light aircraft zipping around to watch.

The kids had a good time playing and we took a short walk to the control tower where you can climb up to a balcony with views across the runway. We also had a peek inside the tiny museum situated in a portakabin across the car park. It's filled with aviation memorabilia and a couple of RAF uniforms for the children to try on. There's no cost to visit City Airport so it's great to drop in for a flying visit – we've landed there so often, we're now frequent flyers!

Daily 27 Oct 2013 - 29 March 2014 9am-sunset, 30 March - 25 Oct 2014 8.15am-8pm. Light aircraft may not fly in heavy winds, snow etc. Admission and car parking is free The Airfield Lodge: Daily from breakfast till late.
City Airport & Heliport, Liverpool Road, Eccles, Manchester M30 7SA
Tel: 0161 789 1362 cityairportandheliport.com

Dragon Miniature Railway

As we turned into the car park at Marple Garden Centre, my three-year-old daughter Eleanor got very excited on spying the mini Flying Dragon train tootling past with mini passengers on board! We headed to the platform "Otterspool Junction", purchased our tickets and waited for our turn. Just before setting off, the friendly driver invited Ellie to have her picture taken in the driving seat – which she adored. And then we were off, speeding (not really!) down the tracks. The journey lasts about eight minutes and takes you through a tunnel, over bridges, and alongside displays of fairytale gnomes amongst other things. Halfway along, you'll see a large picnic and play area where in good weather you can alight and have your packed lunch, and the children can go on all the climbing frames, swings and trampoline. It's a scenic spot by the river – you can only access the play area by train which is just a little bit exciting for young children!

Sat & Sun plus school holidays (weather dependent) 11am-4.30pm. £1 per person.
Dragon Miniature Railway, Marple Garden Centre, Dooley Lane, Marple, Stockport SK6 7HE
Tel: 07748 581160 dragonminiaturerailway.co.uk

East Lancashire Railway

Arriving at Bury's Bolton Street Station is like stepping back in time. There are traditional ticket booths, lovely signage, and helpful staff. We decided to go from Bury to Ramsbottom, but for a longer ride you can take the train from Heywood all the way to Rawtenstall.

At Bury Station, The Trackside pub on Platform 2 does children's meals and they will warm up bottles or baby food. Baby-changing is in the disabled toilets at the end of the platform, there are also facilities at Ramsbottom Station. There are steps at Bury but staff are happy to help with pushchairs. Alternatively there is access to the platform by The Trackside and staff will accompany you across the track.

Ramsbottom is a 15-minute journey through some gorgeous countryside. We've travelled on both diesel and steam trains. Both are good but I think the romance of the steam train wins. The boys loved it and had their heads pressed against the window for the entire journey. There is a buffet car on board as well as toilets.

Ramsbottom station is only a five-minute walk away from shops and cafés including the wonderfully indulgent Chocolate Café. There are plenty of picnic tables by the station too, as well as a children's park. A traditional country market can be found every Saturday, and on the second Sunday of each month, a farmers' market.

The railway hosts a number of family friendly events throughout the year, including Days Out With Thomas™ and the Santa Specials in December; pre-booking is essential for the latter. Do stick your head into the **Bury Transport Museum** (see page 26) directly opposite – it's recently had a super refurbishment.

Weekend Full Line Returns: Adult £14, Child £9, Family £36, under 5s free. Includes free entry to Bury Transport Museum. Check website for up-to-date information on seasonal dates and opening times. Steam trains only run on certain days. The Trackside food available Weds-Fri 9am-3pm, Sat & Sun plus Bank Holidays 9am-4pm.
East Lancashire Railway, Bolton Street Station, Bolton Street, Bury BL9 0EY
Tel 0161 764 7790 eastlancsrailway.org.uk

Fire Service Museum

The Fire Museum is a treasure trove of old fire engines, photographs and uniforms. Laid out as a Victorian street scene, it's aimed at older children, but never underestimate the appeal of a big red fire engine to a small child. Whilst you aren't really allowed on the engines, once you get chatting to the very friendly volunteers, they'll be happy to let you take a closer look. Volunteers from the brigade have restored most of the exhibits and they also run the museum. On the first Sunday of every month, special events for families are held. Parking wise, there is plenty on Richard Street, which is ideal as the entrance to the museum is here and not on Maclure Road.

Every Fri and the first Sun of every month 10am-4pm. Admission free. No café.
Greater Manchester Fire Service Museum, Maclure Road, Rochdale OL11 1DN
Tel: 01706 901227 manchesterfire.gov.uk

The Heights of Abraham

The long and winding road through the Peaks is a worthy journey to reach this highly unusual destination. The Heights of Abraham begins with a cable car ride to the top of Masson Hill – its flat top aloft in the Derbyshire countryside. The hill is home to caverns, woodlands, adventure playgrounds, a fossil factory, a tower to climb, and an amphitheatre, all complete with spectacular views over the beautiful surrounding countryside and villages.

The trip up in the cable car is thrilling and exhilarating but don't forget your head for heights, it's a long way down passing through the deep limestone gorge. Safely at the top, we went straight into a guided tour through the Masson Cavern, which included a light display. With many steps and narrow passages, this 40 minute tour wouldn't be possible with a pram but my two boys, five and eight, loved it. Back out in the daylight we ate a picnic by one of the superb play areas before enjoying a cuppa in the terraced café (again, great views, this time down the Derwent Valley). Disappointingly we ran out of time to fit in the second cavern but did manage the indoor exhibitions and the spiral staircase to the top of Prospect Tower. Both were well worth the visit.

Heading down on the cable car we all decided that The Heights of Abraham got our vote and we would definitely be back again.
10am-4.30pm, later at peak times.
Daily 15 Feb-2 Mar & 29 Mar-2 Nov 2014.
Sat & Sun only 8-23 Mar.
Adult £14, Child £9.50, under 5s free (1 per adult), Family £42 Pay and display car park.
The Heights of Abraham, Matlock Bath, Derbyshire DE4 3PD
Tel: 01629 582365 heightsofabraham.com

The Heights of Abraham – An unusual way to travel over the Derbyshire countryside!

On the Buses at the Museum of Transport.

Museum of Transport

Honestly, if you haven't visited this museum yet, do! Even if you don't think you have a passion for buses, it's hard not to be wowed by the sight of over seventy of them, lined up in gigantic old garages in Cheetham Hill. The dedication and passion of the enthusiasts who help run this museum is so impressive. With no modern museum-style interactive technology in sight, the thrill is simply that of climbing onto some of these vintage buses and trams. So, if you have a child who is touch button crazy, then this probably isn't the place for them.

Newly available are the children's trail activity sheets, a collection of six images that you have to locate around the museum. Kept my kids happy! There's a table for colouring and a little wooden bus where the children can change the destination signs and dress up in costumes. The majority of our visit was spent simply wandering around these historic vehicles: from the elaborately painted Victorian open-top horse-drawn bus and vintage trolleybuses; past the bright orange livery of the 1980's Manchester buses; and finally up-to-date with the prototype for the trams that run in Manchester city centre today. Throughout the year a number of special events are held where some of the vehicles are fired up and you have the chance to go for a ride on them.

There are also replica period offices, preserved like time capsules; complete with antique decor, furniture and old ticket machines. Some of the collection, displayed in a glass cabinet next to the tearoom, was actually used in one of the Harry Potter films.

We stopped in the friendly café for a Kit-Kat and an Eccles cake. 10 out of 10 for this quirky museum. *Weds, Sat, Sun and Bank Holidays. Every day in August. 10am-4.30pm. Adult £4, Children free.*
Museum of Transport, Boyle Street, Cheetham, Manchester M8 8UW
Tel: 0161 205 2122 gmts.co.uk

National Railway Museum in York

This is a terrific museum for everyone – not just train fans! From Mallard, the world's fastest steam locomotive to a working replica of Stephenson's world-changing Rocket, you can explore giant halls full of railway legends. The best bit about the National Railway Museum is that you can see, touch and hop aboard most of the awe-inspiring locomotives.

Over in The Great Hall are the collection's prized pieces, including the royal carriages, the Japanese Bullet and the RA36, used in construction of the channel tunnel. There are hundreds of railway treasures to look at throughout. You can also watch live engineering at The Workshop – including the latest conservation work on The Flying Scotsman, which is fascinating.

The Station Hall is like stepping back in time. The self-service restaurant is here, and it's lovely dining on the platform surrounded by enormous engines; they serve both children's hot lunches and meal bags. There is a picnic area in the South Yard which

29

An aviation icon – Concorde at the Runway Visitor Park.

has a railway-themed play area for children to let off steam, plus a miniature railway (weather permitting, 11.30am-12.50pm and 1.30-3.30pm.)

The Learning Platform in The Station Hall had fun science shows on when we visited – demonstrating steam pressure by firing a doll out of a cannon! With daily demonstrations, tours and a special events programme in school holidays, there's plenty here for the whole family.

Daily 10am-5pm. Admission free.
NRM York, Leeman Road, York YO26 4XJ
Tel: 08448 153139 nrm.org.uk

Oulton Park

If you have children who like cars or motorbikes, then visit Oulton Park racing track in Cheshire. It makes a good family day out and is bound to be a hit with dads.

On entering the park at the main entrance, we drove to the interior of the track and parked on a grassed bank at the trackside. We were then able to unpack our binoculars, lay out a picnic rug and food and watch the racing. Formula 3 cars were soon whizzing by. As we were watching time trials, it was difficult to follow who was in the lead; but the speed and appearance of the vehicles were enthralling enough. I was also

impressed by the picturesque countryside in which the circuit is set.

After watching a few different classifications of car race we decided to take a stroll. We were surprised and delighted to be able to enter the paddock and get up close with the cars, the drivers, and mechanics. We kept expecting to see Lightning McQueen drive out of Mack!

There is a large modern building in the middle of the circuit with a gift shop, toilets and baby changing, plus a self-service restaurant selling reasonably-priced meals, snacks and drinks. The results of the races are shown on a screen whilst you eat.

The Hollies Farm Shop and Café (see page 134) is close by to pick up tea on the way home.
Overnight camping is available at the trackside. Open on various dates of the year. Before visiting check online if there is a race event on.
Adults £13 upwards, depending on event, children free.
Oulton Park, Little Budworth, Tarporley, Cheshire CW6 9BW
Tel: 01829 760301 oultonpark.co.uk

Runway Visitor Park

We visited on a sunny April afternoon which was great for watching the planes from the specially-designed viewing mounds. There are over 600 planes on the move

---

OUR TOP FIVE

Museum of Transport
10 out of 10 for this quirky museum!

Heights of Abraham
A fab alpine-style cable car ride over the Derwent Valley.

Runway Visitor Park
Take off and see the world's most iconic plane – Concorde!

Anderton Boat Lift
A sight to behold and a unique ride...

National Railway Museum
Terrific destination for trainspotters!

every day, so you definitely won't miss out on the thrill of a massive jet whooshing past you.

The whole park is easy for prams with a great play park and climbing frames. My kids aren't at the age where we can all cycle, but there is a family-friendly Airport Orbital Cycleway that looks well worth checking out.

The star attractions are Nimrod and that most noble of aircraft, Concorde – it simply screams speed, glamour and elegance. Set in a palatial glass-fronted hangar, the flagship of the supersonic era is visited via a pre-booked tour (£13.50 per person). If you've ever flown or wanted to fly this work of art then it is an absolute must. Our guide spoke passionately and knowledgably and the fact Concorde will never fly again actually brought a tear to my eye! The Nimrod tour (£13) is available too but you must be at least 1.3m tall.

If you're happy without a tour, there'll be at least one plane (DC-10, Trident or Avro RJX) you can hop on and view free of charge (weekends only).

For lunch, the Ringways Restaurant is large with a well-priced children's selection. Not only that, but it offers a brilliant view of Concorde. There's also a more casual take-out café with coffee, hot and cold snacks and ice cream. We took advantage of the weather and had a picnic at one of the many tables scattered around the park. Finally, don't forget to check out the gift shop. It has more aeroplane-related items than you would ever imagine possible!

Parking £3 per hour.
The Runway Visitor Park, Sunbank Lane,
Altrincham WA15 8XQ
Tel: 0161 489 3932 manchesterairport.co.uk

Walton Park

This little park just off the Washway Road in Sale has had a much needed face lift. As well as keeping the old-fashioned but fun play structures, there are now some new features such as wooden climbing posts, spinning discs, a swinging net and a climbing frame.

The best thing though, needed no improvement – the narrow gauge steam train that operates every Sunday come rain or shine. The quarter-mile circular route is run by members of the Sale Area Model Engineering Society, and has been running for more than 30 years!

Another attraction is the narrow boat Brew Boat café that pulls up alongside the tow path on the Bridgewater Canal most Sundays during the warmer months. Serving through the side hatch – bacon butties, organic soup and delicious hot chocolate – it's a lovely addition to the park.

Train: Sundays 12-4.30pm Adult and Child 30p
Walton Park, Raglan Road, Sale M33 4AN
waltonparktrains.co.uk

Animals, Nature and Wildlife

Whether your children like getting up close to wildlife, or watching from a distance – you'll find something furry, slimy or even spiky here that they will adore.

Blackpool Zoo

We had a fantastic trip to Blackpool Zoo where there's so much to see and do. It is nonetheless a manageable size, especially if you're taking the children on your own.

On arrival we were given a timetable of talks and so we headed off to catch the sea lion show. The set-up was impressive, a lovely beach-style arena; and the talk was informative, but not too long for children.

The indoor and outdoor facilities for the primates (orangutans, monkeys, and gorillas) were full of fantastic activities. We spent ages watching them climb around. The overhead walkway around the giraffe enclosure is an impressive feature, giving a better perspective on just how tall these beautiful creatures are.

We brought our own picnic and sat on a lawn with a play area surrounded by picnic tables, perfect for a rest while they ate and ran off some steam. Lake View Café is open during the summer and serves hot and cold children's meals, they are also happy to serve a small portion of the daily special. A café by the entrance serves toasties, sandwiches and coffee and a miniature railway runs in the holidays and at weekends.

I couldn't wait to get to the lemur enclosure as I'd heard how funny they are but, lo and behold, they were all asleep! With full volume "move it, move it" from the boys, and some cajoling from me, we managed to wake them for a photo opportunity.

The highlight of our day was Amazonia. Naughty squirrel monkeys hide above the entrance and dive bomb unsuspecting visitors as they arrive, rooting around for leftover food and titbits. A staff member is on a never-ending mission with a water spray to keep them at bay, while kids and photo-hungry parents (myself included) encourage them closer!

Lastly we watched the bird display, another creatively-planned outdoor theatre show with lots of close shaves as owls and parrots flew low over our heads.

Blue Planet is one of the biggest aquariums in the country.

There are many more things to mention including a children's farm and a dinosaur safari. Blackpool Zoo is great value, loads of fun and I would highly recommend it.

Daily from 10am. Check website for closing as times vary.
Adult £15.99, Child £11.50, under 3s free, Family £49.50
Book online for 10% discount. Car park £2.50
Blackpool Zoo, East Park Drive, Blackpool, Lancashire FY3 8PP
Tel: 01253 830830 blackpoolzoo.org.uk

OUR TOP FIVE WILD THINGS

Chester Zoo
One of the UK's top zoo's with over 11,000 animals – a great day out for the whole family.

Chestnut Centre
Visit the giant otters at this wildlife park in the Peaks.

Martin Mere
Discover these wonderful wetlands and don't miss the fab Canoe safari!

Sea Life
Manchester's brand new aquarium with Europe's first Sea Bed Walk.

Stockley Farm
Lots of 'hands-on experiences' for the children. Little ones love it.

Blue Planet Aquarium

Blue Planet is one of the biggest aquariums in the country and so has plenty to offer. It's worth allowing a couple of hours, as you can go round as many times as you like, and all kids seem to want to see that blasted clown fish one last time! The 70 metre moving walkway through the Aquatunnel is the best part for us – with huge sand tiger sharks together with mantra rays floating around you. When it's busy though, this section can be a bit of a nightmare with a pushchair!

We enjoyed the Aquatheatre, a partially-seated auditorium with a large picture window, through which you can watch divers perform daily shows, feeding the fish in the enormous tanks. Blue Planet also run special junior

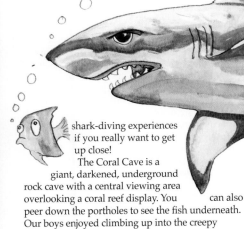

shark-diving experiences if you really want to get up close!

The Coral Cave is a giant, darkened, underground rock cave with a central viewing area overlooking a coral reef display. You can also peer down the portholes to see the fish underneath. Our boys enjoyed climbing up into the creepy crawly section and getting a 360 degree view of spiders and other nasties. I was more "Get me out of here!"

Outside you'll find a play area, along with the otters – which are gorgeous. The boys spent ages out here, and there are a number of picnic tables (if it's raining, you can eat in the Aquatheatre). The café seating area is large, and sandwich boxes and hot meals are available; but it can get very busy.

Overall I was impressed with the layout of the tanks in the aquarium. And there were steps and benches to clamber up onto, to ensure that even smaller children could see into the higher-up tanks, so everyone could have a good look at the sea creatures. However I was taken aback by the entrance fee. £52 for a family is definitely not cheap – but as a family ticket to the cinema is around £34 maybe I'm just out of touch! Discounts and vouchers can be found online, and are definitely worth searching for. Inevitably Blue Planet does get extremely busy on rainy days and bank holidays, but you can fast track the queue by booking online.

Mon-Fri 10am-5pm, Weekends 10am-6pm
Adult £15.50, Child £11.50, Family £52
Blue Planet Aquarium, Cheshire Oaks,
Cheshire CH65 9LF
Tel: 0151 357 8804 blueplanetaquarium.com

Bowland Wild Boar Park

We visited the Forest of Bowland and the Wild Boar Park on a spectacular autumn day – the forest was at its loveliest. I had to quickly feed the baby when we arrived, so got to sample the homemade food in the café very early on. All the food was very reasonably priced and included wild boar sausages as a speciality. There was also great entertainment,

as behind the café they've rigged up a large branch with loads of bird feeders.

Despite the wonderful ornithological display, my boys' eyes had wandered to the wooden play area, all the usual swings and slides, plus a zip wire and tractors to climb on.

The Wild Boar Park is set in 60 acres of woodland and children can wander pretty freely, stroking rabbits and chicks, and feeding deer with food costing 25p a bag. We walked a brilliant circuit along the riverbank around the edge of the park. It's approximately 1km and probably took us about half an hour. It is pushchair-friendly but could get muddy (we were all wearing wellies). The walk took us past meerkats, owls, prairie dogs, wallabies and of course hundreds of wild boar. You'll also find wonderful wood carvings of animals and birds dotted around. There are loads of other walks into the woodland behind the park, and during the summer you can hitch a ride on a tractor and trailer.

Peering at the wild boar in the Forest of Bowland.

33

Park: Easter-Oct Daily 10.30am-5pm. Nov Closed.
Dec-Easter Daily 11am-4pm. Café: Summer Daily 10.30am-
5pm, Winter Fri-Mon 11am-3pm.
Summer: Adult £6.50, Child £6, under 2s free, Family £23.
Winter: £5 for everyone over 2 years old. There is an Honesty
Box if no one is in attendance.
Bowland Wild Boar Park, Chipping, Preston PR3 2QT
Tel: 01995 61554 wildboarpark.co.uk

Brockholes

Brockholes is a relatively new nature
reserve in the Ribble Valley. The
approach offers your first glimpse of the
stunning floating visitor world; a cluster of buildings constructed largely of wood, centred on a huge
lake. It resembles an ancient marshland village.
Imagine the joy of my children when they realised
that access to the village is via a series of basic
wooden walkways across the water!

The land around the lake (120 football pitches in
size!) was rescued from development by The Lancashire Wildlife Trust. Now you will see restoration
of the wetlands, creation of ponds, seeding of
meadows, planting of new hedgerows and trees,
proper bird-watching hides – a wonderful testament
to so many people's dedicated hard work.

Our two weren't quite up to the various walking
trails. However they absolutely loved the activity
room. They got to look at lots of (real) moths,
pressed buttons to hear different birds singing, and
played animal-related games.

There's a large and very nice looking café serving
a great variety of food for adults plus a 'Bugs &
Slugs' children's lunch box. You'll also find a couple
of lovely shops selling gifts, cordials, preserves and
cakes. Before heading home the kids ran off some
steam in the brilliant playground next to the car
park. All in all, a very successful day out and we're
looking forward to returning year on year to see all
the planting properly taking shape.
Free but car parking charges apply. Visitor Village and restau-
rant: Apr-Oct 10am-5pm, Nov-Mar 10am-4pm
Brockholes, Junction 31, M6. Preston PR5 0UH
Tel: 01772 872000 brockholes.org

Cedar Farm

Beautifully-converted farm buildings surround a
stone courtyard housing independent shops, a café,
craft workshops and a small farm. See page 151 for
full review.

The Chestnut Centre – Otter, Owl and Wildlife Park

I had heard many good things about
The Chestnut Centre but for one reason
or another I hadn't managed the trip until this year.

There's a whole new floating world to discover at Brockholes Nature Reserve in the heart of Lancashire.

Down by the waterhole with the elephants at Chester Zoo.

Chester Zoo

We can revisit Chester Zoo over and over again and the entertainment never ceases. The variety of animals, exotic planting, constantly-updating exhibits and efforts for conservation make this a world-class zoo.

It is also vast. Form a plan. Don't simply glance at the map and then run off like a headless chicken into the lion's den! Last time, we decided to visit everything. Really, I mean everything! Using the numbering on the map, me and my six and nine-year-old engaged in a military-style approach – No Dawdling Allowed! We staggered through the gates at closing time, satisfied smiles on our faces, ticking off No. 68, The Condor Cliffs. If you have younger children, or simply want a more leisurely day, pick out some must-sees to get you started.

Despite our pace, we had many magical moments – a baby black rhino kissing its mum, jaguars dramatically play-fighting, penguins gliding and butterflies dancing. We spent ages observing the orangutans, our favourite being an enormous shaggy male who we christened Mr Bombastic! Of course there was a dark moment when Oliver dragged me into the fruit bat forest. I lasted about 20 seconds – it was time to move on!

We ate our picnic in a yurt overlooking the cheetah enclosure, an excellent choice of location as Felix got nose to nose with a cheetah cub – I think it liked the look of his ham butty! The Jaguar Picnic Lodge looks a cosy place to picnic, and has a small coffee house nearby if you've not packed a flask. For warmer days, there are lawns and benches. If you'd rather not carry a rucksack around all day, there are two main restaurants offering self-service meals. We had juice and a cake in June's Pavilion in the afternoon. It was busy, noisy and quite expensive, but plenty of seating was available

As it got chilly we took pleasure in the warmth of the tropical houses – the boys were wowed by a display of cacti in Plant Paradise, a more recent addition to the zoo. There are so many interesting indoor animal houses here, that a day trip would still be worth doing in the rain.

A monorail circumnavigates the zoo, allowing a birds-eye view of the park. It's a chance to rest weary legs too! Another different perspective can be seen from the water bus. These (and crazy golf) are not included in the entry price; but when you consider that the zoo have 11,000 mouths to feed, you can't blame them for trying to make more money!

A wonderful highlight for me came when we got home. As the boys told Dad their tales of the day, about painted dogs and poisonous blue frogs – they were so animated and enthused I could tell that they had loved their day at the zoo. It had been worth every penny.

Daily from 10am. Check website for up-to-date information on closing times, seasonal dates and events.

Low season: Adult £16, Child £13, Family £54.

High Season: Adult £20, Child £16, Family £67.

Book online more than 7 days in advance for 10% discount.

Free Parking. Pushchair Hire available.

Chester Zoo, Caughall Road, Upton-by-Chester, Chester CH2 1EU

Tel: 01244 380280 chesterzoo.org.uk

City Babies & Kids in the LOVE

The Giant Otters – Manoki and Panambi with their cubs at The Chestnut Centre.

This fantastic little gem is set in 50 acres of beautiful Peak District, and it's perfect for children. Even as we were simply paying to go in, Ted was squealing with delight, having spotted a very cute baby barn owl fidgeting on a branch behind the till!

Starting the circuit from the top of the wildlife park, we walked down through parkland, past deer to the otters and owls. The Giant Otters – Dad Manoki, mum Panambi and cubs Kaituma and Meamu are probably a highlight of the park. Native to South America, they are an endangered species and rare to see in captivity, so getting as close as you do at the Chestnut Centre is a real treat. The large enclosure has lots of viewing points and big glass panels, so even little ones get a good view. You also get to sneak a peek into their sleeping quarters. On our visit the otters were on particularly good form, with lots of running in and out of the water with the babies coming up to the glass to check out our little cubs too!

As well as otters there are 16 species of owls, polecats, foxes and Scottish wildcats too. The setting is beautiful. Wooden bridges and pathways guide you through the woodland circuit. Our children loved running around here. The centre is pushchair-friendly but the last bit, back up the hill, can be hard-going if it has been raining. Alternatively, if you've got a baby sling, it's worth bringing it along.

The Chestnut Coffee Shop on site sells simple good food – jacket potatoes, sandwiches and soup. *Jan weekends only, Feb daily, 10.30am-dusk. Last entry 3pm. Spring/Summer 10.30am-5.30pm. Last entry 4pm. Adult £7.75, Child £5.50, under 3s free, Family £23.50* **Chestnut Centre, Chapel-en-le-Frith, High Peak, Derbyshire SK23 0QS** *Tel: 01298 814099 chestnutcentre.co.uk*

Cobble Hey Farm and Gardens

This small farm is set high up in the stunning Trough of Bowland. We were fortunate to visit on a crystal clear sunny day and were wowed by views of big blue skies meeting the sparkling waters off the North West coast, interrupted only by fields and trees. Binoculars were available to rent and so the boys could enjoy spotting ships out at sea too.

On arrival we were greeted by a medley of chickens and cockerels, cooling down with a dirt bath; the boys fancied joining them of course! Over at the barn we met Bonnie and Clyde, a pair of Pygmy goats, along with some of their friends. Next, we headed through the shop and tearoom, collecting an ice cream en route, and into the beautiful gardens. A walk along the paths revealed colourful beds of hostas lining the bank of a bubbling stream, and plenty of open grassed areas to run in.

A super play barn has been added which kids (and indeed grown ups!) will love. It's got a home corner, ride-on tractors, a sand pit, table tennis and a pool table! We sat outside a lovely summer house, taking in the views and chatting to passing walkers. There was just enough time for a clamber on the outside play area and large wooden tractor before we headed back to the barn for animal feeding.

The farmer and his family are very friendly and on hand to answer questions and have a chat. Cobble Hey has a really lovely feel – like you've visited friends who live on a farm, rather than a visitor attraction.

Feb-early Dec, Thurs-Sun 10.30am-4.30pm
Adult £4.50, Child £4, under 2s free
Cobble Hey Farm and Gardens, Off Hobbs Lane, Claughton on Brock, Garstang, Nr Preston PR3 0QN
Tel: 01995 602643 cobblehey.co.uk

Cuddling the kids at Cobble Hey Farm.

Cotebrook Shire Horse Centre and Countryside Park

Escape the city to this little beauty spot in the Cheshire countryside – the only Shire horse stud farm in Britain open to the public, and winner of Cheshire's Small Visitor Attraction in 2013.

We visited on a sunny spring day and were immediately greeted by a very cheerful herd of piglets scurrying round our ankles! As we turned a corner we then met the first of the enormous, beautiful Shire horses being groomed by a member of staff.

We continued to tour the farmyard, meeting Hebridean sheep, ducks, hens, peacocks and very cute Shetland ponies, one of whom my son groomed. After washing hands we ate our picnic at a table by a small lake, overlooking the fields of horses, surrounded by blossom trees and daffodils.

Re-energised we sallied forth once more along the nature trail, which took in three lakes; a fox earth and badger sett; bird boxes; otters; a woodland maze; red deer and of course the most gigantic, elegant horses you've ever clapped eyes on! This close they were awe-inspiring – my kids were dumbstruck. The walk took us about an hour. It's not perfect terrain for a pushchair (muddy after bad weather and full of divots) but was certainly manageable, and all flat.

Daily 10am-5pm
Adult £7.95, Child £5.95, Family £23, under 4s free
Cotebrook Shire Horse Centre and Countryside Park, Cotebrook, Tarporley, Cheshire CW6 9DS
Tel: 01829 760506 cotebrookshirehorses.co.uk

Farmer Ted's Farm Park

This farm park set in open countryside, is a fun day out for children of all ages – there's non-stop action with indoor and outdoor activities from the moment you arrive until the end.

If it is animals you want, there are cows, pigs,

llamas, goats, guinea pigs, birds of prey, and ponies (to say nothing of loads of bugs and reptiles in their own jungle-themed reptile house). Animal handling sessions are held throughout the day if you want to get a bit closer. The boys loved the opportunity to tickle a millipede, and found the sheep racing absolutely hilarious.

If you fancy a bit of time out whilst the kids hare around, nab one of the picnic tables; positioned perfectly to overlook the outdoor play areas, go kart circuit and covered sand pit. For lunch try the enormous indoor café where we were very pleasantly surprised to find a large soft-play area – perfect for a cold or wet day. Afterwards we took in an amusing magician's show. It was a little tame for my seven year old, but the younger ones were riveted.

We now had two choices, the barrel ride (£1 extra, weather-dependent) or the tractor trailer ride. As I wanted to join in too we opted for the latter, and laughed as we were bumped around the farmer's field, waving at passers by. Just enough time left for the indoor climbing frame before heading home after a very enjoyable day.

Open all year round but check website for up-to-date information on opening times and prices.
Farmer Ted's Farm Park, Flatman's Lane, Downholland, Ormskirk L39 7HW
Tel: 0151 526 0002 farmerteds.com

Greenacres Animal Park

This is a sweet little park, just an hour from Manchester. It's perfect, in my opinion, for under fives. There are lots of animals you can stroke, touch and feed in the animal petting area. On the day we visited, my children were lucky enough to get close to a magnificent owl and delighted in being able to touch his feathers. As well as bottle feeding the lambs, you can also buy bags of food and feed other animals such as goats and pigs through chutes next to their enclosures.

Margot meets a wise old owl at Greenacres.

After a good look at the animals, the children were ready for a run around the play area which had plenty to keep them entertained. They especially enjoyed climbing in and out of the huge piles of tractor tyres. There is also an indoor soft-play barn.

The tractor ride with the farmer, around the outskirts of the park, was a great success. Emus and alpacas trotted after us, sticking their heads in for a photo close up, they clearly know where the food comes from! If your tummy starts to rumble, head to the Hungry Horse Café which serves bacon and sausage baps and children's meals such as chicken nuggets, fish fingers, sausages and chips. You can also bring a picnic as there are plenty of tables dotted around outside.

Finally, the icing on the cake was the Victorian-style fairground. The rides were scaled down for young children and included a 'mini' big wheel, an octopus with a whirlwind spin, mini jets and a hand-cranked mini-roundabout. My kids adored it.

An added dimension to Greenacres is the avail-ability of on site camping (campers get free access to the farm). A great idea for those who want to try a family camping trip!

Low season: Adult and Child £5 each, under 2s free
The funfair is open at
weekends and during
school holidays. All rides
£1 per go.
Greenacres Animal Park,
Cottage Lane, Deeside,
Flintshire, Cheshire
CH5 2AZ
Tel: 01244 531147
greenacresanimalpark.co.uk

Home Farm at Tatton Park

Tucked away on the edge of the Tatton estate is this small Victorian farm. It's home principally to rare breeds, so you can brush up on your Gloucester Old Spots and your Angora Goats. What that means in practice is the most extraordinary collection of chickens clucking around your feet if you're a small child with a bag of goat food in your hand. I swear, one chicken was the size of my daughter!

We took the land train from the car park and happily spent an hour laughing at the greedy goats, patting the donkeys, admiring the pigs and playing with the chickens. The farm has been extended to include a play barn. It isn't the biggest, and only contains small pedal tractors, so I imagined it wouldn't hold much appeal. How wrong I was. They, and a dozen others, would have spent all morning careering into one another in the tight space if I hadn't prised them away.

Also relatively new is a play area with a mini activity course through the woods, a den-building zone, two mazes (one a seasonal maize maze), and an al fresco story tent (there's another story area at the farm in a barn) where stories are told (May-Sept) on Sundays. We had a ball in the woodland park, and if that wasn't enough, the walk to and from it involved stroking some pretty friendly reindeer – always a winner!

28 Oct-28 March 2013 Sat-Sun 11am-4pm, 29 March-26 Oct 2013 Tues-Sun plus Bank Holidays 12-5pm. Closed during RHS Flower Show in July. (See page 76 for full review of Tatton Park)

Adults £6, Child £4, under 4s free. Family £16.
National Trust members half price. Car parking £5
Tatton Park, Ashley Road, Knutsford,
Cheshire WA16 6QN
Tel: 01625 374400 tattonpark.org.uk

Knowsley Safari Park

Strap yourself in, gird your loins, and check your insurance policy – it's time to brave this five mile drive through big game country! Well, whilst it isn't the savannah, this park on the outskirts of Liverpool is one of the North West's major attractions.

From our experience choose your day carefully as it can be a sweltering traffic jam fraught with the danger of a child needing the toilet just as you arrive at the tigers! We went out of season and had the luxury of driving the route twice with plenty of time to linger alongside some pretty exotic creatures. Honestly, there is nothing more awe-inspiring than sitting twenty feet from a pack of lions.

That said, and anyone who has ever been

Our Amazonian Adventure: The brilliant Canoe Safari at Martin Mere.

Martin Mere Wetland

I can honestly say that this day trip was one of the highlights of my year! On arrival, the first thing my kids laid excited eyes on was the super new play area – an enormous wooden climbing frame, zip wire and water feature. We were in there for ages – thankfully there's a café hatch so you can grab a quick coffee.

After dragging the kids away, with the promise of returning, we bought bird feed from reception – £1 a bag. There are also feed-dispensing machines on the way round if you run out. Martin Mere is home to 100 species of rare and endangered ducks, geese, swans, cranes and flamingos. We ambled through, enjoying our children's delight as they watched the birds and stopped frequently to let ducks nibble grain out of their hands.

In addition to our feathered friends, you can watch otters playing and swimming in a huge beautiful glass-fronted enclosure. You can also see them being fed twice daily (11.30am and 2.30pm).

We soon set our sights on the Canoe Safari; small rowing boats which you can hire to glide around the wetlands. This is also a great spot for a picnic as there are tables, a kiosk, a smaller play area, plus the opportunity for den building. Perfect if you've got a couple of landlubbers who don't fancy the boats.

Though the literature says three in a boat, our guide was very accommodating as there were four of us (including two toddlers). After a safety briefing, we headed to our canoe, kitted out in life jackets. They even had little wooden paddles for young ones who like "helping" to row the boat. This is the perfect opportunity to recreate Swallows & Amazons. It took a bit of teamwork to row in a straight line, but we soon got the hang of it as we coasted around the mile-long reed bed circuit, along with ducks and the occasional warbler. It was absolutely brilliant. I can't recommend it highly enough.

The remainder of the day was spent wandering down walkways and alongside lakes, feeding more varieties of birds. This culminated in the Harrier hide which had amazing views. If you've got time and patience this is great, but there were some committed twitchers when we arrived, so we didn't stay long with our noisy brood!

November sees the arrival of up to 2,000 whooper swans, migrating from Iceland to spend the winter in Lancashire. This "Swan Spectacular" is unique to the North West and, being creatures of habit, they all feed every day at 3pm – quite an event!

This summer sees the opening of a new Wild Walk in the wetland habitat, perfect for little ones to mooch through the muddy meadows.

The Mere Side Café is a good stop for lunch with a wonderful view; selling hot and cold meals, and kids' sandwich boxes. And there are so many family activities at Martin Mere throughout the year, from pond dipping to Toddler Thursdays. Definitely one for your 'To Do List'!

Daily 9.30am-4.30pm (6pm in the summer)
Adult £11.80, Child £8.70, under 4s free, Family £31.60
Canoe Safari £6 per boat, Boat Tour £3 per person Easter - October half term. Binocular hire £5 (from In Focus)
WWT Martin Mere Wetland Centre, Fish Lane, Burscough, Lancashire L40 0TA Tel: 01704 895181 wwt.org.uk

The City Babies & Kids in... LOVE

Plenty of monkey business at Monkey Forest in Staffordshire.

to a safari park will agree, whilst the big cats have a definite wow factor, nothing beats the monkey enclosure. The monkeys can be avoided if you are the car polishing type – but that definitely isn't us, so in we headed and were met with mayhem and chaos, both inside and outside the car. We will never forget the unexpected appearance of a massive, highly coloured baboon's bottom on the windscreen! Though laughter did turn to tears when a monkey's head suddenly popped into view just an inch or so from our two year old's face!

Once out of the car there are still other animals to see: otters, elephants, warthogs and more, all of which can be viewed at reasonably close proximity. There are sea lions who at regular times throughout the day put on a spectacular show. And we adored the eerie walk-in bat house. You'll also discover a small but well-stocked farm with all the usual suspects, plus the odd llama and a bug house. So, all in all, animal-wise, Knowsley has it pretty well covered. As if that isn't enough fun for one day, there's also an amusement park, and a high ropes course for six-year-olds and over; both of which are an additional cost to the entrance fee.

15 Feb-30 Oct Daily 10.30am-5pm, 1 Nov-14 Feb Weekends and school holidays 10.30am-3pm (amusement rides seasonal).
Low season: Adult and Child £10 per person, under 3s free.
Peak season: Adult £16, Child £12, under 3s free.
Amusement rides £2, unlimited ride wristband £10.
Knowsley Safari Park, Prescot, Merseyside L34 4AN
Tel: 0151 430 9009 knowsleysafariexperience.co.uk

Monkey Forest at Trentham

Monkeys are great aren't they and our little monkeys (groan….!) were very excited about the prospect of walking amongst over 140 of them in a forest in Staffordshire!

Monkey Forest is home to the endangered Barbary Macques species, originally from Algeria and Morocco and now part of a very successful conservation project allowing them to roam free in this section of Trentham Estate. Following a short briefing about how you should behave (no monkey business!) a maintained pathway takes you through the forest. At first you feel slightly apprehensive; each time you hear rustling in the trees, is something about to leap out? The anticipation of all the kids around us was palpable! Who's going to spot the first monkey???!!!!

Quite used to seeing tourists, the monkeys sit and pick, roll in the grass, wiggle their bottoms at you, climb trees and generally watch you wander by. Some of the younger ones love to perform and their antics will have you giggling in no time. Then suddenly you'll hear a shriek and roar and everybody rushes to watch the older monkeys get grumpy and fight, more than likely over food. All great fun and all part of the experience.

The circular route is just under one mile, so an easy walk for all the family and I would say fine for a pram bar a few steps here and there. There are guides throughout to answer questions and every hour, a feeding session to watch. Our walk round took just over an hour.

At the end, the landscaped area has two adventure playgrounds; a centre playing a documentary film about the monkeys; picnic tables; shop and the pleasant Banana Café, selling hot meals and sandwiches, with space to sit inside and out. It's an interesting and unique place to visit though probably not a full day out so you may want to consider combining with a trip to **Trentham Gardens** (see page 77).

Open Daily Feb half term plus Sat & Sun in March 10am-4pm; 1st April-18th July 10am–5pm; 19th July-31st Aug 10am-6pm; 1st Sep-25th Oct 10am-5pm; 26th Oct-2nd November and weekends in Nov 10am-4pm. Adult £7.50, Child £5.50, under 3s free.

Trentham Monkey Forest, Trentham Estate - Southern Entrance, Stone Road, Trentham, Staffordshire ST4 8AY Tel: 01782 659845 monkey-forest.com

Reddish Vale Farm

For the under-fives, Reddish Vale is the perfect farm. Because of its small size it feels secure – nobody can wander off and get lost. And this is why I like it so much.

There are plenty of farmyard animals – ducks, pigs, horses, sheep, donkeys and goats; plus a lovely petting area with guinea pigs and rabbits. All the animals are easy to see. They even have low windows in the pigsty, and buckets of carrots to feed the animals are 50p. If you want to give the kids a workout then there is a bouncy castle and slide, also 50p. Plus there is a selection of free ride-on tractors and trailers. On Sundays from 1-3pm there are pony rides for £2.

The tearooms are open every weekend throughout the year, and daily in the school holidays. Children's meals start from £2.50 for a burger, nuggets or a hot dog and chips.

Farm: 15 Feb-20 Apr Weekends and school holidays 11am-4pm; 21 Apr-1 Sep Weekends and school holidays 11am-4pm, Mon-Wed 11am-4pm, Oct & Dec Weekends 11am-4pm Adult £4, Child £3, under 3s free. Cash only.

Reddish Vale Farm, Reddish Vale Road, Reddish, Stockport SK5 7HE Tel: 0161 480 1645 reddishvalefarm.co.uk

Sea Life Manchester

The brand new Sea Life Centre in Manchester boasts over 5000 sea creatures, an underwater ocean tunnel and Europe's first seabed walk. It might not be as large as some aquariums but the exhibits are colourful, dramatic and well laid out, and my children found them fascinating.

First off you are taken in a group to 'Turtle Beach' where a guide explains the behaviour of turtles – laying eggs, hatching and scurrying to the sea – whilst you watch a visual projection of this taking place before you. It lasts about five minutes, which

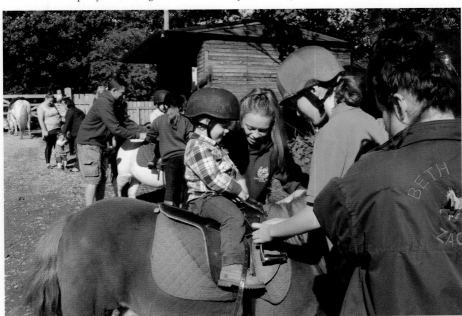

Learn to ride at Reddish Vale Farm.

was perfect to hold the interest of my nine and six-year-old. After this, you are left to wander through the exhibits at your own pace.

Children are provided with a paper diving mask and a passport to stamp in different zones. There's a prize if all nine stamps are collected. I could tell you what it is, but that would be spoiling things!

Throughout the day there are feeding times and talks where you can learn more about our fishy friends and their habitats. As there is nowhere to eat here, we popped out for lunch in the Trafford Centre. Tickets allow re-entry all day so we decided to come back to watch the stingrays feeding at 3pm. Arriving at their tank five minutes early, we found the rays animated with excitement of their anticipated lunch.

There are opportunities to touch starfish or crabs and watch fish swimming over your head; you can take part in interactive games, and even climb through a soft play area if you're small enough. At the huge main tank – home to sharks, a green turtle named Ernie and thousands of exotically-coloured fish – you could spend hours watching, from one of the large windows or the tunnel. If you are brave enough (and eight years plus) you could even get in and walk about! This seabed trek is an opportunity to spend ten minutes diving with a breathe easy helmet. This isn't included in the entry price, and must be booked in advance, but would make a super treat.

Daily 10am-7pm
Adult and Child £16.50 per person, Family £14.50 per family member, under 3s free. £8.25pp after 4pm entry. Book online up to 24hrs in advance, £12pp. Or buy a Combi ticket to Sea Life and next door's Legoland Discovery Centre.
Sea Life Manchester, Barton Square, The Trafford Centre, Manchester M17 8AS
Tel: 0871 221 2483 visitsealife.com

Smithills Open Farm

Smithills in Bolton is an impressively-stocked open farm with baas, grunts, moos and quacking deafening you from the moment you hit the car park. The main attraction is the big barn which seems to have every animal imaginable side by side. I learnt this to my cost when one of the staff asked for a volunteer to hold one of the animals. The children were beside themselves when I, expecting a cuddly bunny or something, found a twelve foot python thrust onto my lap! Snakes aside, feeding and petting the chicks, guinea pigs and lambs was great fun for all ages. Then, at the opposite end of the barn, a herd of cows trooped in for the 1pm milking parade!

Outside there are open spaces, climbing frames and pedal tractors if your kids need to let off steam, and up in the top fields you can see llamas, alpacas and deer. Donkey and tractor-trailer rides are available too at a cost of £1 each and if it's wet there are plenty of indoor attractions. Don't miss the brilliant, free bouncy assault course and the cosy café that serves cheap tasty children's meals with a smile.

Daily 10am-5pm
Adults £7, Child £6, under 2s free.
Smithills Open Farm, Smithills Dean Road, Bolton, Lancashire BL1 7NS
Tel: 01204 595765 smithillsopenfarm.co.uk

Stockley Farm

I have a huge soft spot for Stockley Farm. Having visited many times with my older boys, I was looking forward to taking my third child Ted and his best friend Ellie.

Lots of improvements have been carried out over the years but the tractor ride from the car park to the farm remains as fun as ever and the warm welcome you get at the farm has not changed either.

We started our day grooming Shetland ponies Flare and Babe. Ted looked a little nervous but Lesley, the lovely helper, soon encouraged him to have a go. Next we were taken over to the goats and each given a huge baby bottle to feed the kids – which Ted and Ellie adored. Onto pets' corner, where they both enjoyed snuggling up to the rabbits and guinea pigs. Thankfully neither could read the "Guinea pigs for sale" sign!

A quick pit stop at the café for lunch saw the children tuck into picnic boxes (£4.75) while I enjoyed a huge homemade vegetable bake. If you have brought a picnic, there are plenty of tables outside and in the barn. Here you'll also find a large hay stack and an enormous inflatable to climb on, perfect if it's raining.

The sun appeared so the little ones spent the rest of the day exploring the outside play area which includes climbing frames, an old tractor and two large sand pits, along with diggers. Our last stop was to feed the hens and the pigs with our remaining food bags – Houdini, the incredible

Bottle feeding the goats at Stockley Farm.

Look out for a green turtle named Ernie amongst the thousands of fish at Manchester's Sea Life.

escaping goat who thinks she's human, joined us for the trip and Ted and Ellie loved holding her lead.

15 Feb-2 Nov & Dec, Weekends 10am-5pm (peak), 10am-4pm (off peak), Weds 1-5pm, school holidays Daily 10am-5pm (peak), 10am-4pm (off peak)

Off peak (until Easter): Adult £8.95, Child £7.95, under 2s £1.50, Family £32. Peak: Adult £9.20, Child £8.20, under 2s £1.75, Family £33. Joint Tickets for Stockley Farm and Arley Hall & Gardens (see page 70) are available.

Stockley Farm, Arley, Northwich, Cheshire CW9 6LZ
Tel: 01565 777323 stockleyfarm.co.uk

Windmill Animal Farm

A trip to Windmill Farm is not going to disappoint. It's got everything from outdoor and indoor play areas, a train, and of course animals, including birds of prey. All the usual suspects are here, such as cows, goats, pigs, Shetland ponies, plus a favourite of mine – Shire horses. A brilliant new addition in 2012 is a wooden goat bridge linking two fields together. A great opportunity to play the part of the troll as the goats 'trip trap' overhead!

Our group of six boys dived into the enormous outdoor playground, with its huge wooden climbing frame, along with a zip wire and a big basket swing. Even in wet weather Windmill Farm is good – its indoor soft play area is the largest I've seen on a farm, plus you'll find roller racers and pedal tractors as well! There is a café on site serving the usual selection of hot and cold food.

There are a number of benches indoors and out,

and you are very welcome to bring your own picnic.

Windmill's pride and joy is its own miniature railway. Both steam and diesel engines run on the 15-inch gauge track that crosses the farm, and is more than a mile long. The train stops halfway round at Lake View and there are more picnic tables if you want to have your lunch here. To occupy the children while you wait for the next train you'll find another climbing frame.

If you've got a range of ages of children to entertain, I'd say that Windmill Farm caters for all.

Open half term (15-23 Feb) and weekends to 5 April, then Daily until Sep 10am-5pm

Adult £6, Child £5.50, under 2s free, Family £20.

The Windmill Animal Farm, Red Cat Lane, Burscough, Lancashire L40 1UQ
Tel: 01704 892282 windmillanimalfarm.co.uk

"Manchester's got everything except a beach" Ian Brown, Stone Roses

But head to the west coast and you'll find a terrific selection of beaches – perfect for a day trip.

Ainsdale Beach

On a glorious summer's day we set the satnav for Ainsdale, one of the largest areas of wild duneland left in Britain. You actually drive on to the beach to park your car, which was great fun, though I was concerned we'd get stuck! (There is a jeep going up and down pulling out any stranded vehicles!)

The refreshment van and toilets are located where you drive in. This is also the swimming area so don't drive too far! We were woefully unprepared without breakers or a picnic but thankfully we had remembered buckets and spades so the kids soon got digging.

The dunes are magnificent, and the children loved rolling down them. I don't think you'd bother with a pram round here, although nearby is the Sand Lakes Nature Trail which has access for prams and wheelchairs and takes you round a small pool. The award-winning beach at Ainsdale is stunning and we even went for a paddle. A cliché yes, but it felt like being abroad!

Beach entrance toilets open daily throughout summer, ad hoc in winter. Cars £5.
Ainsdale Beach, Shore Road, Merseyside PR8 2QU
Tel: 0151 934 2967 visitsouthport.com

Formby

This reserve is National Trust owned and includes a pine forest squirrel reserve and Formby Sands. This is uncommercialised stunning natural coastline without a pier or prom in sight. If you're heading to the reserve first, then park under the trees but if you are intending to take a Crackerjack-worthy collection onto the beach then it is better to park a little closer, and walk back to the squirrels unladen.

A short hike over grass-covered sand dunes from the car park takes you to the wild open beach of Formby Sands. The dunes are great for 'sand sliding' and the firm sand is equally as good for football as it is for making sandcastles. With its exposed position, kite-flying is popular but the wind eats its way into everything so be prepared for sand sandwiches! Even with a three-wheeler it is difficult to push a pram over the sand dunes but the squirrel reserve is very pram-friendly.

The reserve borders the dunes and is home to one of the UK's last remaining colonies of red squirrels. You can purchase bags of nuts at the entrance lodge to encourage the squirrels down from the trees. Toilets are next to the reserve, which is some distance from the beach. On a warm day there is an ice cream van and a coffee van but nowhere else to purchase refreshments so pack a picnic.

Car park: 9am-4.30pm. Cars £5.
Formby, Victoria Road, Formby, Liverpool L37 1LJ
Tel: 01704 878591 nationaltrust.org.uk

Llandudno

A good friend persuaded me that Llandudno (yes, in Wales!) was manageable in a day. As we set off in the car during half term, I was praying she would be right!

Set between the Great and Little Orme headlands, the scenery really is spectacular. The peninsula has a sweeping beach either side. The West Shore beach is rugged and quiet – I loved it! Plus, parking is free. There is a great playground and even the walk back to the car via the sand dunes took some time as they hid in the long grass playing army games.

For lunch we drove back to the centre of Llandudno, with its Victorian and Edwardian B&Bs and wide promenade. There are lots of independent cafés plus your familiar chains to choose from. After lunch we headed down to the North Shore beach where parking is pay and display. Once again the boys loved digging in the wet sand and built a dam off the slipway. The sun had disappeared by now so we thought we'd take a quick turn along the pier before heading to take the cable car to the summit of the Great Orme. With lots of rides and games to

Snuggling in the sand dunes at St Annes.

Buckets and spades on Ainsdale Beach.

spend your money on it was a struggle to get off the pier. By the time we got to the cable car the last car had just left. The views by the bottom of the lift were beautiful so I think a trip to the top would be worthwhile. There is also a dry ski slope, a toboggan run and a lovely park here. A beautiful funicular tram runs to the summit from Llandudno Victoria Station.

All in, we had a fantastic time – Llandudno has loads to offer a day tripper.

Cable Car: Easter to October 10am-6pm.
Adult £6, Child £4.
Llandudno, Conwy, Wales llandudno.com

St Annes-on-Sea

St Annes is a smaller, quieter beach resort than neighbouring Blackpool, but still has the pier and promenade, plus all the attractions that young children love at the seaside. A day trip here is a regular occurrence in our household.

We usually park in the pay and display car park by the Beach Terrace, a lovely stand-alone café with great views. It's about 500m south of the pier – ideal for a quick cup of tea before you start. Then we head along the prom towards the pier. Spoilt for choice the children begin on their favourite, the little train,

which takes a circular route around the crazy golf, taking in a tunnel along the way. From there it's onto the trampolines; or one of a number of attractions including boats and a bouncy play area, all suitable for under fives. If the tide is out, there is a purpose-built paddling pool to cool down in.

The pier is a bit tired, but full of the type of rides that small children adore. Most of them are open from Easter until the October half-term. For lunch we either return to the Beach Terrace Café or, more commonly, pack a picnic.

The beach itself is beautiful. On the north side of the pier it is bordered by sand dunes which can either be explored or used as shelter from the wind. During the summer months the tide is low during much of the day, so it is a long walk to the sea. After an afternoon spent building sandcastles on the beach, we lure the boys off with a ride on the donkeys before finally they fall asleep in the back of the car!

Beach Terrace Café: Mon-Sun 9am-dusk.
Beach Terrace Café, South Promenade (at jct with Fairhaven Road), St Annes-on-Sea FY8 1NN Tel: 01253 711167 beachterracecafe.co.uk
St Annes Pier, South Promenade, St Annes FY8 2NG

45

Airkix – an indoor skydiving simulator, is as close as you can get to flying without sprouting wings!

Attractions and Theme Parks

From roller coasters to walking the tightrope, and flying down the luge to racing your BMX at top speed – we've found plenty of exhilarating ideas to get their hearts racing.

Airkix

Probably one of the most unusual experiences we've reviewed for *Babies & Kids in the City*; here, children aged four years and upwards can fly! Airkix, an indoor skydiving simulator, is frankly as close as you get to flying without actually sprouting wings.

We were all very excited on arrival – both the spectators (mums!) and the flyers (four boys plus one dad who'd wangled his way out of work early!) You arrive an hour ahead of your flight in order to fill in the appropriate forms and to take part in a safety briefing with your instructor. Whilst waiting for the briefing, we went upstairs to the viewing area alongside the simulator – this was our first proper look at it…. wow! It's a large cylindrical wind tunnel that is clear-sided so you can see all the skydivers taking their turns. The fans are in fact at the top, well out of the way of the flight chamber – a safety net (phew!) provides a sort of 'floor' and then way below that, you can see the 'inlet contractor' where the air is drawn in at the bottom. Quite a

sight if you've not seen anything like this before.

Josh, our cheerful instructor came to go through the procedures and how everything would run – what was going to happen, correct flying positions and hand signals that you needed to try and remember in order to communicate with him when you're in the simulator.

Then, in a scene straight out of Top Gun, our four boys plus Dad donned their flying suits, helmets, goggles and ear plugs before taking their places around the wind tunnel. Josh took each person in turn: one step through the door, lean into the wind, and whoosh, you're flying horizontally five feet above the safety net. It's great fun, and perfectly safe because the instructor guides you constantly in the column of air. And until you're really capable, he won't let go of you!

All but one of our group managed to fly on their own – the one that didn't was a little overcome with the sheer noise level together with the sensation of breathing in such high-velocity wind. Josh did a brilliant job of reassuring him, and he was ready to try again when his second turn came around.

Each flight (our group had two each) lasts one minute – this might not sound a long time but to put it in perspective, on a 12,000 ft real skydive, you'd free fall on average for about 45 seconds.

In a crowning moment (for an extra fiver and only if you wish it to happen), the instructor will take you careering upwards, right to the top of the tunnel at a rate of knots as the fan is turned to full blast. Quite incredible.

Airkix is about as exhilarating as an attraction for kids can possibly be. It's an utterly unique experience and one you'll be talking about for weeks.
Daily – booking essential.

Kix-Start taster session (peak-time) £45.99. off-peak £39.99 Family Flight for 5 people: Peak-time £179.99. Off-peak £159.99. Kix-Start Super Saver (week days before 11am or term-time 4-6pm) £29.99 each.
Airkix, 9 Trafford Way, Trafford Quays Leisure Village, Manchester M41 7JA
Tel: 0845 331 6549 airkix.com

Alton Towers

The mere fact of telling the *Babies & Kids in the City* guinea pigs that we were planning a trip to Alton Towers was enough to create a frenzy of excitement. And no surprise really, it is massive; made up of 11 different zones with a collection of dizzying roller coasters, water rides that leave you dripping wet, scary houses, fun houses, the Shark-bait Reef designed by Sea Life, and new for Summer 2014 they have teamed up with the BBC to produce a CBeebies Land for little ones.

The hours spent here resulted in giggling, occasionally petrified kids and a host of soaked, dizzy adults. For my five-year-old, the Runaway Train – a fast roller coaster, was a bit like being thrown in at the deep end as he screamed with panic all the way round the ride, but he then swelled with pride in front of the older kids at the end and announced "That was epic!"

Harry the eldest child and his Mum, needing another rush of adrenalin, were both tall and brave enough for Thirteen, a roller coaster in the nearby Dark Forest Zone. Whilst they went off, the rest of us opted for nearby Hex, billed as a multi-media journey inside the legendary Towers. This proved to be a big mistake... we should have read the small print which said 'Be careful not to unearth the Curse of the Chained Oak'... it was far too frightening for our bunch and we had to bail out through an emergency exit! Cloud Cuckoo Land was a good choice for the younger ones in the group as were the Charlie and the Chocolate Ride, Driving School, Frog Hopper, and Carousel. The queues all day had been small but the queue for the Ice Age 4D cinema

experience here ate up about 45 minutes and, whilst very good, I don't think it was worth the wait.

We took the Skyride to travel around the park. This was brilliant with spectacular views. Definitely recommended. Finally, don't be overwhelmed by the scale of Alton Towers. Do your homework, decide what appeals most and throw yourself in. It may not be the cheapest of days, but it will be one that the kids beg to go back to.
Open Feb half term 10am-4pm, 22 Mar-3 Nov 2014 check website for seasonal opening times.
Adult £48, Child £40.80, Family £41.40 per person. Book online for discounts. Car park £5.
Alton Towers Resort, Alton, Staffordshire ST10 4DB
Tel: 0871 222 3330 altontowers.com

Blackpool Tower

When we make the trip to Blackpool, the landmark that raises our excitement to fever pitch, indicating that we're nearly there, is the Tower. In fact, in our car, the first person to spot the Tower wins a prize!

The first stop for us had to be a trip to the top of the 380ft tower. Before our ascent we enjoyed a short film about Blackpool, which comes complete with water spray and wind. Some children might be a little scared by this experience, but my two loved it! Then, like Charlie in *Charlie and the Chocolate Factory*, we headed skywards in a glass elevator – where we were met with breathtaking views of the piers and funfairs of Blackpool, and across the Irish Sea. If you haven't got a head for heights you might find the

I can hold Blackpool Tower! Great views from the end of the pier.

The boys loved the Total Wipeout style 'Eliminator' at Apple Jacks.

Apple Jacks Adventure Park

If you're looking for a fun outdoor venue that caters for children across a range of ages, then I recommend you try Apple Jacks. We rocked up mid-morning on a beautiful sunny day in half term.

The older boys spied The Eliminator immediately, a tall inflatable with a giant swinging inflatable ball; the idea being to knock your opponents off their perch. They thought this was just brilliant. The best moment was when four-year-old Ted insisted on getting up and having a go with the big boys...and managed to stay on, bless him!

The enormous Bouncy Pillow (a 40-foot-long yellow rubber inflatable) beckoned next. The kids all spent ages on here whilst we basked in the sun on adjacent benches. Jack's Ball Blast was a big hit – literally! You shoot sponge balls out of Nerf-style guns at your friends...and then duck as they fire back. From there we took in roller-skating (outside), archery, a tractor ride, Go Karts, Quad Karts (£1 extra a go), and a spot of pig racing! There's also a huge adventure playground, complete with sandpit, which all the kids enjoyed. Every year, from July onwards, Apple Jacks is famous for its massive Maize Maze. Our spring-time visit was too early, so we missed out, but I've heard it's a goody. Apparently families can end up spending ages in here, searching for clues to help them escape!

It's worth mentioning that Apple Jacks is all on the flat, so dead easy for prams; and also it's not overwhelmingly big. You feel that you can pretty much see everything around you so, at certain points when our children wanted to play in different zones from each other, we could still keep an eye on them all. We'd taken along our own food and set up a picnic blanket on the field near the Go Karts. There is a café on site though and a good-looking barbecue was blazing nicely, serving up burgers and hot dogs, so next time I might take that option!

Undoubtedly, we experienced Apple Jacks at its best, a glorious day without a cloud in the sky. As the majority of the activities are outside, I'm not quite sure how you'd fare here in very wet weather, so pick a sunny day and give Apple Jacks a whirl!

Check website for up-to-date information on seasonal dates, opening times and prices.

Apple Jacks Adventure Park, Stretton Road, Warrington WA4 4NW
Tel: 01925 268495 applejacksfarm.co.uk

Ellie catches air on the enormous bouncy pillow.

glass floor a bit unnerving, otherwise it is a fantastic photo opportunity. Outside there is a guarded 360-degree balcony where you can really blow away those cobwebs.

Back down at sea level we took in the 4D cinema experience and Jungle Jim's play centre. And don't miss the circus, it's fantastic – fast paced, with plenty for grown ups and kids.

Also worth a 'quick-step' into is the Tower Ball-room. An amazing room, complete with organist in bow tie and several couples cha-chaing away – less *Strictly*, more *Come Dancing*, which was originally filmed here in the Seventies!

Entry to the top subject to weather conditions.

Check website for up-to-date information on seasonal dates, opening times, online discounts and combined tickets.

The Blackpool Tower Eye: Adult £12.95, Child £9.95. Jungle Jim's and Circus tickets are extra.

The Blackpool Tower, The Promenade, Blackpool FY1 4BJ Tel: 01253 622242 theblackpooltower.com

CBBC Interactive Tour

MediaCityUK in Salford, the stunning waterfront home of CBBC and CBeebies, is the perfect place to take your aspiring Spielberg or Helen Skelton. Recommended for chil-

dren aged six to 11-years-old, the CBBC Interactive Tour takes in a working set, a mock-up of *Newsround* and *A Question of Sport*, and the CBBC links studio.

My children loved taking turns as a presenter, reading from the autocue, and presenting the weather. And there were shrieks of delight as they played a Horrible Histories game, particularly when they pulled a brain out of a mummy!

My friend was lucky enough to see the *Blue Peter* working set on her visit. On our tour however, the *Citizen Khan* set was assigned to us – not a show my kids have ever watched. Still, they found it interesting to see all the different rooms laid out, the lighting rigs, cameras and props.

A fascinating part of the 90 minute tour was an insight into radio drama production, and how they create sound effects for radio. We learned how to make the rustle of leaves, the sound of horses' hooves and how to produce a vomiting noise using a hot water bottle! The highlight for me though, was the dead room. Lined with pointed foam, to deaden echoes and eliminate all sound, I could definitely do with one of these in the back of my car!

The tour guides were young and bubbly, and really connected with the kids. Don't forget to take your camera as there are loads of photo opportuni-

Harry fishes around for the brain on a Horrible History mummy on the CBBC Tour.

ties. And remember to visit the Blue Peter garden afterwards, with its bronze statue of Petra. (But avoid reminiscing about the dog, you'll only show your age!)

Tours take place Mon-Weds and weekends. Booking is essential. Adult £9, Child £6, Family £26.50. under 6's not admitted.

BBC, MediaCityUK, Salford M50 2EQ
Tel: 0370 9011227
bbc.co.uk/showsandtours

Cheshire Farm Ice Cream

The farm is situated near Tattenhall and we drove down deserted country lanes anticipating a quiet day. How wrong we were – we turned the corner to face a large grassy car park with well over 100 cars already parked up! There is loads to do here and, apart from the indoor soft play which was very busy, everywhere else was absolutely fine.

Outside, under threes will be entertained by a wooden play area which is a small version of a larger one for older kids. You'll also find mini golf, quad bikes and a gold panning area that cost £1 each. Once you've had a play, there's a viewing area to watch the cows getting milked (every day at 3pm) and a model cow on which the children can practise milking.

As you move inside to the tearooms and ice cream parlour, there are all the ice cream flavours imaginable – from rhubarb and custard to sticky toffee pudding. The kids of course had theirs sprinkled with all sorts of horrible, brightly-coloured, sugary stuff!

Don't miss the small farmyard – in the barn you can get close to Shetland ponies, goats and rabbits. Outside you'll find some chickens, pigs and alpacas. All in all, a great afternoon out, just make sure you allow enough time!

Admission free, no picnics allowed. Small charge for soft play area, though free for children under 90cms. Daily 10am-5.30pm.

Cheshire Farm Ice Cream, Drumlan Hall Farm, Newton Lane, Tattenhall, Cheshire CH3 9NE
Tel: 01829 770446
cheshirefarmicecream. co.uk

OUR TOP FIVE ATTRACTIONS

Airkix
Skydiving in Manchester. Wow!

Stonerig Raceway
Fast-paced scalextric over seven incredible tracks. Every Dad's dream!

Apple Jacks
A fun outdoor venue for the whole family.

Ski Rossendale
Inspired by Jenny Jones' Olympic triumph? Try Rossendale for size.

Manley Mere
Mud, mud, glorious mud! Perfect for all kids.

Chill Factore

Let it snow, let it snow, let it snow. Particularly in mid summer! What could be better than turning your back on the tropical Manchester sunshine for a spell on the piste – nothing short of delightful. The Chill Factore is one of Britain's foremost indoor ski centres operating all year round at sub-zero temperatures with skiing, tubing (sliding down a slope in a huge rubber ring), luge, and snow play for the very little ones. The snow park is only small but with soft play penguins, sliding rubber rings and building blocks to make igloos out of, it was perfect for the allotted play period for our younger children. Personally I think any child older than five might get bored quite quickly in this section. Meanwhile, we'd taken advantage of one of Chill Factore's many enticing ski lesson offers and booked our seven and eight-year-olds into a taster session over on the beginners' slope which was a great success. We finished off our visit with a trip upstairs to the Alpine-themed restaurant, Mont Blanc, where we tucked into a very good pizza and hot chocolates.

Chill Factore is exciting, exhilarating and a giggle. Before you know it, your three-year-old will be whizzing past you, a Chemmy Alcott in the making.

Snowplay: Daily 9.30am-6.30pm. Main slope, Tubing & Sledging: Daily 9am-11pm.

Snowplay (2-10 year olds) from £6 each for 1 hour. Tubing & Sledging (4+ years), Luge (6+ years): Snowpark Pass: 1hr £20, 2hrs £25.

Trousers, jackets, socks and boots can be hired, or take your own.

It is compulsory to wear suitable gloves (you can buy them at Chill Factore). Pre-booking advised.

Chill Factore, Trafford Way, Trafford Quays Leisure Village, Manchester M41 7JA
Tel: 0843 5962233 *chillfactore.com*

Crocky Trail

The magic of the Crocky Trail is in its simplicity – and that it is just good old-fashioned fun! Run free in the playground and on the trail, get muddy and wet, and have an adventure while scaring yourself

Screams and thrills on Chill Factore's awesome luge.

just a little bit! On arrival my boys excitedly changed into wellies and waterproofs and immediately ran off towards the enormous slides and mechanical rides. Imaginatively designed, the rides in the play area are refreshingly anti-health and safety, complete with heart-in-your-mouth vertical slides and spinning barrels.

Highlights included a Surfer Slide, rocking and sliding the boys around as it moved back and forth like a huge wave; a Total Wipeout inspired beam and a roundabout with a difference, in that it spins you off at speed! When higher slides beckon, Titanic awaits; a slope that rises slowly until it is almost vertical. Stay on as long as you can – if gravity doesn't get you, the judder at the end will! Even the youngest member of our party had plenty of fun on the mini-diggers.

Lunch time was soon upon us so we grabbed our picnic from the car and as it was a drizzly day found a table in the covered area. A small café sells a selection of hot and cold drinks, lunches and ice creams.

After lunch we headed off to the trail. It is possible to negotiate a pushchair around, but if your toddler is inquisitive they won't stay in it for long, there's too much fun to be had! Starting as a well-trodden muddy path, the trail presents challenges along the way including precarious swinging rope bridges, underground tunnels, muddy pools and swings. At each obstacle we encountered groups of

muddy giggling children; muddy giggling mums too! The trail took an hour or so to complete. My eldest son declared that this was the best place he had ever been to.

We drove home completely exhausted, with the children planning a return trip! Next time we will remember to pack a change of clothes!

Summer: Daily 10am-6pm, Winter: Weekends and school holidays 10am-5pm.

Adult or Child £12, under 5s free.

Check website for discounts and family tickets.

The Crocky Trail, Cotton Abbotts, Waverton, Chester CH3 7PH

Tel: 01244 336161 crockytrail.co.uk

Getting muddy on the Crocky Trail.

51

Ride the Buffalo-coaster at Drayton Manor...if you dare!

Drayton Manor Theme Park

Once the home of Sir Robert Peel, Drayton Manor is now an action-packed theme park split into six thrilling zones; together with **Thomas Land** (see page 63), perfect for those with younger children. We visited on a sunny (busy!) day in the summer holidays.

We plunged straight in at the deep end, heading for the extreme rides of Aerial Park. After queuing for over an hour (ouch!) for the Ben 10 ride I began to regret our decision, particularly when my six-year-old buckled at the last minute, refusing to get on! After this tricky start things picked up, and we were able to hop straight onto The Drunken Barrels, The Big Wheel and Apocalypse; a terrifying vertical drop ride where you feel you've left your stomach back at the top!

If you want something slightly tamer, that's guaranteed to result in howls of laughter, then Splash Canyon in Action Park is a must! Seating six people in a raft, it spins as it rides through a torrent of water. And whilst you're getting

A more sedate ride for all the family!

soaked, head for Stormforce 10, a log flume that even goes backwards for a while – just don't forget your cagoule!

Varying height restrictions apply throughout the park, they're indicated on the handy map that you're given as you go in. Be aware of these to avoid kids' disappointment after they've waited excitedly in a queue.

For lunch we managed to get a picnic table by the lake at the heart of the park. Alternatively The Grill Inn has an à la carte menu from 12pm onwards, or you could stop off in one of several cafés which offer a variety of hot dogs, pasta, chicken and pizzas.

Every good theme park has a haunted house, and Drayton doesn't disappoint. The Haunting comes complete with a simulator, making a room spin at high speed, and a finale of vampire bats rising from a grave. There was also the ubiquitous rocking pirate ship, rollercoasters of varying magnitude and speed, dodgems, a carousel, boats, a zoo, Dino trail, and much more.

My six-year-old finished off his day feeling so proud for braving the Buffalo-coaster, an easy-going rollercoaster with a few sharp bends; and my nine-year-old took his first steps onto an upside down ride, Pandemonium. It looked terrifying, but left him with a flushed face and a big smile.

Whatever the age of your children, we're sure you'll find something at Drayton Manor to delight everyone. You will go home wanting more!

29 Mar-2 Nov Daily 9.30am-5pm.
Adult £36, Child £27, 2-3 year olds £5, under 2s free. Car Park £3.
Check website for online discounts. Buggy Hire available £6 per day, nappies for sale in the toy shop.
Drayton Manor Theme Park, Tamworth, Staffordshire B78 3TW
Tel: 0844 472 1960 draytonmanor.co.uk

Diggerland

So it's a theme park where kids get to ride lots of real full-size construction machinery... no, I'm not kidding you. Diggerland claims to be the UK's most unique attraction and I think they're probably right. There are a variety of rides and often younger children need to be accompanied by an adult (wahey!) It's a fun and unusual place to bring family and friends for a day out.

From the minute you arrive, Diggerland is impressive – there are lots of different sized yellow JCBs lined up just waiting for someone to have a go. They are all static but you can move the arm and bucket around and there are levers to play with.

Other attractions include the Sky Shuttle – where a digger lifts you 50 feet into the air, Ground Shuttle where you sit in the bucket of a digger and are driven at speed around a patch of wasteland, and Spin Dizzy – an enormous digger that spins you round until you literally plead to get off! For a more sedate time, try the tractor that pulls a long line of trailers slowly around the park, or Dig-a-round – a carousel with buckets instead of seats. There are also coin-operated dodgems and a rather good indoor soft play area. The absolute favourite for our lot was driving the child-sized motorised land rovers around a road course.

the City Babies LOVE & Kids in

Foodwise, a couple of burger vans serve the usual. There are plenty of tables outside and some inside, so I'd suggest taking a picnic if you're there for the day.

We've visited in sunny and slightly wet weather and on both occasions we've not had to queue for terrible amounts of time. If you're after a theme park with a bit of wow! factor then Diggerland's definitely the one for you!

15 Feb-Nov Weekends, daily during school holidays.
Feb 10am-4pm, Mar-Nov 10am-5pm.
Adult and Child £19.95, under 3s or under 90cms free.
Check website for online discounts.
Diggerland, Willowbridge Lane, Whitwood, Castleford, West Yorkshire WF10 5NW
Tel: 0871 227 7007 diggerland.com

Gulliver's World Theme Park

Whether you are the kind of mum who revels in the highs and lows of a theme park screaming louder than any child on a roller coaster, or whether, like me, you dread the whole thing – kids love 'em and theme parks are here to stay. So when my theme park-loving friend suggested a day trip to Gulliver's World, and my children all whooped with delight; I smiled through gritted teeth and agreed to go along.

I'd say Gulliver's World is aimed at the under 10s. Parts of the park looked past their best, but my kids were certainly oblivious to this and had an absolute

Diggerland is impressive – lots of different sized JCBs ready for you to hop on and have a go!

ball; taking in the rickety wooden Antelope roller coaster, the Pirate Ship, rotating Dinosaur eggs, the carousel, dodgems, a train ride and the Log Flume.

And I think I might have found the worst theme park ride in the entire world... The Snow Toboggan! Sounds good? It's actually a large inflatable ring sliding down a big ramp on dirty carpet. The attendant kept shouting enthusiastically to "wiggle and it might go faster!" It doesn't.

There are height restrictions on many of the rides at Gulliver's World. Bear this in mind if you've got several little ones with you, most will need to ride with an adult if they're under 1.2m tall.

We'd brought a picnic and there were plenty of places outside to tuck in. There were a couple of cafés on site, but they got very busy during the lunchtime rush. They all have microwaves for bottle warming, and baby food is available too.

When we were there the ZingZillas were doing a turn on stage, but our lot were happy enough racing around planning what thrill to drag me onto next. By the end of the day, we were all exhausted and happy. For a first step into theme parks with small children, Gulliver's is ideal!

Also at Gulliver's, you'll find Splashzone – best described as soft play meets waterpark, with loud disco music thrown in for good measure. The idea is that you stay on the sidelines enjoying a drink and staying dry, while your hair goes frizzy and your children disappear into a haze of water jets and slides (there is a one metre height restriction on the larger two slides). For older or more independent children this is great, but when accompanying

younger ones you should go prepared to get wet! There is no standing water, it's constantly draining away under your feet, so you don't need to be able to swim. Adults can wear shorts and T-shirts or you can don your cossie if you want! Unfortunately you still won't be allowed on the slide.

Gullivers: Opens 15th February, check website for up-to-date information on seasonal dates, opening times and online discounts. Adult and child £22.50, under 90cm free.

Splashzone: Opens 6th February, check website for up-to-date information on seasonal dates and opening times. Booking is essential and is for a two hour time slot.

Adult £2.50, Child over 90cm £5.95, Child under 90cm £3.95.

Gulliver's World, Warrington WA5 9YZ
Tel: 01925 444888 Splashzone Tel: 01925 230088
gulliversfun.co.uk

Hathersage Pool

It's a shame that old-fashioned lidos are a thing of the past as a trip to Hathersage open air pool is absolutely wonderful. It's great to be swimming outside, and with stunning views of the surrounding Peak District to boot. The water is kept at a very warm 28 degrees centigrade and you'll find a grassed area to lay out your towels. If you need shade, there is a covered veranda and even an old-fashioned bandstand.

There are two swimming sessions a day if you're not a pass holder, so it's best to get there early as entry numbers are limited. It does mean the possibility of long queues, but also ensures the pool doesn't get too crowded.

Access to the poolside is via about 20 steps and

Who needs the Med when you've got Hathersage open air pool?

Chasing the baddies in Forest Pursuit at Legoland.

there is no lift so be aware of this if you're taking a pushchair. Excellent separate changing rooms are available for men and women, together with a family changing room with baby changing facilities. You'll also find outside hot showers by the pool.

A nice touch is the Pool Café, where you can buy a take-away and eat by the pool. Hot food, including portions of chips, drinks, ice creams and sweets are available all day. An aqua fun session is held a couple of times a week at no extra charge with a variety of floats and pool toys.

Adult £6, Child £3, Family £16. Pay and display car park. Apr-Sep times vary, check website for details.
Hathersage Swimming Pool, Oddfellows Road, Hathersage, Hope Valley S32 1DU
Tel: 01433 650843 hathersageswimmingpool.co.uk

Legoland Discovery

Arriving at Legoland Discovery is like jumping into a big box of Lego. You walk in via Lego statues and into a lift where you're met by Professor Brick-a-Brack! The professor introduces the kids to the wonders of Lego and asks a couple of youngsters to pull a lever or two and out pops a Lego brick.

From there it was Kingdom Quest, a five-minute journey with mounted laser guns where you can shoot skeletons and trolls and rescue the princess. The kids loved this and wanted to get straight back on. Eventually we made it to Miniland, a model of famous local sights like Blackpool Tower, Old Trafford and Chester Races. However, this couldn't compete for my boys' attention as they were drawn to an enormous Lego pit alongside a soft play climbing frame with slide.

You'll find a super race track where you can design and build your own car and then test it out on the track. We were at this one for ages as you can imagine. They also had a master model builder class which was interesting for older children.

Forest Pursuit is a popular driving adventure for children aged four plus, where they get to chase

baddies and ride their own police car (bit slow!) around a themed track. It got a big thumbs up from us, as did Merlin's Apprentice, a circular spinning ride in the air. The highlight for us though was the 4D cinema where we were buffeted by the effects of rain, lightning and even snow during a short Lego character action film.

All in all, my kids had a great time and are desperate to go back – however I was surprised at how small the whole indoor centre was, given the cost of entry. There's no doubting the quality of what's there, but I would say that you're talking about no more than a couple of hours entertainment.

Daily 10am-7pm, last admission 5pm.
Adult or Child £16.95, under 2s free. Check website for online discounts. Café on site.
Legoland Discovery Centre, Barton Square, The Trafford Centre, Manchester M17 8AS
Tel: 0844 844887 legolanddiscoverycentre.co.uk

Madame Tussauds

It was approximately 24 years ago that I last visited Madame Tussauds. It was in London with my parents but I vividly remember loving it, in fact I still have a slightly yellowing photo of myself and 'Manuel' of *Fawlty Towers* fame. This time, my boys and partner were strangely less keen about going than me but I assured them they would love it.

My boys are eight and five, so the right age to recognise the celebrities. The attraction took us on a walking route through different genres. It started with an opportunity to sit on the *X Factor* panel alongside Louis Walsh and Simon Cowell, then do sit ups in the England dressing room with David Beckham, and a little later, a walk across Abbey Road with The Beatles. None of the waxworks are behind barriers or glass so you can get up-close and personal with them. It's amusing comparing your hand or nose size with Cheryl Cole or Lady Gaga and you can take as long as you like doing so. Dotted around are activities for children and adults alike such as the 'I'm a Celebrity' challenge, golf-putting with Tiger Woods, a mirror maze and games

Ollie's the new judge on X Factor!

True Blue fan Sam relaxes in the hospitality chairs at the Etihad Stadium.

against the clock – all of which my boys found fun and engaging.

Whilst the attraction is housed over several levels, the staff can arrange to transport you from floor to floor by lift, so a buggy could be taken round.

We allowed two hours for our visit, which was about right and whilst you could stay for longer, it's probably not a full day's activity. Nearby are Sea Life and **Blackpool Tower** (see page 47) so you could combine your visit with one of those or just take a stroll down the prom.

Daily from 10am. Check website for up-to-date information on seasonal closing times and online discounts.
Adult £15.95, Child £12.95, Family £48.
Madame Tussauds, 89 Promenade, Blackpool FY1 5AA
Tel: 0871 282 9200 madametussauds.com

Manchester City Stadium Tour

As we entered through the main doors of the Colin Bell stand, we just knew that we were in for a treat. And the Manchester City Stadium Tour doesn't disappoint – even if you're not a true blue!

Our host Paul was very enthusiastic and knowledgeable. For example, did you know the stadium sits on the former Bradford Colliery? Or that the three lines on the City badge represent the three rivers running through Manchester? No? Me neither!

Our tour started in the chairman's lounge, where VIPs are wined and dined before watching the match from heated luxury leather seats in the stadium. I'm sure I could get used to this level of comfort! And, for the benefit of those who prefer to stay in the lounge, I have never seen so many TVs to watch the footy on in one room.

We then headed downstairs to the players' warm up room with bikes, weights and mats; plus a mini football net for the crossbar challenge. This is where children get the opportunity to show off their skills, chipping a football onto the crossbar. Next door is the home changing room, complete with players' shirts; there's a fab photo opportunity to be had here, sitting in your hero's chair.

A recording of the crowd noise, from the legendary game in May 2012 when City won the league, is played in the tunnel as you walk out onto the pitch. You get that little tingle down your spine as you begin to dream! And in the technical area alongside the pitch, I had a real sense of what the atmosphere would be like when the 50,000-seater stadium is packed full of fans.

In the press room we posed in the manager's chair, holding an important press conference, whilst watching ourselves on the TV monitors! You can take photos everywhere, and we weren't ever rushed.

A tour of the Etihad Stadium is great for football fanatics, young and old. There's plenty of free parking on site and the tour is accessible to pushchairs. There's an outdoor picnic area by the club shop and a café in the nearby National Squash Centre (open weekdays and for weekend tournaments).

Stadium & Club Tour Adult £14, Child £10, under 4s free
Mon-Sat 10.30am-3.30pm Sun 10.30am-3pm
Manchester City FC, Etihad Stadium, Sport City,
Manchester M11 3FF
Tel: 0161 444 1894 mcfc.co.uk

Manchester United Museum & Tour

If you're a Manchester United fan, then this is an absolute must of course. If you're a football fan but the Reds aren't your team, then this is still a great tour. We revisited following the unveiling of the new colossal bronze statue of Sir Alex Ferguson, which is positioned by the stand of the same name and conveniently the museum and tour entrance.

First off is the museum. You're advised to arrive an hour and a half before your tour so you can really do it justice. Split over three floors, it covers every detail of the club's history; from the Busby Babes to Juan Mata. We spent most of our time in the trophy room which, as you can imagine, is pretty big!

The 70-minute tour starts off in the stadium and you can't fail to be impressed. As we emerged from the players' tunnel, we could easily imagine how fantastic it must feel to walk onto the pitch with 76,000 spectators cheering. United have been playing at Old Trafford since 1910 and the old players' tunnel is the only part remaining of the original stadium, the rest was flattened in World War II. There's also the opportunity to sit in David Moyes' seat; although when we tried it, the under-floor heating hadn't been switched on!

Down to the wood-panelled dressing room: the star attraction here is finding your favourite player's shirt, hanging where they changed at their last match. A great photo opportunity, particularly for mums who had a schoolgirl crush on Giggsy!

Time it right, and you can have lunch or a coffee in the Red Café following the tour. You may find yourselves swapping chairs to find your favourite

Brothers Ollie and Felix are huge Reds, yet remain good friends with Sam (opposite)!

seat, as they all have a player's name on them. A Little Devil's meal, such as Rooney's Ravioli, was reasonably priced at £5. Alternatively, if you are planning to eat, it is worth knowing you can book the Old Trafford Experience; a combination package of a tour and a meal in the café (£18 for juniors, £25 for adults, under fives go free).

If you want to make a day of it, book the Leisure Cruise Tour. A canal boat collects you from Castlefield Basin in the city centre at 9am, taking you through Media City to Old Trafford, where you depart for the Museum and Tour; before heading back to Castlefield at 3pm. Advance booking only, it is recommended for older children.

Daily (except weekend match days) 9.30am-5pm.
Museum only: Adult £11, Child £8.50, Family of 4 £36,
under 5s free. Museum and Tour: Adult £18, Child £12,
Family of 4 £54, under 5s free.
Manchester United, Sir Matt Busby Way, Old Trafford,
Manchester M16 0RA
Tel: 0161 868 8000 manutd.com

Clever friends took their wetsuits to Manley Mere!

Manley Mere

Are you stuck for something to do in the holidays? Are your children going stir crazy? Is the day grey? Is it raining? Then try out Manley Mere Adventure Trail, where you will have fun getting soaked and filthy whatever the weather! Take wellies. Take clothes that you don't mind getting dirty beyond hope. And take a towel, spare clothes and spare shoes – and a bin bag to pile the dirties in.

On arrival we ate our picnic overlooking a rather lovely sailing lake (they run holiday courses in watersports such as sailing and windsurfing) while the children played on a rustic wooden climbing frame. So far so clean! Once you set off on the adventure trail, however, it all starts to get very messy! Early on, I gave up trying to keep mine dry as they repeatedly jumped into muddy ponds with such delight.

The adventure trail is 1.5 miles long, with obstacles en route through woodland and over streams. Around each challenge there is a pathway offering the option to simply walk past, making the trail suitable even for cautious little ones. An all-terrain pushchair would have negotiated the trail no problem. Highlights included a seat on one end of a see-saw which you can drag over a muddy pond, eventually dropping its victim in, and the zip wire which passes across a stretch of muddy water.

At the end of the trail there is a cold water hose to spray the children down. At this point my boys became water-shy and decided that they would just dry off and have a warm shower back at home!

We popped into the Chameleon Café, by the car park, for a warming hot chocolate. There was a good selection of food on offer: paninis, toasties and pasta dishes, and children's meals were priced around £4. The **Travellers Rest** (see page 106) is only a five minute drive away if you want something more substantial.

This is a fantastic day out, appealing to all ages, so take some mud-loving friends with you! It's definitely on our list of things to do again next summer holidays.

Summer: Daily 10am-6pm, Winter: Thurs-Mon 10am-5pm. Adult or Child £8, under 5s free. Car park £2.
Manley Mere Sail Sports and Adventure Trail, Manley Lane, Manley, Frodsham WA6 0PE
Tel: 01928 740243 manleymere.co.uk

National Cycling Centre

Wow – what amazing facilities we have on our doorstep. The Centre has a velodrome that regularly plays host to major championships and a brilliant BMX Track.

I took my boys to the BMX Track, on an under 16s starter session in the summer holidays. With a starting age of five, you need to be able to ride standing up, the gradients are pretty steep, and if you fall off it really hurts! Wearing long trousers, a long-sleeved top and sturdy shoes, they were fully kitted up with pads and a helmet, then measured for a bike. After a safety briefing you start by cycling on the flat, getting used to the bike. Harry loved it and was soon flying off round the dirt track. Sam is a less confident rider, but the coach was brilliant and really encouraging. By the end of the session Harry was starting from the raised start ramp, a thrilling drop down to the main track. For Sam we'll be back next year for another go – if I've not put him off for life!

For those with little ones they run fab strider sessions on balance bikes twice a week. It's aimed at two to five-year-olds and no experience is needed as there are loads of coaches on hand to help.

On the back of our successful visit, when friends came to stay with teenage boys, both keen cyclists, we took the opportunity to book them onto a starter session (from nine years plus) at the Velodrome. Again, after being measured for a racing bike you get a full safety briefing – there are no brakes, you only pedal forward, and your feet are strapped in! The boys had a great time attempting to be the next Sir Chris Hoy and got pretty competitive trying to get higher and higher up the banks on each lap, and then speeding down the straights. For parents, watching at the top of the bank, it's pretty hairy!

Wow! The BMX track is brilliant and right on our doorstep. If you fall off though, it really hurts!

New in 2013, the Clayton Vale 12km mountain bike trail has graded trails, from easy to severe. They start at the centre, where there is a skills zone so you can practise your moves if you're not sure what level to attempt. Riding the trail is free, or you can book taster courses to get you going.

Before your first session, you'll need to register in advance. It's free and you can download a form online.
BMX Starter Session: Adult £6, Child £4 plus bike hire of £2. Strider Session £3. Velodrome Taster Session: Adult £11, Child £8.60 includes bike hire. MTB Taster: Adult £10.50, Child £7.50 includes bike hire
The National Cycling Centre, Stuart Street, Manchester M11 4DQ
Tel: 0161 223 2244
nationalcyclingcentre.com

Nickelodeon Land

If your kids are fans of Linny, Tuck & Ming-Ming (too), Dora the Explorer, Diego and the wonderful SpongeBob Squarepants, then the arrival of Nickelodeon Land will have them squealing with delight.

This six acre colourful site within the Pleasure Beach has 12 rides themed according to your favourite characters. It is possible to combine this part of the park with a visit to the main Pleasure Beach. You can also buy wristbands for Nickelodeon Land only. Our boys were irrepressible, heading straight to SpongeBob's Splash Bash where they took huge delight in manning the onboard water guns. All of us were soaked within an instant, a fact which thrilled the boys.

Fortunately, getting dry was as much fun as getting wet: we all stood in front of a large dryer, limbs outstretched.

Next up was Dora's World Voyage which delighted Felix so much, he went around the world three times in succession.

This was followed by Avatar's Airbender – spinning and soaring through the air on a giant disk, and the Blue Flyer – a roller coaster they could ride unaccompanied. The Rugrats Lost River is a fun flume ride where you look for the Temple of Spoon.

Nickelodeon Land was a real hit for our boys. They spent the day running from one ride to another, only pausing when they spotted a Nick character off the telly... SpongeBob being the star

YOU MUST BE AT LEAST THIS TALL TO RIDE

59

attraction. The park is just the right size for younger kids. We were able to do everything in a day, including multiple trips on favourite rides, and have a pretty decent lunch in the Big Pizza Kitchen.

Opens from 8 Feb 2014 weekends 11.30am-5pm.
Daily from 29 Mar-3 Nov 2013. Check website for up-to-date information on seasonal opening times and online discounts.
Pleasure Beach & Nickelodeon Land: Adult wristband £29.99, Junior wristband £26.99, Family wristband £70.50, free for under 2s if they don't ride.
Nickelodeon Land, Blackpool Pleasure Beach, 525 Ocean Boulevard, Blackpool, Lancashire FY4 1EZ
Tel: 0871 222 1234 nick.co.uk/nickelodeonland

Red House Farm

Red House Farm gives you the option to have lunch in the country, buy some delicious local produce from the farm shop and entertain your children as well. There is a courtyard complete with small play area, a sand pit, motorised diggers (£1) and a number of rabbits and chickens, all great for younger children within view of the award-winning tea room.

In the summer months there is a Maize Maze, which my eldest son and I tried out. We were given a flag (to denote our position), a map, and a themed competition sheet to complete as we made our way round. Red House Farm changes the maze design

annually based on various themes; in honour of the Queen, we experienced a Jubilee maze. It took an hour to complete. It was slightly muddy in parts but would still be easy to negotiate with a pushchair.

Paying for the maze also allows free entry to numerous fun activities set out around a field. Oliver loved the (supervised) climbing wall. There were also pedal quad bikes, an inflatable bouncy slide, a football area and a whopping haystack. A laser quest game can be played for a further charge. Some centrally positioned picnic tables overlook these, so it is perfect for mums to set up base with a coffee whilst the children can tear around.

BBQ stall available in summer.
The courtyard area, tea rooms and shops: Daily 9.30am-5pm.
Maze & Laser Quest: July-Sept 10am-6pm. Check website for up-to-date information on seasonal times and prices.
Maze: Adult £5.95, Child £4.95, under 5s free.
Red House Farm, Red House Lane, Dunham Massey, Altrincham WA14 5RL
Tel: 0161 941 3480 redhousefarm.co.uk

Sandcastle Waterpark

This is the UK's largest indoor waterpark and it has something for everyone. As soon as you leave the changing rooms you feel like you are on holiday, with the temperature at a tropical 84 degrees! You

Armed with a red flag in case they get lost – the Maize Maze at Red House Farm.

Like me, Ski Rossendale is 40 years old. It's where I learnt to ski (in the 1980s!) and my boys love it just as much as I did.

Ski Rossendale

City Babies & Kids in the LOVE

Jenny Jones and the Bell brothers all started skiing on dry ski slopes, as did many of the skiers and snowboarders representing Great Britain. Whatever your ambitions for your children, whether you're hoping for a future champ, getting ski-fit for a forthcoming holiday, or simply trying out a new sport, you are bound to have fun at Ski Rossendale.

I took my boys there, who have both skied before on snow, one Sunday afternoon. They were super excited as I explained that Ski Rossendale, also 40 years old like mummy, was where I learnt to ski! As we pulled into the car park at the foot of the main slope, they couldn't believe how big it was.

We didn't book ahead, but if you haven't skied or boarded before, you need to book a lesson before being let onto the slopes. I had brought salopettes, jackets and ski gloves; but waterproof pants over comfy trousers and a pair of thick gloves, a must on a dry slope, would be fine.

All booted and suited, the boys were advised not to go on the nursery slope which has a snow fleck surface, as it was busy with beginner lessons. Instead they were directed towards the large matted slope. A little nervous initially, once they had set off on the pommel lift there was no stopping them.

I advised that they get off midway for a few runs whilst they found their ski legs but, after doing this once, they were soon heading straight to the top with huge smiles on their faces. To make the slope faster there are small jets spraying a water mist; the boys were delighted and reported that it felt just like real skiing. With the backdrop

of the Rossendale hills, and the wind in their faces, it was easy to understand why.

After I realised they had got the hang of it, I took myself off to enjoy a hot chocolate in the mountain restaurant, complete with terraces overlooking both slopes.

As daylight disappeared and the floodlights came on, the boys discovered a third slope – the freestyle park. They were soon testing their skills here, fearlessly catching air on the smaller jumps. Next time they've set their sights on the quarter pipe!

Tues-Fri 1-9pm, Sat Morning Kids Club, Sat 1-5pm, Sun 9am-5pm. Beginners 45 mins taster lesson £10. Ski or Board session: Adult £20 for 2hrs, £30 for 4hrs; Child £15 for 2hrs, £20 for 4hrs; Family of four £55 for 2hrs, £75 for 4hrs. Includes ski, boot and helmet hire.
See classes and activities section on page 143 for ski club information.
Ski Rossendale, Haslingden Old Road, Rawtenstall,
Lancashire BB4 8RR
Tel: 01706 226457 skirossendale.co.uk

Enjoy a hot chocolate overlooking the main slope, set in the Rossendale Hills.

Make a splash at Sandcastle – the UK's largest indoor waterpark.

pay to enter whether you go on the slides or not so you may as well join in. You can even hire swimsuits and a towel so there are no excuses.

There are more than 18 slides and attractions with great names such as Typhoon Lagoon and HMS Thundersplash! Definitely worth a try is the world's longest indoor roller coaster waterslide at 250 metres called the Masterblaster – if you are brave enough and over eight years old! Note that some of the bigger rides (Hyperzone) require an additional wristband to be purchased before you ride. For younger kids there is everything from a wave pool to a pirate ship play area, lazy river, bumpy slides and several tunnels. As long as younger children sit on your knee they can also go on some of the more adult rides.

The waterpark opens at 10am and the car park next door was full by 9.30am. We parked behind the Pleasure Beach and walked round. There are lots of tables to eat lunch at and various fast-food outlets, but be prepared to queue. If you don't want to carry cash in your bikini, you can load up a wristband with virtual money when paying to enter.

So go, make a splash at Sandcastle – we were there for over six hours and had a blast!

Weekends and school holidays from 15 February 2014, and daily in Summer season from 10am. Check website for up-to-date information on seasonal times and online discounts. Adult: £13.50, Child £10.95, under 3s free (Hyperzone wristband £2.50-£6 age dependent). Lockers available.
Sandcastle Waterpark, South Beach,
Blackpool FY4 1BB
Tel: 01253 343602 sandcastle-waterpark.co.uk

Scale Models Scalextric

This is a fantastic place to come and test your once-perfectly-honed scalextric skills. After all, who isn't a big kid at heart? Set in an old spinning mill, it's a climb up the stairs or a test of faith in the rickety lift

to this fab little gem. There's an eight lane computerised scalextric track, some tea and coffee making facilities, a few snacks available, and that's about it.

Julie made us feel very welcome and soon had us on the starting grid. With an electronic start system, you're penalised if you try and jump the gun; the atmosphere soon starts to get tense. The kids were quick to figure out which car was the speediest and which lane was the easiest to race on, so desperate were they to beat their friends. There were even some professional eight-year-olds who had brought their own cars!

If you're not racing there's still plenty to do, as out-of-control drivers (usually the adults!) take corners far too quickly, and cars constantly fly off the track. In fact, as the competition hots up, suddenly yours is the most important job – getting the cars back on track and racing as fast as they possibly can!

Monday 6.30-8.30pm is family night and, although a bit late for our boys during term time, this is fine in the school holidays. They also run family fun days throughout the year (10am-3pm).

And for the champions at the end of an evening's racing, there's the chance to stand on the podium, basking in glory! Every boy racer's dream!
Mon 6.30-8.30pm Adult & Child £5 each
Scale Models, 5th Floor, Goyt Mill, Upper Hibbert Lane, Marple, Cheshire SK6 7HX
Tel: 01625 876325 scalemodels.co.uk

Stonerig Raceway

If you want some time to yourself, some much needed R&R, then send the man in your life to play scalextric at Stonerig Raceway with the kids. They will think you are the best mum ever! Run by enthusiast Gareth, Stonerig is a brilliant place, tucked away in an industrial unit near Oldham.

There are seven brilliantly-themed tracks: choose from landscapes such as Ice Mania, Crazy Valley or The Rocks. I particularly loved the overhead cable car in the Alpine Valley, and the attention to detail is amazing! We went on a weekday evening and were lucky to have the place to ourselves. But even if it gets busy at weekends, there are so many tracks to choose from that you shouldn't have to wait long for a turn.

Stonerig quickly won my three boys over (aged from four to nine years), keeping them all entertained and interested for a full hour, with no arguments! The youngest even won on the 120ft pro-track. I'd like to say his older brothers let him, but I don't think they did!

I thought the super-fast Nascar track would be their favourite, but funnily enough they loved the

A labour of love – Stonerig Raceway has seven brilliant tracks available to race on. On your marks...

smaller Crazy Valley best as they kept crashing into each other, and thought this was hilarious!

Guys are on hand to help put your cars back on the tracks when you inevitably spin off; the tracks are so big, and often mountainous, it can be hard to spot where the cars have gone! There are lap counters, false start detectors and speed gauges so you can have loads of individual races or try to beat your own personal best.

Wed 11am-6pm, Thurs-Fri 11am-7.30pm,
Sat and Sun 11am-5pm
Adult or Child Arrive and Drive 1 hour £9.50,
1.5 hours £13, 2 hours £17
Stonerig Raceway, Unit 2 Milking Green, Hartshead Street, Lees, Oldham OL4 5EE
Tel: 0161 478 2184 stonerigraceway.co.uk

Thomas Land

Having taken my eldest child for a day at Thomas Land when he was three, it seemed only fair that his younger sister should have the treat of a visit here too. And so, before she started school, I arranged the trip for June. Deliberately going on a week day in term time to avoid the crowds, I also took advantage of the well-priced "Adult & Toddler" ticket. In spite of not being a mad Thomas fan, Ellie was beside herself with anticipation about going to her first ever theme park. And when we arrived at the hallowed gates of Thomas Land, on spotting Harold the Helicopter gliding through the air, I thought she was going to pop with excitement.

Thomas Land is a relatively new attraction. The park is well-designed, clean, fabulously shiny and colourful, with the appealing faces of those familiar train engines beaming out at you everywhere. There are 12 themed rides to amuse the children including what turned out to be Ellie's favourite, The Troublesome Trucks; a 220 metre (quite nippy!) roller coaster that runs up and over Thomas Land. Generally, you'll find that you need to accompany your little ones on all the rides: I had a whale of a time! There's also Emily's Indoor Play area to discover – we happened to catch it on a very quiet moment, so the kids had a fantastic time in this huge play zone. (Note: no adults are allowed at all on the structure in here, so your child needs to be happy enough to allow you to simply watch.)

We brought along our own picnic, and grabbed some coffees from the little café which I noticed did well-priced kids' sandwich packs (£3.95). The main area of Thomas Land was rather busy at lunchtime, so we climbed aboard Percy and took the little train down to the other end of the park. There we found an empty picnic table and the brilliant Spencer adventure playground, it was almost impossible to

63

The magic of Sodor with all your favourite characters at Thomas Land.

tear the kids away from this!

We ambled back through Drayton Park Zoo (as Thomas Land is located within the vast grounds of **Drayton Manor Theme Park** (see page 52), your ticket allows you access here too). We did a quick diversion via the pretty Carousel and got wet on the water rapids of Splash Canyon, before concluding our visit with a few re-runs on the kids' favourite rides back at The Island of Sodor!

Thomas Land open: 15-23 Feb 11am-4pm,
March Weekends 10.30am-2.30pm, 29 Mar-2 Nov.
Daily 9.30am. Closes approx 5pm.
Adult £36, Child £27, Child 2-3yrs £5, under 2's free.
Adult and Toddler (under 4 years) deal available weekdays during Staffordshire term times £20. For discounts, book online in advance.
Thomas Land at Drayton Manor Theme Park, Tamworth, Staffordshire B78 3TW
Tel: 0844 472 1960 draytonmanor.co.uk

WaterWorld

If you love water slides, then this is the place for you! With more than 30 different rides, there is something for young and old alike. On first arrival, the place did feel slightly tired, but that was soon forgotten once we got stuck into the thrill of the rides.

Our two favourites were the multi-lane slide where you can race each other to the finish, and the water roller coaster with its 375ft of ups and downs. With the Black Hole Flume, Python Flume, and the Space Bowl where you plunge into deep water at the end, there is plenty to keep any adrenalin junkie child or adult amused.

Whilst our seven-year-old went off with his dad, exploring the extent of their bravery; our four-year-old enjoyed pretending to be a frog on floating lily pads, part of the park's assault course. There is also a small toddler area with gentle slides and a pirate ship with climbing nets, buckets and jets of water everywhere! We loved getting swept along and jumping waves in the beach effect wave pool. If you do get chance to relax, there's a Jacuzzi, bubble pool and lazy river ride to take advantage of. Needless to say, we had no such joy!

There's plenty of poolside seating, where many parents, armed with reading attire, watch their older children happily swimming with friends. Poolside, there is also a café selling fast food and drinks; although we ate in 'Subway' by the entrance, once we'd changed back into our clothes. There is also a small soft play area for the very young in the entrance hall and a shop selling swimming essentials. WaterWorld run an Aqua Disco (Fridays 6-9pm) where you can swim and dance in time with the music! All in all, it is a fun-filled morning or afternoon out, and a surefire hit with kids.

Open daily from 10am during peak times
Online prices Adults & Children £11.49, under 1.1m £8.49, Spectators £5.49, Family of four £40.45, Family of five £50.50
WaterWorld, Festival Park, Etruria, Hanley, Stoke-on-Trent, Staffordshire ST1 5PU
Tel: 01782 205747 waterworld.co.uk

A destination with a difference...

Somewhere you can spend the whole day come rain or shine with something for everyone to enjoy.

Children can immerse themselves in another world as they discover the many delights of our adventure play area and **'Inspiring Children To Do'** workshops.

Conveniently located next to our play area, our new Caffé Lago offers drinks, homebakes and children's lunch bags, perfect refreshments when keeping an eye on the little ones.

Visit **bents.co.uk** to find out more about our extensive programme of events.

On site at Bents, Wild Wings Birds of Prey. Fees Apply.

bents

For beautiful living

Bents Garden & Home, Warrington Road, Glazebury, Cheshire WA3 5NT. Tel: 01942 266300.
Open 7 days & Bank Holidays. Check online for seasonal opening times.

SHOP ONLINE www.bents.co.uk

Climbing Centres

Whether you're pro or just having a go, you'll be made to feel welcome at one of the brilliant climbing centres in the area.

Awesome Walls

If you want to be seriously wowed, then a trip to Awesome Walls in Stockport is a must! Based in the engine room at Pear Mill, it's the largest climbing centre in England, and it impresses as soon as you walk in!

The boys had an hour long taster session within a small group during February half term. After a warm up and traverse on the practice wall, it was time to get strapped in. The instructor took the safety aspect very seriously, actively encouraging the children to start learning to tie their own ropes. They were harnessed in and shown how to belay for someone else; thankfully, on this occasion, the instructor was always at the bottom of the rope! He was extremely supportive of those who seemed nervous of heights, and didn't push anybody beyond their limits.

The boys successfully climbed 'The Fin', a great beginners wall offering a range of heights from 6 to 9.5 metres; but for enthusiasts the 'Tall Wall' reaches the dizzying heights of 23.5 metres! I was extremely impressed at how well the kids did. If the situation had been reversed, I'm not sure how well I would have got on!

As well as parties, Awesome Walls run Little Angels Kids Club: Mondays & Fridays 6-8pm and weekends 10am-12noon. There's a mezzanine café area overlooking the climbers, where you can sit safely with a cake, a coffee, and your own feet firmly on the ground!

Mon-Fri 10am-10pm, Weekends 10am-8pm
Taster Session: Adult £19, Child £15. Little Angels Kids Club: £9.50
Awesome Walls, The Engine House, Pear Mill, Lower Bradbury Road, Stockport SK6 2BP
Tel: 0161 494 9949 awesomewalls.co.uk

Sam successfully climbs 'The Fin' at Awesome Walls.

Manchester Climbing Centre

My boys love to climb- up the bannister, along the back of the settee…they're not fussy! Manchester Climbing Centre, housed in the impressive setting of a Victorian former church, offers both taster sessions and beginner courses; so I decided it was time to channel some of my kids' energy into a family trip here.

Enthusiastically, we clad ourselves in running tights and thermal tops, and set off – looking rather like The Invincibles! Rob, our friendly instructor, kitted us out with climbing shoes and harnesses, then imparted a quick lesson in how to tie a figure of eight knot. The kids were absorbed, but I was sidetracked by the wonderful stained glass windows, until I remembered that this knot might save my life! Concentrating, and firmly attached to a rope checked by Rob, my seven-year-old headed up his first wall. Rob belayed (the technique used to anchor the climber's rope to prevent them falling) for him, promising that we would be doing this ourselves soon. First off, a climb halfway up the wall, then an abseil back down. Felix is fairly athletic and mastered this no problem, but he was unsure of heading straight to the top on his first go.

My turn arrived…I set off eagerly. Unafraid of heights, I was surprised when I felt a bit shaky three quarters of the way up. Urged on by my children and husband I reached the summit to great applause. Faintly embarrassing as we were only on the small wall, but satisfying all the same!

We moved on to something bigger, but with a kinder gradient, and this is where we learned the belay technique. Rob attached the belay device to my harness, and instructed me on technique. I saw my husband's face whiten as he realised that I would be responsible for taking the strain when he abseiled back down, or fell! I'm about half his size and there was a lot of 'walking' the rope with my hands that I needed to concentrate on. Rob taught me well, and confirmed that the belay device would be taking the strain, it was simply down to physics! (Although Rob actually held the end of the rope too, just in case!) For the boys he used a method which gave them less responsibility, again holding their rope for good measure.

Climbing in pairs we raced to the top and everybody made it up to the dizzying heights of the vaulted ceiling. Everybody except me. I thought I'd save the glory for next time!

Mon-Fri 10am-10pm, Sat & Sun 10am-6pm
Taster Session: £15 per person for one hour if booked in a group of 4, Kids Club £8 per session.
Manchester Climbing Centre, St Benedicts Church, Bennett Street, Manchester M12 5ND
Tel: 0161 230 7006 manchesterclimbingcentre.com

Manchester Climbing Centre is set in a former church with a café overlooking the enormous climbing walls.

Rock Over Climbing

If you fancy a go at rock climbing with the kids but you're not sure about heights, ropes and harnesses, then Rock Over Climbing is a brilliant place to start. Technically called bouldering, there are no ropes involved; the floor is fully cushioned throughout so no problems if you fall or jump off the wall as you never get too high. Sam hates heights so this place proved to be ideal!

We went for a family induction over the holidays and, after being kitted out with climbing shoes, we were soon traversing the practice wall. The instructor recommended 15 minutes warm up for the oldies or we'd soon be feeling it in our arms. He wasn't wrong! My first thoughts were that it didn't look too hard, but how wrong I was and, despite sticking to the beginner climbs, my legs just don't stretch that far!

An hour later we were left to our own devices, Sam and I enjoying a steady climb at our own pace. Meanwhile Harry loves anything extreme and was soon off, climbing an overhang.

Upstairs there's a newly-designed kids' play area with slides, mini walls and more toys than you can imagine – this place is great. It's also perfect if you want to climb while your kids take a break, as there is no time limit on your visit. Harry enjoyed it so much we went back on Sunday to the kids' climbing club session which was excellent, and very well run. There are three clubs aimed at different ages of children, all fast-paced and fun, plus they run loads of outdoor climbing trips over the school holidays

Once here, families seem to be in no hurry to leave and, with tea and cake available, plus an amazing log burner, I can see why!

Mon-Fri 12-10pm, Weekends 10am-10pm
Non-Members: Adult £9, Child £5.50, under 5s £3
Rock Over Climbing, Clarence Hat Works, 45 Julia Street, Manchester M3 1LN
Tel: 0161 288 1218 rockoverclimbing.co.uk

Bouldering at Rock Over Climbing requires no harnesses or belaying.

Castles and Ruins

Step back in time and let your imagination run free as you explore castles and ruins dating back to medieval times. If only these ancient buildings could speak, what a tale they would tell.

Beeston Castle

The once mighty Beeston Castle now lies in ruins at the top of a hill in the rolling Cheshire countryside. In its day this was a royal castle, most famous as the site from which Richard II embarked on his Irish campaigns of 1399. Legend has it that Richard left 200,000 gold and silver marks at the castle that were never reclaimed. So keep your eyes peeled as they're rumoured never to have left the site!

The entry staff at the base of the hill will provide a choice of walking routes up to the keep; plus you can circumnavigate the base and take in the sandstone caves, allegedly home to a Cheshire Dragon... sadly entrance to these is prohibited. Whilst there's not much more than the outer walls left standing, the walk up to the castle and the views on all sides are brilliant. They stretch from the Pennines in the east to the Welsh mountains in the west. Whilst there's no doubting it's a steep hill, the walk proved easily achievable for our three year old.

There's no café but hot drinks and snacks are available from the museum at the entrance or on a sunny day you might prefer to bring a picnic. All told, if you're looking for a spectacular castle visit, you might prefer some of the less dilapidated monuments listed elsewhere. However, if you want a walk with great views and a healthy dose of atmosphere and romance, Beeston's the one for you.

Check website for up-to-date information on seasonal dates and opening times.
Adult £5.90, Child £3.50, Parking £3. Admission free for English Heritage members.
Beeston Castle and Woodland Park, Chapel Lane, Beeston, Cheshire CW6 9TX
Tel: 01829 260464 english-heritage.org.uk

The boys look for treasure at Beeston Castle.

Clitheroe Castle

Towering above the charming town of Clitheroe is the 800-year-old Norman keep of Clitheroe Castle.

The keep itself is small, in fact the second smallest in Britain – but considering its age, it is pretty much intact. There are two ways up, either by climbing about 100 steep steps, or via a buggy-friendly path to the museum entrance and then approximately 10 steps. It is worth the climb, as the views of the town and surrounding Ribble Valley are breathtaking. Just below the keep is a beautifully-designed outdoor activity space that wouldn't look out of place at a French chateau. My children enjoyed listening to the pan pipes, communicating through a pair of funnels and looking into a periscope. There are several benches in this area, where we sat and ate a picnic whilst admiring the view.

After lunch we headed into the Steward's House (dating from the 1700s) and modern atrium, which together house the two-storey museum, café, shop and gallery. At the entrance to the museum the boys were delighted to be provided with activity backpacks which contained a full explorer's kit of pith helmet, magnifying glass, pencil case, clipboard and a sheet of items to spot. Key exhibits included: fossils, telling of elephants and hippos in the area; a brilliant audiovisual display presenting the castle's history; costumes ranging from lords to serfs, to try on; and an Edwardian kitchen and collector's study to explore. There are plenty of hands-on exhibits for little ones throughout.

There are 18 acres of formal gardens surrounding the castle, and we finished our visit by taking a stroll through the rose garden, down to the children's play area.

Nov-Mar Closed Wed & Thurs, Fri-Tues 12-4pm, Daily Apr-Oct 11am-4pm.
Adult £4, children free.
Clitheroe Castle Museum, Castle Hill, Clitheroe BB7 1BA
Tel: 01200 424568 lancashire.gov.uk

Norton Priory Museum & Gardens

A trip to Norton Priory this summer was a true highlight for me. These monastic ruins date back to the 1100s. Low stone walls delineate the original priory; but the beautiful arches and columns of the undercroft, once used as the storage area for the monks, remain intact.

After an informative chat with the very nice lady selling us our entrance tickets, we were all set, armed with activity sheets. Look out for the

Ringing the giant Priory bell at Norton Priory.

spectacular 14th century statue of Saint Christopher, watching over the foyer.

First off we explored the museum. Stone carvings and other excavations reveal the story of the Augustinian community who lived there; and, following the dissolution of the monasteries, Norton Priory's reincarnation as a manor house owned by the Brooke family. There were hands-on exhibits, story sacks and interactive screens. Climb the viewing tower outside for a stunning panorama and a birds-eye view of the site. There are activities up here too, including brass rubbing and jigsaws.

The kids were keen to get outside to find more of the "treasure" depicted on their trail maps. After clambering excitedly over the ruins, we followed Norton Priory's sculpture trail, a pleasant walk around extensive grounds and through woodland. We found picnic benches to eat our packed lunch by the enormous bell. Which, inevitably, the children relished ringing, a lot!

After lunch we wandered through tunnels of quince trees in the beautiful 18th century walled garden. Flowers, herbs and vegetables lined the paths, and much produce was for sale in the shop. A wildflower meadow buzzed with life. It was one of the best walled gardens I've ever visited.

The day ended with a cuppa and homemade ice creams in the Courtyard Tearoom. My

companion walked away with something a little stronger – three bottles of the famous Norton Priory Ale!

Apr-Oct Museum & Café Daily 10am-5pm, Walled Garden & Tearoom Daily 12-4pm; Nov-March Museum & Café Daily 10am-4pm, Walled Garden Closed.
Closed 24-26 Dec & 30 Dec-10 Jan.
Adult £6.75, Child £4.75, under 5s free, Family (5) £19.25.
Norton Priory Museum & Gardens, Tudor Road, Manor Park, Runcorn, Cheshire WA7 1SX (Don't use the postcode for sat-nav.)
Tel: 01928 569895 nortonpriory.org

Skipton Castle

Skipton Castle sits proudly at the top of the main street, and is heaven-sent for every little boy and girl who can't wait to get sword in hand and helmet on head.

Once through the gatehouse we headed straight into the keep, noticing the 'mason's marks' on the walls. These are the initials or symbols of the people who carved the stones. It made a good game trying to spot all the different marks throughout the castle. My eldest son even drew some in his notepad. Next was the Conduit Courtyard with its beautiful yew tree. We sat under the tree and imagined ourselves back in time. From here there are several doorways off to various parts of the castle. Pick whichever one you want as, once inside, all the rooms meet up.

We took the staircase up to the banquet hall and then on to the kitchens where, contrary to modern day building regulations, a medieval toilet overhangs the side of the castle. Sitting on this was a source of great hilarity to two young boys, particularly when they were told that they would have wiped their bottom with some moss on a stick. Next up was the watchtower, with a terrific view over the town, but the highlight had to be the dungeons, particularly when a guide switched out the lights!

Back outside there are a few benches in the castle grounds where you could eat a picnic, but sitting on the lawns is not permitted. There's no café here, but the town is full of them. You could try The Bull at Broughton, a Ribble Valley Inn which is a ten minute drive away, with a menu by Michelin-starred chef, Nigel Haworth.

Mon-Sat opens at 10am, Sun 12pm.
Mar-Sept last admission 6pm,
Oct-Feb last admission 4pm
Adults £7.30, Child £4.50,
under 5s free
Skipton Castle, Skipton,
North Yorkshire BD23 1AW
Tel: 01756 792442
skiptoncastle.co.uk

Sam and Ted getting wet under The Emperor Fountain at Chatsworth House.

Country Houses and Estates

The North West has an impressive selection of some of the country's finest stately homes. Most are imaginatively geared up to catering for children, making them fabulous places to visit.

Arley Hall & Gardens

Although this stately home is open for guided tours, the principal reason for our visits is always the gardens. They are renowned for their beauty and have a reputation as being amongst the finest in Europe. Our last visit was on one of the rare sunny days over the summer break. Three mums with six children – we packed a humongous picnic, armed the kids with a few lightsabers for charging around with when they got there, and headed down the M56.

Looking for frogs on the lily pads at Arley Hall.

You come in the back way at Arley, through the gift shop, across the cobbled courtyard, passing under the clock tower, then... you turn around and the fabulous Victorian, Jacobean-style mansion greets you. Countryside views roll out in front of the house. It's very pretty. If you turn right through the iron gate, you enter the 12-acre gardens. Situated in the gardens and surrounded by shrub roses is a little half-timbered cottage, built in the mid-19th century as a place for the family then living at Arley to enjoy afternoon tea. There are plenty of open spaces as you walk around where the children can run. If you want something a bit more rugged, there is a woodland walk on the other side of the hall, which we found manageable with prams.

Although on this occasion we'd brought our own food, we have eaten at Arley in the past and it's always been good. The restaurant is in The Tudor Barn, a terrific building which between 11am and 5pm serves a wide selection and includes a kids' menu. Outside there's also a pleasant picnic area situated round a wooden play area.

On the way out, you'll walk past the Nursery selling plants propagated from the estate's gardens and I'm sure your day will have inspired even the least horticulturally-minded mums!

Stockley Farm (see page 42) is a few minutes walk from Arley Hall so you may want to consider combining the two.

Arley Hall opens 1st March-31st Oct 2014. Check website for up-to-date opening times.
Gardens: Adult £7.50, Child £3, Family £18;
Hall & Gardens: Adult £10, Child £4, Family £25.
Joint Arley Hall & Stockley Farm tickets available.
Arley Hall & Gardens, Northwich, Cheshire CW9 6NA
Tel: 01565 777353 *arleyhallandgardens.com*

Chatsworth House

Set among 1,000 acres of Capability Brown-designed parkland on the banks of the River Derwent, the majestic descent towards Chatsworth (one of the finest stately homes in Britain...or Darcy's Pemberley, if you've been watching its most recent ITV appearance!) takes your breath away.

A walk near the roaming deer at Dunham Massey.

First stop for us was a tour of the gardens. Our knowledgeable guide told some wonderful stories, our favourite was about the Great Conservatory. Designed to be heated by underground coal tunnels, it became too costly to run during the Great War and all the plants died. The unbelievable outcome of this was an order from Duchess Evelyn Fitzmaurice to demolish the conservatory! An absolute travesty, as the glass-house had been designed by the then Head Gardener, Joseph Paxton, who went on to replicate it on a grander scale with the wonderful Crystal Palace, built for the 1851 Great Exhibition. To add insult to injury it was his grandson Charles Markham, an explosives expert, who actually blew it up! You don't have to look far from the maze to still find large shards of glass in the flower beds.

Paxton also designed and built the impressive gravity-fed Emperor Fountain in the lake – now only on half pressure as too many visitors (and guests of the Duke) got a soaking! Three-year-old Ted managed to get wet without the help of a fountain, sitting on his bottom in the water as we walked down the 24 steps of the impressive Cascade waterfall! The view of Chatsworth House from the monument overlooking the waterfall is simply stunning.

There are no signs in the gardens to 'keep off the grass' and

you are positively encouraged to explore as much of the grounds as possible, at every turn there are delightful hidden features to find.

After grabbing a picnic box lunch from the café by the house (there is a much larger café by the farm with more choice and space) it was over to the farm and adventure playground which I had saved for last. It is a brilliant aspect of Chatsworth – the farm is immaculately clean with all the usual suspects to pet, stroke and feed. My boys wanted to spend the majority of their time in the playground. As it was late in the afternoon it was starting to quieten down, but I imagine on a warm midsummer day it would be extremely busy. It is fantastic though, and one of the largest and most imaginative I've seen. From high wires, trampolines and climbing frames to water features, diggers and sand to play in – it is a child's paradise. And Chatsworth is my paradise too! I can't recommend it highly enough.

Chatsworth House opens from the 10th March until the 23rd Dec. Check website for up-to-date opening times. Park: All year round. Shops & Restaurant Daily 7 Jan-23 Dec.
Complete Ticket: Adult £19, Child £13, Family £55, or tickets are available for each separate attraction. Car: £3 Pushchairs and prams aren't allowed into the main house but they do lend out baby slings.
Chatsworth House, Bakewell, Derbyshire DE45 1PP
Tel: 01246 565300
chatsworth.org

Lyme Park has a huge wooden play area, but when you're with some friends, nothing beats your own den!

Dunham Massey

The grounds of this country estate are a stunning mix of parkland and maintained gardens. There are plenty of deer roaming free and they tend to mooch quite close so children are usually transfixed!

A moat surrounding the early Georgian house is full of ducks and swans to feed, whilst nearby, rabbits hop around. There are no steep hills and the wide paths make ideal pushchair terrain.

There's a designated picnic area close to the entrance by the main car park which is improved by its proximity to the The Log Pile – a recent addition where you'll find fallen trees and stumps to climb on. During the summer holidays there are den-making materials and a rope swing. We enjoyed tucking into our packed lunch whilst the children played for well over an hour stacking logs, making a fern canopy and simply messing about.

If you haven't brought a picnic, the self-service restaurant in the converted stables does great home-cooked food, lunch boxes for kids, and baby food. There's a large separate room just off the main dining area specifically aimed at families with highchairs and toys.

The house is well worth a look. There are front-carrying baby slings and hip-carrying infant seats available for loan. The gardens are good for all ages as there is space to roll around, a fabulous evergreen tree whose branches sweep the ground, as well as quiz sheets to take round with you. Check out the sawmill too, the giant waterwheel has been restored to full working order.

2014 sees the transformation of Dunham into Stamford Military Hospital. To mark the Centenary of the First World War – Dunham will tell the story of the convalescent hospital that treated 282 soldiers in the hall between 1917 and 1919. It promises to be a very different experience.

Also newly opened is the visitor centre, reception area, large shop and café with indoor and outside seating. It's a super design and a great enhancement. *Check website for up-to-date information on seasonal dates, opening times and prices.*

Dunham Massey, Altrincham, Cheshire WA14 4SJ
Tel: 0161 941 1025 nationaltrust.org.uk

Gawthorpe Hall

The National Trust has embarked upon a policy of ensuring family fun is an essential part of a visit to their properties. Gawthorpe Hall is no exception. We went at half-term and this grand Elizabethan stately home was host to a simple indoor quiz trail that enthralled our six-year-old. We've really noticed a difference with NT properties recently – our kids now can't get enough of them. Outside there's a formal garden together with woods to explore and the chance to spot some woodpeckers there!

A pleasant café in the stable yard serves the usual refreshments.

Grounds: Daily 8am-7pm.
House: 29 Mar-2 Nov Wed-Sun & Bank Holidays 12-5pm.
Adult: £4, Children free.
Gawthorpe Hall, Burnley Road, Padiham, near Burnley,
Lancashire BB12 8UA
Tel: 01282 771004 nationaltrust.org.uk

Lyme Park

Lyme Park is a stunning mansion house that closely resembles an extravagant Italianate palace surrounded by gardens, moorland and ancient deer park. The park is rolling countryside with loads of open space and if little legs will allow there are plenty of substantial walks.

First stop for us was Crow Wood, an enormous playscape built primarily from wood. The two huge towers, the tallest being 12 metres, had to be helicop-tered in, which is no mean feat considering the play area is on a steep slope and surrounded by mature trees! When you're ready for a break, head to the Timber Yard where you'll find a coffee shop, toilets and a plant shop. It is set by a lovely stream and pond but Lyme Park advises against playing in the water as it can be deep in parts and, because it runs off the moor, it may contain Weil's disease.

A manageable walk with younger ones is to the Cage, an old hunting lodge on a hill to the east of the approach driveway. It isn't open all the time and the route to it is not pram-friendly, but if you take the spiral staircase to the top, the views back to Manchester are fabulous. It also contains a large wooden 3D jigsaw of the Cage for children to play with, which fascinated my four-year-old.

The house itself is as beautiful as you'd imagine it to be and the Victorian garden around the house is a lovely short walk, with its roses, sunken parterre, hothouse and a reflection lake.

If you are looking for somewhere to take the children where they can run around in wonderful surroundings then Lyme Park fits the bill, and with all the slopes here it is the perfect spot to head for sledging when it snows.

Check website for up-to-date information on seasonal dates,
opening times and prices.
Lyme Park, Disley, Stockport, Cheshire SK12 2NR
Tel: 01663 762023 nationaltrust.org.uk

Quarry Bank Mill & Styal Estate

We've made it to Quarry Bank Mill twice in the last year. First we came with Grandma who isn't so steady on her feet so we opted for a look round the 18th century working cotton mill, which is very impressive. There are plenty of hands-on exhibits and the kids were enthralled by guides in traditional costumes giving demonstrations and potted histories of the mill equipment. Be warned, if you have a child who doesn't tolerate volume, when the machines start up the noise is fierce. At the bottom of the mill is the most powerful waterwheel in Europe in operation; it was hypnotic. You can't take a pram round as there are lots of narrow staircases, but shoulder seats and

The fabulous mill at Quarry Bank. The grounds and nearby walks are great for kids.

hip carriers are available for a small deposit. We finished with a visit to the child-friendly restaurant where they serve kids' lunch boxes and meals.

Our second visit was on a hot summer's day so we decided to take advantage of the extensive grounds. We ate our picnic and played football close to the cars in order to deposit our bags and other detritus once we'd finished. Then a big walk through Styal Village and down to the river. Whilst mums kept to the paths the kids scrambled along the banking, climbed on trees and fences, investigated bugs, leapt over streams and got very muddy and wet.

If you have time the Apprentice House is worth a tour. See where the young apprentices slept and lived, and even get to peer at some leeches in a jar. Your children will learn what priviledged lives they lead today!

Check website for up-to-date information on seasonal dates, opening times and prices.

Quarry Bank Mill and Styal Estate, Styal, Wilmslow, Cheshire SK9 4LA
Tel: 01625 527468 nationaltrust.org.uk

Rode Hall

Grade II listed Rode Hall and Gardens is a beautiful example of an 18th-century country house containing fine furniture and an important porcelain collection. While the Hall itself is probably not of interest to little ones, the gardens are a beautiful setting in which to while away a few hours with toddlers and children. There is a manageable walk (approximately one mile) with plenty to unearth and discover.

The busiest time of the year is February for the

February is the perfect time of year for the Snowdrop Walk at Rode Hall.

Snowdrop Walk. It is a perfect winter's walk (generally suitable for pushchairs) and you'll feel justified rewarding yourself in the tearoom afterwards.

The gardens are constantly changing throughout spring and summer. Early daffodils give way to carpets of bluebells in May. Then from mid-June the magnificent walled working kitchen garden really comes into its own. Many types of fruit and vegetables are grown here and much of the produce is used in the kitchens. Buy a jar of Kelvin's Gooseberry Chutney from the shop next to the tea room. It uses Rode's own gooseberries grown by its head gardener, world-champion gooseberry grower Kelvin Archer.

The rustic tearoom is situated alongside a cobbled courtyard. In winter a cosy fire is lit in the grate. All the soups and cakes are homemade, usually by Lady Baker Wilbraham herself, and the highlights include the flapjack, cream teas and homemade elderflower cordial. The children's menu is simple, with sandwiches or beans on toast. The hugely popular farmers' market is a day out for the whole family. There are children's activities (previously mine have enjoyed decorating biscuits and pumpkin carving), unbeatable hot sausage sandwiches and live music – plus you can buy great quality local produce while you're there!

Check website for up-to-date information on seasonal dates and opening times.
Snowdrop Walks: Feb-mid March Tues-Sun 12-4pm.
House and gardens: Adult £7, Children free.
Gardens and Snowdrop Walk: Adult £4, Children free.
Christmas: House opens for one weekend in December.
Note for the diary: Just So Festival at Rode Hall Gardens – a wonderful family festival 15-17 Aug 2014.
Rode Hall, Scholar Green, Cheshire ST7 3QP
Tel: 01270 873237 rodehall.co.uk

Speke Hall

When the devoutly Catholic Norris family built this magnificent Tudor timber-framed manor house over 400 years ago, they would never have imagined groups of children buying ice creams from a van in their garden, and running along the coastal path to watch aeroplanes land at John Lennon Airport next door. It's certainly a strange contrast!

It was a blazing hot day when we visited with friends, so we wanted to make the most of being outside. The kids, ranging in age from three to ten, spent the first hour tearing between the playground and the adjacent maze – created in 2011 by one of the world's leading maze designers. Meanwhile, mums and dads set up camp on blankets between the two, and were occasionally disturbed by rosy-faced children demanding a drink or snack.

City Babies & Kids in the LOVE

The Tudor manor house at Speke Hall was a huge hit with Ollie and his friends.

At lunch-time we headed for a little bit of shade, armed with our picnic, but there's a café on site if you've come unprepared.

With suncream reapplied, we ambled along the cool coastal path lined with blackberry bushes, perfect on a late summer's day. From here we looked on at a few Boeings coming in to land, and beyond to the glistening panoramic views of the River Mersey and North Wales. The track circled us back through woods, past a large pond, to the foot of a splendid lawn in front of the house. With plenty of space, and lots of sporty kids, we took it upon ourselves to have a ball-throwing competition. Embarrassingly, only a three-year-old threw a shorter distance than me!

We ventured into the house, which proved to be a hit! Armed with clipboards and pencils we hunted for an eavesdropper and spy holes, played on the billiard table, admired the William Morris wallpaper, dressed up as maids, and listened in raptures to tales of ghosts and priest holes from the amazing jovial and informative staff.

With time marching on we just had time to stroll through the grounds where we found borders pulsating with colour, scent and bees; a kitchen garden; an orchard and a fragrant rose garden.

Speke Hall is a really beautiful place to visit, to have fun wandering back through the ages.

Check website for up-to-date information on seasonal dates, opening times and prices.

Speke Hall, Speke, Liverpool L24 1XD
Tel: 0151 427 7231 nationaltrust.org.uk

Tatton Park

Simply driving down one of the long majestic carriageways that dissect Tatton's 1,000 acres or so of deer parkland is guaranteed to lift your spirits. You're instantly transported to a more elegant world, one where you might expect to find Hugh Bonneville lurking behind every tree... Obviously the kids in the back of the Golf quickly snapped me out of my favourite daydream!

Tatton Park has lots to offer for all ages – it's got a huge playground, a working farm, a neoclassical mansion, a Tudor Old Hall, award-winning formal gardens, parkland, farm-shop, café and usually a few small fairground rides – plenty for a day trip! On our last visit, we spent the bulk of the day exploring the gardens – hiding under tree canopies, looking for the Magic Faraway Tree! We rolled down small hills, threw pennies in fountains and played hide and seek amongst the trees. Once little legs were well and truly worn out, we took lunch at the café, though usually I prefer to bring along a picnic. A beautiful old-fashioned carousel is usually running in the cobbled courtyard just by the shops and café. Inevitably it's impossible to escape without the children having at least one ride. All of this makes Tatton a real favourite for us.

Finally, being such a large estate, Tatton plays host to a barrel-load of events throughout the year, from classical music with fireworks to country shows, right up to being the northern site for the annual RHS show, so it's worth checking the event site. There will definitely be something for you.

Check website for up-to-date information on seasonal dates and opening times.

Mansion, Gardens or Farm: Adult £6, Child £5.50, Family £16. Totally Tatton Ticket (Entry to Mansion, Gardens & Farm): Adult £11, Child £5.50, Family £27.50 (Ticket can be used on another day if one or more of Tatton Park's attractions not visited). Car: £5. National Trust members – Free entry to the house and gardens and 50% discount to the Farm.
See review of Home Farm on page 38.

Tatton Park, Knutsford, Cheshire WA16 6QN
Tel: 01625 374400 tattonpark.org.uk

Towneley Hall, Park and Gardens

I was delighted to discover Towneley Hall in Burnley. The 500-year-old hall and extensive parkland serves as a walking destination, a museum, a place to play sport, children's play space and simply somewhere to come and lunch.

On arrival, you are taken aback by the large vistas and dramatic avenues that span out from the beautiful house. The children were drawn to the large duck pond, with its jet fountain at the front. Their groans when we mentioned our intention to look round the house soon subsided as they discovered the treasure hunt for kids; the hunt for 'mice' took us through the kitchens, bedrooms and dining rooms. Also of interest was Towneley's art gallery and museum rooms complete with mummies! For lunch, try the café in the old stable. There is a full menu and plenty for kids, all at reasonable prices. Outdoor seating under parasols overlooks the hall and grounds.

We then began our exploration of the estate. After a ten minute walk towards the river down one of the avenues, we came to the children's play area, conveniently placed by the Rotunda which houses toilets, baby changing and, at busy times, a refreshment counter. We stopped here but could have continued along Deer Park Road to another pond. There is also a woodland trail, pitch and putt, football pitches, bowling green and a war memorial to explore. The highlight for us was the walled permaculture site, which contains a magical collection of eco-friendly buildings, wood carvings and allotments. With smoke emitting from the grass-covered rooftops we felt as though we'd walked into a scene from *The Hobbit*.

Hall: Sat-Wed 12-5pm, Thurs 12.30-5pm.
Adult £4, Children free. Car park 70p.
Towneley Hall, Towneley Park, Burnley BB11 3RQ
Tel: 01282 477130 towneley.org.uk

Admire the Italian gardens at Trentham before getting your shoes off for the Barefoot Walk.

Tatton Park is one of our favourites and James and Katie had a great time by the lake

Trentham Gardens & Adventure Play

There is a huge amount on offer at Trentham and my visit with a friend and our five kids barely scratched the surface! There are award-winning gardens with a Barefoot Walk, a shopping village, a **Monkey Forest** (see page 40) and Aerial Extreme high rope adventure, all within the estate. I'd been desperate to try out the children on the Barefoot Walk so we decided that our trip would simply consist of entry to the gardens together with a lunch. As it turned out, that filled the day perfectly.

You'll find the entrance at the centre of the shopping village and once through the turnstile the vast, verdant landscape of the estate stretches out. At its heart is the mile-long Capability Brown designed lake. You can take a two-mile circular lakeside walk (for little girls there's a pretty Fairy trail to follow!) and in the spring and summer there are boat rides or you can go on the miniature train that runs alongside the water's edge (£2). Adjacent, you'll find the stunning Italian Gardens – their patterned formality combined with lots of paths to run amongst intrigued the kids well enough for us to enjoy the planting.

The Italian Garden Tearoom is a modern, curved glass-fronted building with lots of indoor and outdoor seating and lovely views. Whilst we waited for the food, we were able to sit outside with coffees – the older kids enjoyed playing on the adventure playground which is right next door, complete with assault course, zip wire and young drivers' zone.

After lunch we embarked on the Barefoot Walk; for the uninitiated, you take off your shoes and socks, roll up your trousers and walk along a 1km trail of woodlands and meadows. It's suitable for all ages and the underfoot textures include bark, logs, hay, grass and pebbles, but by far everyone's favourite is the mud. Watching the anticipation on our boys' faces as they prepared to step down into the large mud bath was brilliant – the brown gloop instantly went up to the knees of some little leggies and they giggled and squealed as they squelched through. Even though the day was chilly, nothing dampened the kids' spirits as they charged through the walk once and then ran back to the start, begging to do it again. Foot showers are available at the end, but it may be advisable to have a spare set of trousers stored away!

Summer: Daily 9am-6pm. Winter: Daily 10am-3pm. The Barefoot Walk will re-open 31 March 2014.
Summer: Adult £9.25, Child £7.75, Family £32.
Winter: Adult £7, Child £5.25, Family £23.
Check the website for offers.
The Trentham Estate, Stone Road, Trentham, Stoke-on-Trent, Staffordshire ST4 8JG
Tel: 01782 646646 trentham.co.uk

Strolls and Picnics

You're never too young or old to don a pair of wellies and get out for a brisk walk or gentle dawdle. Here is a selection of our favourites... and they are all perfect for younger children.

Scrabble joined Ted on our trail round Blaze Farm.

Blaze Farm

In the Wildboarclough region on the edge of the Peak District, Blaze Farm nestles in a beautiful location. Hovis filmed their advert here in 2011 and you can absolutely see why! Blaze is a traditional dairy farm and the Hilly Billy Ice Cream sold in the little shop is made using milk from their own herd – the ice cream alone is worth making a detour for!

There aren't loads of animals to see but enough to please most toddlers; a donkey, a couple of pigs, goats, calves and a few hens. The main attraction for us was the nature trail. We enjoyed a 20 minute amble round the clearly-marked trail admiring the views accompanied, much to Ted's delight, by Scrabble the farm's cat. There is a longer trail for older children which splits off about half way round; the walk is mostly pushchair friendly but due to a stile, you will have to turn back at one point. A duck pond signals the end of the walk – don't forget the bread! You can also purchase bags of chicken feed in the shop for 20p.

There is a freshwater stream to wash your wellies before heading inside for a cup of tea and cake. The tea rooms offer a delicious-sounding menu of soup, toasties, a traditional ploughmans lunch and apple pie. The new 'Afternoon Tea' looks fab and worth popping in for! This is a lovely family-run working farm which doesn't charge an entry fee; they make money from the tea rooms and ice cream so no need for a picnic. Events run through the year, including lambing and sheep-shearing

Tues-Sun & Bank Holidays 10am-5.30pm. Admission free
Blaze Farm, Wildboarclough, Macclesfield,
Cheshire SK11 0BL
Tel: 01260 227229 blazefarm.com

Bramhall Park

Bramall Hall is a splendid black and white timber-framed manor house. It now functions as a museum with public access (available at certain times) to sixteen rooms including The Great Hall, chapel and servants' quarters. With younger children, however, it provides an inspiring backdrop for beautiful walks in the grounds and adjacent woods.

Grass terraces lead downhill to three substantial man-made ponds and a river that snakes through the grounds. There are bridges, so crossing between the sides of the river is easy and a leisurely stroll takes less than an hour. The park's full of good climbing trees and the river itself has gentle shelving banks so children can play at the water's edge – wellies are strongly recommended! It's one of my favourite places to hook up with fellow mums and toddlers as it provides the opportunity for easy ambling at a snail's pace!

We always end up in the playground which is pretty basic but again keeps the children happy. The café in the courtyard with seating inside and out is worth trying for lunch.

Pay and display car park.
Bramhall Park, Hall Road, Bramhall,
Stockport SK7 3NX
Tel: 0161 474 2020 stockport.gov.uk

Chorlton Water Park, Chorlton Ees and Sale Water Park

Chorlton Water Park is a very easy one mile walk around a lake, with flat paths that lend themselves to pushchairs or bikes. There are a couple of gentle sandy slopes down to the water, ideal for feeding the ducks or poking around in the mud with a stick.

The landscaped parkland of Bramhall Park is perfect for prams and scooters.

Cycle or walk along the River Mersey from Chorlton to Sale and grab some tea and cake at Café Ark.

Take detours off the path and you'll find black-berry bushes; and across the lake from the main entrance, over the River Mersey, you'll discover a path on your left leading to Kenworthy Woods – a secret orchard, where you can help yourself to apples, plums and pears. We made some delicious crab apple jam this year from our pickings.

If you fancy a more strenuous walk then continue along the River Mersey through Chorlton Ees to Sale Water Park. Here you can grab a coffee and snack at the fabulous **Café Ark** (see page 115). Just ask one of the many dog walkers for directions.

If you've made it to the café, you will also have found the Mersey Valley Visitor Centre. With a car park and toilets, this is an alternative starting point for exploring.

Chorlton Ees and Ivy Green are a network of mostly pram-friendly pathways, through woodland and open fields which link to Chorlton and Sale Water Park. As there are several pathways it is a case of taking your pick and having a bit of a wander. You are only a stone's throw from Beech Road where you will find a plethora of places to eat.
Toilets for Chorlton Water Park are in the car park. Baby changing in the disabled toilet.
Information desk Sat & Sun 9.30am-midday
Chorlton Water Park, Maitland Avenue, Chorlton, Manchester M21 7WH
Tel: 0161 881 5639 *merseyvalley.org.uk*

Clifton Country Park

Bound by the Manchester to Bolton railway and the M62 motorway, with a pretty lake at its heart, Clifton Country Park is an oasis of woods, meadows and ponds; a sharp contrast to its urban neighbour, Salford.

It's worth a trip here, simply to step back into the area's rich industrial heritage, as within Clifton

you'll also find the remains of the Wet Earth Colliery which dates back to 1740. In the centre of the park stands the old Gal pit, a 100 metre circular brick shaft which was used for extracting coal, access for the mine workers, and pumping out flood water.

The name of the pit comes from Galloway pony, the traditional name for pit ponies or Galloways (from the North and Scotland – now an extinct breed). There is a reconstruction of a horse gin, the structure that harnessed the horse power plus a metal Galloway. It's quite fascinating, and is certainly an unexpected surprise on your walk.

We followed a 3km trail, starting and finishing at the visitor centre, which took in the major parts of the colliery, the lake and woodland. Our two four-year-olds managed it really well, the lure of ducks to feed and a play area at the end was more than enough to keep them trotting along! The visitor centre is extremely helpful and the rangers run a Tiny Tots ramble every Friday morning.

Ellie takes a ride on the metal sculpture of a Galloway pony at Clifton Country Park.

Only five minutes drive from Ikea is Daisy Nook Country Park, in the heart of Medlock Valley.

If you fancy a quick bite to eat, **Slattery's** and **Roma** in Whitefield are a 10 minute drive away, see page 125 for details.

Visitor Centre: Thurs-Mon. Check website for times.
Clifton Country Park, Clifton House Road, Clifton, Salford M27 6NG
Tel: 0161 793 4219 salford.gov.uk/cliftoncountry

Daisy Nook Country Park

Daisy Nook Country Park is in the heart of the Medlock Valley between Oldham, Failsworth and Ashton-under-Lyne. It is quite easy to find if you follow the signs to Daisy Nook Garden Centre; and is very accessible, being only five minutes from the motorway and Ikea.

At the bottom of the hill there's a free car park; visitor centre with displays and murals; toilets with baby changing; and a friendly café, with tables inside and out, selling welcome staples such as bacon barms, toasties, cups of tea and hot Vimto. It is worth grabbing a map and a History Trail booklet to help you choose between a short stroll within the park, or one of the longer trails linking up with other areas including the Park Bridge Heritage Centre. There's also a pushchair-friendly orienteering course and the opportunity for day-fishing in one of the ponds here. Our kids loved "Tots' Lock", a barge-themed sandy play area next door to the centre. Further on into Daisy Nook, we found another play area designed for slightly older children; with log balancing, scrambling boulders, cradle swing and a slide.

Despite being so close to the M60, the park is beautiful and diverse, with woodland, lakes, canals, rivers and a meadow. Most of the walkways from the visitor centre, although nice and flat, are along unfenced waterways, so take care with young children. It is also only when you look over the edge of the path, about five minutes from the visitor centre, that you realise you're actually on the old aqueduct 80 feet above the River Medlock. In the summer, it's a great spot for paddling.

Mon-Fri 9am-4pm, Sat & Sun 9am-5pm
Daisy Nook Country Park, Stannybrook Road, Failsworth, Manchester M35 9WJ
Tel: 0161 308 3909 oldham.gov.uk

Etherow Country Park

One of Britain's first country parks, Etherow is rich with wildlife, fungi, waterways and plenty of pram-friendly routes. The visitor centre, which sells duck food, aims to be open daily 9am-5pm but they can't always man it so it's a bit potluck.

Hundreds of birds were gathered by the man-made lake at the start of the walk: pink-footed geese, swans and ducks amongst others. We took a path that led past a small garden centre and alongside the waterway through woodland. We walked over a few footbridges perfect for Pooh sticks with a couple of picnic tables overlooking the weir. The circular walk to the weir and then round the lake took just over an hour, and was very manageable for my 23-month-old, who didn't get in his pushchair once. After, we spent some time watching the sailing boats on the lake before heading to the café.

If you want something more substantial than a snack, check out the lovely **Hyde Bank Farm Tea Rooms** (see page 131).

Café: Daily Summer 10am-5pm, Winter 10am-4pm. Pay and display car park. Toilets Daily 9am-5pm

Etherow Country Park, Compstall, Stockport SK6 5JD
Tel: 0161 427 6937 stockport.gov.uk

Fletcher Moss Botanical Gardens

Whether in summer or winter, this park is beautiful. There is a sloping botanical garden that follows a small stream down to a clay pond at the bottom. If you can keep the children quiet for long enough, you can see terrapins sunbathing on the lily pads.

The gentle slopes make it great for scootering, although they do tend to shatter the peace and tranquillity as they fly down the hill! You can continue on into Stenner Wood, although often flooded in autumn, in spring it is full of bluebells and snowdrops. If you carry straight on you reach the River Mersey and Simon's Bridge.

There is a paved path that leads back to Stenner Lane, and across the road you'll find Parsonage Gardens. This is a lovely spot with rare trees and beautiful gardens. It also contains the original orchid house, which is open if the ranger is there.

The Alpine Café is a little cramped for a pushchair but there is a lovely outside seating area. If you have packed a picnic the bowling green is now a pergola garden with wooden arches and roses, making it a lovely spot.

Toilets and visitor centre below café. No baby changing. Limited parking off Millgate Lane.

Fletcher Moss Botanical Gardens, Wilmslow Road, Didsbury M20 2SW Tel: 0161 434 1877

Haigh Country Park

With a huge park and woodland plus some magnificent views towards the Welsh Hills, Haigh Country Park is worth exploring. Haigh Hall stands impressively at its heart and though this Georgian building is essentially used for weddings nowadays, it provides a beautiful focal point to the park (you can book for Sunday lunch and afternoon teas).

If you nip to the information office in the Stables Courtyard, you can pick up a History Route map. This details a 3km stroll round the grounds taking in sights such as Swan Pond where mussels were bred for dinner and the windmill once used to pump water to Haigh brewery.

My last visit was with my sister and her new baby. We enjoyed a pleasant amble with the buggy following the main drive running through the park, but for those with older children there are plenty of nature

Haigh Country Park with views to the Welsh hills.

trails and biking is clearly popular too.

We then headed back to the playgrounds. These are located close to the Stables where you'll find a couple of shops and a café.

After a lengthy stint on the swings, and with tummies rumbling, we piled into the car and drove to nearby pub **Suzannas** (see page 122) for lunch. Another lovely day at Haigh!

Pay and display car park.
Haigh Country Park, Haigh, Wigan WN2 1PE
Tel: 01942 832895 wlct.org

Hare Hill

I think one word sums up Hare Hill completely and that is...charming. I was very taken with it and thought it to be a perfect destination for families with little ones who want to stretch legs, but appreciate that little legs don't actually want to be stretched that far. Essentially it's a tranquil woodland garden, with a walled lawn complete with pergola and wire sculptures at its heart.

We dropped in over summer and were delighted to be able to play croquet and giant Jenga in this area – it felt like we'd just been parachuted into a Merchant-Ivory film. After a few tears had been spilt over the competitive element of croquet, we continued our walk round the grounds. The children amused themselves by hunting down the large, wood-carved

Felix and Dad play croquet in the delightful walled garden at Hare Hill.

hares forming a sort of sculpture trail and peeking out from all sorts of places. We enjoyed looking at the plants, and pondered whether our gardens could ever look even a teensy bit like this one....

There is no café on site, just a vending machine, but you are encouraged to bring a picnic, which we think would be just lovely.

If you're up for a bigger walk, follow the signs to nearby **Alderley Edge** (see page 90) finishing off with a fabulous lunch at **The Wizard** (see page 107).
1st Mar-2nd Nov 10-5pm. Closed Mondays except Bank Holidays. Adult £5, Child £2.50
Hare Hill, Over Alderley, Macclesfield SK10 4PY
Tel: 01625 584412 nationaltrust.org.uk

Moses Gate Country Park

Restored from an old industrial site, this beautiful 305-hectare park is a place of national scientific interest due to its unique wildlife. We parked at the bottom car park, which brings you straight in to the excellent, modern and colourful children's playground and the Rock Hall Visitor Centre.

Moses Gate is centred on three lakes, with miles of scenic parkland to take a walk in. There are pathways and seating everywhere and the area we ambled around was nice and flat, so access with a pram is easy. There's no café but plenty of well-maintained picnic areas. A good place to explore.
Community visitor centre:
Mon-Sun 8.30am-4.15pm.

Moses Gate Country Park, Rock Hall Visitor Centre, Hall Lane, Farnworth, Bolton BL4 7QN
Tel: 01204 334343

Pennington Flash Country Park

With a huge lake (the 'Flash') as its focal point, Pennington Flash is a beautiful country park and nature reserve in Leigh. Joseph Bates, British professional ice skating champion in 1902 used to practise on the Flash when it was frozen!

We started our visit with the obvious favourite, the children's playground, which everyone loved. There was sand to play in, a large net swing, toddler swings and even a metal satellite dish-style spinning ride.

We set off on what turned out to be a lovely hour-long stroll. The well-maintained paths were easy to navigate with scooters and prams and remained pretty much flat all the way around. As this is primarily a bird-watching spot, there are hides and the children enjoyed learning about what they were used for and then, of course, trying to spot some birds. Make sure you take some bread, as there are plenty of ducks to feed on the way.

It's worth combining Pennington Flash with a visit to nearby **Bents Garden Centre** and it's fabulous café and play area (see page 149).
Pay and display car park
Pennington Flash Country Park, St Helens Road, Leigh WN7 3PA
Tel: 01942 605253 wict.org/wigan/parks

A walk with Nana in Smithills Country Park.

Reddish Vale Country Park

Reddish Vale Country Park spans over 398 acres of greenbelt land along the River Tame in the heart of Stockport, linking up with the Goyt, Etherow and Saddleworth trails. The park was bequeathed £82,000 by local man, Frank Bramwell. It was for the use of the Vale and so a marvellous Memorial Trail with pathways, benches and bridges has been built around the duck ponds beneath the viaduct. This is a lovely walk with a pushchair and of course feeding the many ducks is always a winner with toddlers. If you're feeling more energetic, there are lots of walks further into the Vale.

Behind the Visitor Centre you will find a 'Grow your own Grub' community orchard and a butterfly conservation area. The Visitor Centre itself has also benefitted from the legacy and there is a well-equipped children's area with colouring, toys and activities. The staff are extremely welcoming and happy to help you plan out a walk over a cup of tea and a biscuit.

Every Thursday 10am-12noon, a toddler group meet in the visitor centre for walks and indoor activities. There are also regular bug hunts in the Vale and a monthly Art in the Park group.

If you're hungry after your walk, nearby **Ash Tea Rooms** (see page 131) makes for a lovely stop.

Visitor Centre Mon-Fri 10am-4.30pm, Sat-Sun 12-5pm
Reddish Vale, Stockport SK5 7HE (road access is only via Reddish Vale road)
Tel: 0161 477 5637 reddishvalecountrypark.co.uk

Smithills Country Park

We started with a walk around the hall's gardens; they're neither sizeable nor grand, much more country garden style, but in full bloom they're charming – totally enhanced by the backdrop of Smithills Hall.

After this we headed towards the surrounding woodland, following the shorter red-signposted route. A gravelled winding path led us down quite a steep descent to a bubbling stream then back

up again towards the car park, all beneath a huge canopy of trees. It took around 30 minutes and, bar a couple of steps, was perfectly manageable with a pushchair and two toddlers on foot. For those with kiddies in backpacks, you might want something a bit more challenging. Smithills actually comprises over 2,000 acres of woodland and grassland so I'm sure you'll find what you are looking for.

Combining a walk in this country park with a trip to the adjacent **Smithills Open Farm** (see page 42) and, if you're up to it, a tour around the magnificent medieval hall is a good way to pack a lot into a day trip to Bolton!

Smithills Hall: Wed- Fri 10am-3pm, Sun and Bank Hols 12-4pm Adult £3, Child £2, under 5s free.
Toilet facilities are in Smithills Hall.
Smithills Country Park, Smithills Dean Road, Bolton, Lancashire BL1 7NP
Tel: 01204 332812 boltonmuseums.org.uk

Tandle Hill is glorious with plenty to explore for kids – they'll love the super- long slide there!

Tandle Hill Country Park

I was lucky enough to visit Oldham's oldest country park on a sunny winter's day and, as I arrived at Tandle Hill for the first time, I was quite taken aback when confronted by the most wonderful panoramic views of Manchester and the Welsh mountains. It was quiet yet exhilarating, and the children clearly felt the same way as they charged off down the hill towards the dramatic woodlands.

They played for some time on the climbing trail which is set amongst humungous beech trees; next time, it would be great fun to bring a crowd of kids here and settle down for a picnic. After this we ran back up the hill towards the visitor centre and café where there's a second children's play area set in a giant sand-pit; with swings, a timber playhouse, and a tremendously long slide that takes you virtually all the way back down the hill you've just climbed! Will and Ellie just adored this – total giggles over the speed they managed to pick up on their way down.

At Tandle Hill there's a plentitude of walks to choose from, including an ideal two-kilometre circuit accessible with a pushchair. Once into the woods and across a small stream there is a detour along a stone path to the war memorial, which stands at the highest point in the park. The woodland opens into a clearing where there are more fantastic views across the countryside to the Pennines and the southern hills of the Peak District. There are steps back down to the path but, if you've got a pushchair or bike in tow, you'll have to go back the way you came.

If the café is closed when you visit, consider nipping into the village of Royton, a couple of minutes drive down the road, to try out the popular family-run 'Peace, Love & Cake' for coffee or lunch.

Tandle Hill is a beautiful, vast and impressive country park – I would certainly recommend you make the effort to visit, if you haven't already discovered it.

Café open most weekends and school holidays.
Tandle Hill Country Park, Tandle Hill Road, Royton, Oldham OL2 5UX
Tel: 0161 627 2608 oldham.gov.uk

Vernon Park and Woodbank Park

These two parks, set next to each other, are polar opposites yet connected by the sweeping River Goyt. Vernon Park is a beautiful heritage park set on the hillside, so pretty tough with a pushchair! It's beautifully laid out with a replica bandstand, maze and a small museum. Inside this eclectic museum, there is a charming café, serving hot drinks and toasties, with lovely seating outside overlooking the formal gardens.

Next door in Woodland Park is a huge modern play area, lots of pathways for scootering, and it's also where the Stockport Harriers are based. In the summer holidays they run loads of brilliant athletic events for children – worth looking out for. It's also one of the friendliest parks I've visited!

Baby changing in the toilets in the museum.
Vernon Park and Woodland Park, Turncroft Lane, Offerton, Stockport SK1 4AR
Tel: 0161 474 4460 stockport.gov.uk

King of the castle at Vernon Park.

Swings and Roundabouts

Thanks to funding over the last few years, a number of parks have made some great improvements to their facilities. So get out there and start playing!

The wooden pirate ship at Bruntwood Park.

Bruntwood Park

Just a few minutes from the John Lewis roundabout in Cheadle you'll find Bruntwood, personally my favourite children's play park in this area. Recently overhauled, it suits both younger and older children with highlights including a zip wire; a huge circular tunnel slide; and a new beach-themed kiddy climbing frame, complete with golden sand and seagull ride-ons. There's opportunity to feed ducks once the children have exhausted themselves here. And there's a nice café housed in the pretty, original Victorian conservatory. On hot sunny days we love hanging out in the gardens, watching the kids climb fallen trees in the nearby woods. During school holidays there's an inflatable bouncy castle.
Pay and display car park.
Bruntwood Park, Bruntwood Lane, Cheadle SK8 1HX
Tel: 0161 217 6111 stockport.gov.uk

The Carrs

This great park in Wilmslow is a brilliant summer picnic destination. There are two playgrounds, with more than enough to entertain the kids for quite some time. A big plus of this park is that it has the River Bollin running through it. Whatever the weather, it's hard to keep both little and big ones from pulling off their shoes and dipping their toes in. If you're up for a relatively easy walk, then follow the river to the end of The Carrs which takes you up to Twinnies Bridge (about 20 mins). Then it's on to **Styal Estate** (see page 73) for the hardcore walkers.
Pay and display car park.
The Carrs, Cliff Road, Wilmslow, Cheshire SK9 4AA
cheshireeast.co.uk

Heaton Park

Just four miles north of the city centre, there is lots to see and do with little ones here. There are four car parks, so look on a map before you go to work out which one's best for you.

First off we visited the Farm Centre – home to pigs, cows, sheep, rabbits and alpacas; although the animals were slightly upstaged by the tiny outside play area with its wooden tractor. Next up was the land train, which runs every day through the summer and school holidays from 11am. It takes you on a generous circuit around the park for £1 each. Heaton Park isn't short on hills, with its spectacular views over the Pennines, so the train is a perfect alternative to walking. It's easy to take a pram along as well – they have a couple of specially-adapted carriages with built-in ramps so you can just push your buggy in and sit next to it.

After lunch we hit the playgrounds – there are two large children's areas providing a range of activities for 3-14 year olds. Also worth mentioning are the rowing boats, which can be hired daily during the summer, and out of season at weekends. They cost £8.50 for up to four people for 45 minutes. Vintage tram rides operate on selected Sundays and most Bank Holidays (limited winter opening times so check first). They run along a small length of track between the depot and the lakeside (adults £1, kids 50p). During most school holidays you're likely to find a fairground alongside the boating lake.

Also at the park are Heaton Hall, a Grade I listed country house, which has temporary exhibitions in some of its lower rooms; the wildlife garden and pond; a tram museum; orangery; 18-hole 'to scale' pitch and putt; and a garden centre with a café.

If you're visiting the area then see page 124 for some great suggestions of places to eat in nearby Whitefield and Prestwich.
Farm Centre: Daily Apr-Sept 10.30am-6pm,
Weekends and Winter 10.30am-3.30pm. Café on site.
Heaton Park, Off Middleton Road, Prestwich,
Manchester M25 2SW
Tel: 0161 773 1085 heatonpark.org.uk

John Leigh Park

John Leigh Park in Altrincham had an injection of cash a few years ago and it clearly demonstrates why it is important to keep funding for parks in place. Lots of families were out enjoying the last

The City Babies LOVE Kids in

The Carrs playground is really popular – there's usually an ice cream van too which the kids love!

remaining warmth in the winter sun, indicating it is a well-used and well-liked park.

The timber play area is not enclosed and set in a wooded area, it feels very in-keeping with the parkland. There is something for all ages and some challenging pieces including a rope bridge, climbing nets, a basket swing and an extra large see-saw. There is an enclosed smaller play area for under-fives with swings, climbing frame and an aviary containing finches and cockatiels – a lovely feature.

Y... McGregor (see page 117) is just round the corner if you fancy brunch.
John Leigh Park, Oldfield Road, Altrincham WA14 4EQ Tel: 0161 912 2000 trafford.gov.uk

Longford Park

The park dates back to 1850 and still contains the historic coach house and stable buildings; unfortunately the original house built by John Rylands, the famous cotton merchant, has been flattened.

There are two children's play areas – one has been updated in recent years and comes complete with an enormous climbing boulder and a zip wire. The other playground is near Pet's Corner, with baby swings, slides and a sit-on roundabout. Pet's Corner itself is small but there are hundreds of birds to look at, together with rabbits and a goat!

The Pavilion building underwent a full refurbishment in 2012 turning it into a café – **Caffeine & Co**, which is a great addition (see page 126).
Longford Park, Edge Lane, Stretford, Manchester M32 8PX friendsoflongfordpark.org.uk

Moss Bank Park

This is a terrific public park in Bolton with much to offer families. There's a large children's playground complete with swings, climbing frame, slide and a huge sandpit. A separate adventure area, aimed at older kids, has some really fun play equipment that

Longford Park has lots to offer – playground, Pet's Corner and a great new café.

even the most moody young teen would find hard to resist! During the summer months, Moss Bank Park plays host to an assortment of funfair rides and activities like pitch and putt, plus there's a miniature railway. If you get chance, take a quick walk round the walled garden – it's quite lovely.

Moss Bank Park, Moss Bank Way, Bolton BL1 6NQ
Tel: 01204 334121 bolton.org.uk

Stamford Park

This is a lovely, big and popular park boasting a super playground suitable for children aged up to 15 years, with basket swings, zip wires and pyramid slides. There's lots more besides – a duck pond, large boating lake (which operates seven days a week during the summer) and a lovely wooded area known as The Dingle. The dancing water fountains

Walton Hall has a popular free children's zoo.

are a huge hit with the children! Stamford Park now has an aviary featuring chickens, rabbits, guinea-pigs, canaries and finches (open daily 10am-3pm). Plus a restored conservatory contains hot-house plants (perfect to duck into if you need to warm up in winter!) Finally, there's a modern pavilion housing a café and toilets. A lovely day out!

Stamford Park, Mellor Road, Stalybridge
SK15 1QR Tel: 0161 342 3348 tameside.gov.uk

Walton Hall and Gardens

There are two big areas – one for little ones, and one for over-sevens which included a zip wire. I was pleased to see the 70s rocking horse still here, with a shiny new coat of paint!

The parkland itself remains well-kept and very attractive. The children's zoo, which is free, looks in really good shape and is extremely popular. There were peacocks buzzing around, miniature potbel-lied pigs, Shetland ponies and a variety of chickens. Feeding time is 2pm in summer and 1pm in winter.

There is a small heritage centre where you'll also find a revamped café.

Pay and display car park £3.20.
Summer: Zoo Daily 10.30am-4.45pm, Café 10.30am-5pm;
Winter: Zoo Daily 10.30am-4pm, Café Weekends, Bank &
school holidays 10.30am-4.15pm
Walton Hall Gardens, Walton Lea Rd, Higher Walton,
Warrington, Cheshire WA4 6SN
Tel: 01925 601 617 waltonhallandgardens.com

Witton Park

With multiple play zones for children, pretty ponds, and large fields for ball games, this is a gem of a park in Blackburn. I visited ahead of a trip to the nearby **Clog and Billycock** pub (see page 101). The children's areas are fab with a massive assortment of tackle to have a go on: from the traditional swings and slides to the weird and wonderful huge, chunky, wooden adventure equipment in "The Wits" section. Lots of activities and classes are held at Witton.

Old Stables Tearoom and the Pavilion Café: Tues-Sun and Bank Holidays 10am-4pm.
Witton Park, Preston Old Road, Blackburn BB2 2TP
Tel: 01254 55423 visitblackburn.co.uk

Wythenshawe Park

This public park in south Manchester is set around a 16th century hall with a working community farm, a good-sized playground, horse riding and a café. There is even a horticultural centre complete with glasshouses which are fun to explore. It also has historic and ornamental woodlands, formal flower-beds and wildflower meadows.

If you've got toddlers, the small farm is great for a quick half hour. There are cows, sheep, pigs, horses and chickens – the usual suspects. You can buy freshly laid eggs here too.

Simply Cycling, a not-for-profit organisation, run

Simply Cycling in Wythenshawe Park have over 180 specialist bikes and is open to all ages and abilities.

tirelessly by volunteers, have over 180 specialist bikes that have been adapted for people of all abilities to ride. They run sessions at Wythenshawe Park called 'Wythenshawe Wheelers'. The sessions on the athletic track are open to all, very friendly and a lot of fun. They operate Tues & Fri 9.30am-3pm, Weds 9.30am-12noon and Sat 1-3pm. £2 per cyclist. Check website for more details www.simply-cycling.org

Toilets are in the stable courtyard. The hall is open for children's events and activities during school holidays.
The Courtyard Café is open at weekends only.
Wythenshawe Park, Wythenshawe Road, Manchester M23 0AB
Tel: 0161 998 2117 manchester.gov.uk

Sunday Walks

Pack your boots and flasks and head for the countryside – here is a selection of first-class walks that will delight out-of-town visitors and help you to recharge your batteries amid some awe-inspiring natural beauty. Not limited to Sundays of course!

Alderley Edge

Alderley Edge, a prominent wide red escarpment in Cheshire, never fails to cast its spell on me with the towering trees hinting at its rich folklore.

As well as good stories, Alderley Edge has some wonderful walks. We usually follow the wizard's walk, a three and a half mile route passing several landmarks featured in the legend of Merlin the wizard. Not for the faint-hearted is the 'thieves' hole' – a deep circular cave dug into the red sandstone. Elsewhere you'll find a water pump, a tiny wizard's house (a stone hut!) and a beacon marking the highest point of the Edge. Some of the paths are a bit steep – we've managed with a pushchair but you can avoid them if you wish.

An option for more able walkers is the two-hour circular route to **Hare Hill** (see page 81) which takes in some great scenery.

Alderley Edge is also a good place to bring children to play. My most recent visit involved meeting up with a few other school mums – our six-year-old boys climbed trees, became Jedi Knights, and generally entertained themselves solidly for two hours. Us mums meanwhile tried to identify landmarks in the panoramic view from Stormy Point. On a clear day you can see the hills of Derbyshire and Yorkshire with Lyme Cage prominent just in front.

For refreshments, there is a tearoom and a small enclosed wooded picnic area with tables, or alternatively you're right by **The Wizard Inn** (see page 107) if you fancy something a little stronger. There is an

information office offering family tracker packs on weekends containing maps, games and challenges. *Public toilets in the car park but no baby changing facilities. Car park 8am-5pm. Pay and display car park.*
Alderley Edge, Macclesfield Road, Nether Alderley, Cheshire SK10 4UB
Tel: 01625 584412 nationaltrust.org.uk

Beacon Fell Country Park

My sister was visiting from Australia with my two-year-old neice – a very reluctant walker! So, after quizzing friends for ideas on a good place for a gentle Sunday stroll, were recommended Beacon Fell. It is also only a half hour drive from my favourite pub the **Inn at Whitewell** (see page 103)! Beacon Fell was a great suggestion – you can make the walk as short or long as stubborn little legs will allow. There's a very gentle climb leading to a summit which will give everyone a great sense of achievement.

When you arrive, there's a large well-signposted pay and display car park, and an information centre which doubles as a café. The ranger was extremely helpful and planned out a short easy walk for us, the Sculpture Trail, which led us straight up to the summit in about 20 minutes. We set off with gusto and, along the way, saw a number of carved wooden sculptures including an enormous snake winding its way through the trees.

Instead of walking directly to the top, you could take in more of the forest via the Woodland Trail. It takes about 40 minutes and also culminates at the top of the fell. A triangulation pillar sits at the summit, which is 266m above sea level, giving breath-taking views of Bowland Fell and Parlick Fell. Apparently, on a clear day, you can see all the way to Blackpool, and beyond to the Isle of Man and Snowdonia.

Beacon Fell was a super find for us, one that you could easily just head off to and explore. It's not too big and all the trails are well signposted. Despite an early tumble from my two-year-old niece, resulting in her being covered head to toe in mud, we all made it to the top, albeit she had to be carried most of the way!
Daily Summer 9.30am-6pm, Winter 10am-5pm
Beacon Fell Country Park, Goosnargh, Preston, Lancashire PR3 2NL
Tel: 01995 640557 lancashire.gov.uk

"Anyone seen Merlin?" at Alderley Edge.

Whether on two wheels or two legs, Delamere Forest is a perfect child-friendly destination.

Delamere Forest

With my middle child, Sam, having recently learnt to ride a bike, we wanted to go somewhere to cycle and build his confidence. Delamere Forest is absolutely perfect for this. Set in 2,300 acres, it is the largest area of woodland in Cheshire, and is simply stunning.

Lots of dry sandstone paths make it easy for both pushchairs and bikes. There are lots of different routes to try, a variety of lengths and all very clearly marked. Being new to the family biking lark, I don't have a bike rack, so I squeezed the older boys' bikes into the back of the car and hired one with a baby seat for me and Ted. Tracs, the hire place, is next door to the café. They were extremely helpful in kitting us out with bikes and helmets and recommending a novice-friendly route. You can buy a map for £2 but it isn't essential. Adult bike hire is £20 for a half day, plus £6 for the child's seat, a kid's mountain bike was £15.

The forest is beautiful, and every five minutes or so we'd be stopping to admire or investigate somebody's den we'd found. After an hour or so of gentle cycling we headed to The Delamere Café for a well-deserved lunch. There's a kids' corner with books and toys, plus a huge fish tank. You'll also find a microwave for warming bottles or baby food. There is plenty on the menu including pittas, hot baguettes and toasties. For children they'll serve smaller portions of the main meals, which included my boys' particular favourite, sausage and beans. If you want something a bit more special, perhaps for Sunday lunch, the nearby **Travellers Rest** can definitely be recommended (see page 106).

Throughout the year the Forestry Commission run lots of events for kids, ranging from barmy boot camp to fairytale fitness trail. Check website for details, booking is essential.

Whether you're on two wheels or two legs, Delamere Forest has something for all ages and abilities, and is a fabulous place to spend the day. It was perfect for building up Sam's confidence, and he was extremely pleased that he'd managed to cycle the seven mile White Moor Trail.

Beacon Fell, a family walk with a small sculpture trail to look out for.

91

Taking a break with Jossy the lab on the historical Eyam trail.

Delamere Café: Summer Mon-Fri 9am-5pm, Sat & Sun
9am-5.30pm; In Winter the café closes half an hour earlier.
Tel: 01606 882726 delamerecafe.com
Tracs Bike Hire: Daily 10am-6pm Tel: 07949 088477
Delamere Forest Park Visitor Centre, Forestry Commis-
sion, Linmere, Delamere, Northwich, Cheshire CW8 2JD
Tel: 01606 889792 forestry.gov.uk

Dunham Massey

The beautiful grounds of this country estate are a
stunning mix of parkland and maintained gardens
with herds of deer roaming free. See page 72 for full
review.

Eyam

The inhabitants of the Peak District
village of Eyam made the ultimate
sacrifice during the Black Death of 1665.
A parcel of cloths, sent from plague-infested London
to Eyam, brought the deadly disease to the North
of England. Over the following weeks, as villagers
started to die and panic set in, the rector called
a meeting. Bravely imposing a quarantine upon
themselves, allowing no one to enter or leave Eyam,
they stopped the disease spreading beyond the
village. But the sacrifice meant that, over the coming
months, more than half of the population of Eyam
died of the plague. 350 years later, driving through
the picture-postcard village, it's unimaginable to
consider the suffering that took place here.

We picked a bright cold day for our walk, parking
in the free car park opposite the well-signposted
museum. Heading right, out of the village, we
followed signs for the youth hostel, and took the
footpath left, just past the youth hostel, up very
steep stone steps through woodland. The steps eventually gave way to a muddy path… up again! Good
to get the steep bit out of the way first!

From here we followed the footpath 'yellow
arrows', left along the bottom of fields, then up to the
right, with a stone wall on our right. We crossed a
lane, dog-legging to the left, then over another stile.
More field paths brought us to Sir William Hill Road.
We turned right here, walking to a T-junction, then
right again to head downhill towards the village.
Mompesson's Well, near the bottom, is the spring
where neighbouring villagers left food and medical
supplies for the quarantined villagers of Eyam.

After throwing pennies into the well, we passed
between two stones on the left, onto a woodland
footpath, which opens onto a residential lane. We
turned left at the junction, looking for the Riley
Graves, where Elizabeth Hancocke buried her
husband and six children in August 1666. Encircled
by a stone wall, they stand alone in a field on Riley
Lane; a contemplative spot.

Heading back to the village, welcoming tea shops
awaited us. The children loved checking out the
stocks and bullring, and reading the green heritage
signs dotted around on cottages. We even saw the

1666 death register, housed in Eyam church. We didn't have time to visit Eyam Hall and gardens (opened to the public by the National Trust in 2013) but that's a great reason to head back – to explore more of this village's incredible story.

Eyam Museum, Hawkhill Road, Eyam, Derbyshire S32 5QP eyam-museum.org.uk Tel: 01433 631371

Goyt Valley

On one of the rare days of sunshine at the end of the summer holiday, we headed into the Peak District to the Goyt Valley. I'd arranged to meet friends for a picnic and a walk. Arriving from the Rainow direction there is a car park on the right just after the road called 'The Street' splits.

We parked and walked up to the ruins of Errwood Hall, once home to the Grimshawe Family, to have our lunch. The best time of year is June when 40,000 rhododendrons are out in full force. Even so it was a lovely walk up the hill and into the quiet of the woods. The ruins are pretty fab and the kids loved climbing over walls and jumping off the sides of the old building.

After lunch we dropped off the remains of our picnic, walked up the road a short distance and scrambled down the steep bank to the river. In hindsight we should have walked a bit further along and gone down via very accessible pathways. We were a party with a pregnant lady, so getting back

Walking up to the ruins at Goyt Valley.

up the bank proved interesting! Once there though, the boys couldn't wait to paddle in the water in their boxers, you could assume from their screams that it was freezing!

We had a fun and event-filled day. There are lots of walking routes online if you want to take this trip a bit further.

NB: For our walk, my top tip would be to park up and walk along the road until you see the access to the river (it's closed to cars on Sundays and Bank Holidays from May until the end of September). This also avoids the one-way traffic system which

brings you out at the wrong end of the Peak District for the drive back to Manchester, plus it can get pretty treacherous in winter.

Errwood Hall, The Street, Goyt Valley, Peak District National Park, Derbyshire goytvalley.co.uk

Healey Dell Nature Reserve

Much of the beauty of this area comes from the fact that the River Spodden has carved its way through a steep-sided valley. There are waterfalls and well-known sites such as Fairies Chapel, which is at the bottom of a steep descent. It's a dramatic landscape that is impossible to access with a pushchair. On our visit we saw one couple with their baby in a backpack nipping over a narrow stile – they clearly knew what they were doing! For pram users you are limited to the route marked for wheelchair users.

We followed a trail that included a section of the abandoned Rochdale to Bacup railway line and found ourselves on top of a 100-foot high viaduct gazing across the magnificent Spodden Valley. This beauty spot is quite remote in feel, despite the fact that there are houses and streets nearby, so it's definitely one to visit with a friend.

Finish off with a trip to the lovely new tearooms with a friendly atmosphere which has got the locals waxing lyrical!

Tea Rooms: Fri-Sun 10am-4.30pm.
Healey Dell Heritage Centre and Tea Rooms, Dell Road, Shawclough, Rochdale OL12 6BG
Tel: 01706 524425 healeydellheritagecentre.org.uk
Healey Dell Ranger Office: Mon-Fri 9am-4.30pm.
Tel: 01706 350459 healeydell.org.uk

Holcombe Hill

As a child I lived at the foot of Holcombe Hill and therefore I'm rather fond of it, or more particularly of Peel Tower perched at the top. It was built to commemorate Sir Robert Peel, former prime minister and founder of the modern police force. I have since returned with my boys and we have

Hollingworth Lake is a superb walk if you've got toddlers or pushchairs in tow.

enjoyed the spectacular views of Manchester and North Wales from the top.

On first assessment, there isn't anything particularly child-friendly about it – the paths are difficult for pushchairs and there are no toilets or places to eat. I therefore wouldn't recommend it for people who would struggle carrying children some of the way. But it is an achievable walk for older toddlers and for parents with a sling or back carrier. The village is nearby and so is **The Shoulder of Mutton** (see page 105), a great pub for food, so for that reason I would recommend it as a place for a good family walk. My three-year-old felt a huge sense of achievement at reaching the top of the hill and, after our picnic, enjoyed rolling back down parts of it again!

The tower is open on various days of the year, so if you can manage a further 150 steps after the hill climb, try and coincide your visit with an open day. On Good Friday morning it is traditional to roll eggs down the hill, and you will usually find children of all ages taking part.

Car parking available on Lumb Carr Road.
Holcombe Hill, Accessible from Lumb Carr Road, Holcombe Village, Bury BL8 4NN bury.gov.uk

Hollingworth Lake Country Park

The two and a quarter mile flat perimeter path around Hollingworth Lake offers a superb walk if you have toddlers and pushchairs in tow. The lake is man-made (dating back to 1800) but appears natural and has beautiful countryside surrounding it. On a clear autumn day I took my parents, a three-year-old and a baby. The three-year-old managed to walk almost the whole distance without stopping. She was kept entertained by muddy puddles, a bridge over a weir, plenty of wildlife and by throwing pebbles in the lake (not at the wildlife!) from the small beach. If that was not enough there is a small children's playground at the end of the circular route. There are plenty of benches for those who want to sit and take in the scenery or eat a picnic. That said, there's also a great fish and chip shop at the side of the lake.

There is a vast network of paths and woodland (not suitable for pushchairs), which connect to the perimeter walk. These are great for kids who are good at walking or if you are using a papoose. Pay and display parking is available at the visitor centre on Rakewood Road, where there is a café, toilets with baby changing facilities, and the playground. In the summer, rowing boats are available for hire. The ferry service is temporarily suspended as money is raised to repair *Lady Alice*.

A couple of pubs overlook Hollingworth Lake, which offer meals and bar snacks, making a Sunday walk followed by a pub lunch a particularly attractive option.

Felix, Ollie and Dad peeking over the summit of Shutlingsloe. Awe-inspiring views over the Cheshire plain.

Visitor Centre: Sat & Sun 10.30am-4.45pm, Mon 11am-3.45pm.
Café: Daily 11am-3.45pm (4.45pm at weekends).
Rowing boats: weather permitting Daily Apr-Oct.
Hollingworth Lake, Rakewood Road,
Littleborough, Rochdale OL15 0AQ
Tel: 01706 373421 rochdale.gov.uk

Lyme Park

If your kids like a walk, the moorlands and deer park at Lyme Park are perfect. And of course, when it snows, there's nowhere finer for sledging... See page 73 for full review.

Lymm Dam

There are two paths that take you on the mile or so circular route around the lake here, one of which is wheelchair-friendly. We opted for the other one, which was perfectly easy going with two toddlers. If we'd had a pram, bar a few steps, I still think it would have been fine.

As you walk, there are various diversions to keep the children happy. There are fishing platforms jutting out that they can climb down to (under strict supervision) and throw sticks into the water. The path winds through some attractive beech woodland to the Wishing Bridge, a small hump-backed stone bridge under which the water rushes into the main lake – the children were fascinated by the two different water levels on either side.

A little further on is another, smaller bridge,

over the drain – this sluice is made of cement and with wellies on, the boys were able to walk down and paddle at the edge of the water. We continued on, finding a couple of rope swings, and just as Max began to complain of being tired we reached the church, situated close to the road where we had parked. Before we reached the road, however, we came across a sort of rocky out-crop. Formed millions of years ago, this significant geological feature known as the 'bluff' provided the most fun, as the boys clambered up and down the red sandstone. It was far and away their favourite part of the walk.

With plenty of benches and some picnic tables dotted all the way around, as well as the buggy-friendly path, Lymm Dam made for a really pleasant, easy walk. And, if you want to treat yourself to lunch, the award winning **Church Green** restaurant is less than a five minute walk away (see page 132). *Lymm Dam, south of Lymm village on the A56, Lymm, Cheshire WA13 9NJ warrington.gov.uk*

Macclesfield Forest – and the summit of Shutlingsloe

Macclesfield Forest is not well sign-posted from Macclesfield, but it is well worth finding for a family walk or cycle ride in the wild outdoors. Taking the Leek road from Maccles-field (A523), then heading left towards Langley, we set our sights for the Trentabank Visitor Centre.

95

Arriving here felt as though we'd driven out of Cheshire and straight into the Scottish Highlands, the scenery took our breath away. Shining reservoirs banked by forests of pine, giving way to moorlands beyond, all the way to Cheshire's two highest peaks: Shutlingsloe and Shining Tor.

Parking at the visitor centre by Trentabank reservoir, we were able to pick up leaflets setting out five colour-coded routes varying from 1km to 9km. You choose your route and then follow the bands of colour on wooden posts positioned at junctions along the route. The shorter walks are mainly gravel paths and sections of country lane, all accessible to pushchairs. I'd say the longer walks are better left to families with older children.

With spirits high, we took on Shutlingsloe. For a mile this walk lulled us into a false sense of security, before we turned right at a wooden signpost indicating our 'mountain'! It's a fairly steep scramble in parts, and so isn't negotiable to buggies or reluctant toddlers! Our twelve, nine and six-year-olds had no such problems – they loved the challenge. The views across the Cheshire plain are awe-inspiring and are so worth the effort. The journey back down was very easy-going, with the children hurrying ahead to get to the 'Nice Nosh' van.

John serves food, and helpful information, including orienteering maps, from his van in the car park every weekend. It's great stuff; real Stafford-shire oatcakes, locally cured bacon, and loads of homemade cakes – including a gluten-free chocolate one! We settled on John's own ginger beer and parkin – absolutely delicious (my husband also had a bag of freshly made pork scratchings which he said were the best he'd had for 25 years!)

Food: Weekends 10am-4pm nice-nosh.co.uk.
Trentabank Visitor Centre, Clarke Lane,
Langley SK11 0NE visitpeakdistrict.com

Marbury Country Park

Marbury is well worth a day trip to allow the children to run really wild. Its landscape includes parkland, ancient woodland and a mere. It is a haven for a huge variety of wildlife from bugs and dragonflies to bats and wild flowers, so there is a great opportunity for budding Attenboroughs to explore nature. We visited on a sunny day armed with our own picnic, and many other people had done the same. There are designated picnic areas with tables provided, although you can disappear off into the far reaches of the park to set up your rug in the wilderness.

There are several trails of varying length to follow, on a maze of pushchair-friendly paths covering much of the huge park, including along the water-side of the beautiful mere – don't forget your bread to feed the ducks, they were very entertaining!

The park offers bicycle hire, or you can bring

Marbury Country Park has everything from walking trails to bug hunting, plus there's an outdoor lido!

your own. There is a fabulous open-air pool which is open in the summer months. Unfortunately we hadn't come prepared, but there were children (some in wet suits – it's not a heated pool) shrieking with delight, diving off the board, swimming and splashing around.

We had brought our well-thumbed copy of *Jarrold Short Walks: Cheshire and the Gritstone Edge* to tackle a three and a half mile walk from Marbury Country Park. It starts along Budworth Mere, takes in the **Anderton Boat Lift** (see page 25) and a spot of canal-side walking, before re-joining the woodland paths of the park. There are a few stiles on this walk so it is not suited to pushchairs There was so much to look at along the way, from the Boat Lift to fields of tall maize, that it kept even the six-year-olds going without complaint! Our boys loved clambering on logs, making up games and the total freedom that exploring the great outdoors provides. It was one of those magical days when they come home exhausted and happy.

Car park £2.50.

Pushchair access, toilets, Rangers office and snack van. Open-air swimming pool: May 12-6pm, June-Sept 11am-7pm. Adult £5, Child £3, under 3s free. Non-members should call the pool before visiting as on busy days entry is restricted to members only. Pool staff: 07599 702903.

Marbury Country Park, Comberbach, Northwich, Cheshire CW9 6AT

Tel: 01606 77741 northwichwoodlands.org.uk

Middlewood Way and the Macclesfield Canal

Opened in 1985 by David Bellamy, the Middlewood Way is a well-maintained ten mile 'linear park', stretching from Macclesfield to Marple along a disused railway track. Its close proximity to the wildlife and woodland of Poynton Coppice Nature Reserve and the canal path along Macclesfield Canal, and the choice of several car parks along its route, make this an unbeatable choice for a variety of enjoyable family walks.

The Middlewood Way offers lots of walking options for different ages of kids – if you can only tempt your children out with the promise that they can bring their scooter or bike, it's perfect!

The Middlewood Way, Bollington Car Park, Adlington Road, Bollington, Cheshire SK10 5JT cheshireeast.gov.uk.

Pendle Sculpture Trail

Pendle is one of those places... it's synonymous with mystery and intrigue and of course instantly conjures up images of just one thing: witches! Four centuries ago, during an era of religious persecution and with superstition rife, ten innocent villagers condemned

If you go down to the woods today... Pendle Sculpture Trail is steeped in superstition and mystery.

for witchcraft were the convenient scapegoats of their day. Now, inspired by the history of the witches and the dramatic wild landscape of this part of Lancashire, four artists have created the Pendle Sculpture Trail. The setting is Aitken Wood, Barley, beneath Pendle Hill.

Park up at Barley Car Park and arm yourself with a map and the trail quiz from the Visitor Information Centre or download the information ahead of your visit from www.letswalkinpendle.btck.co.uk. This is absolutely imperative if you do wish to follow the Sculpture Trail because, firstly, there are zero sign-posts directing you to the trail from Barley and then once you're up in the wood there's no information in situ to read what it's all about – and it's a long way back to the start!

Once you've left the car park, turn right and walk through Barley Village (if you're planning a lunch or cuppa, it might be worth checking out the cute looking tea rooms which you walk past – they even have a children's menu!) and then first right past The Methodist Church, signposted "private road", leading up towards Lower Black Moss Reservoirs. The countryside here is immediately gratifying but one thing we hadn't quite gathered is that it's actually a mile walk (including one uphill stretch and one steep path) from the car park to Aitken Wood itself so this is a 'proper' walk!

Upon reaching the woods, we encountered the first of the ten ceramic plaques etched with symbols to represent each of the Pendle people who were hanged as witches. The idea is to identity the

Climbing Rivington Pike makes for a great family walk.

witches listed on the Trail map with the clues given on the plaques. The sculptures made out of stone, wood and metal serve to add to the wild and eerie atmosphere.

I have to warn you, finding the plaques and sculptures is not as easy as it sounds (it took the grown ups and our six, seven and nine-year-old boys a good hour or so to find and then work out the clues) but blimey it was worth it! We were in splendid isolation – the only ones in the woods and the woods were immense – huge tree canopies with not a sound in the air. It was majestic and the kids had enjoyed a great time – as well as learning bucket loads! The walk back to the car was exhilarating – a chance to soak up more of the stunning views.

If you've not discovered this beautiful part of England yet I strongly recommend you go, and the Pendle Sculpture Trail is a perfect starting point. Some tips: wear hardy boots/trainers or wellies – it will be boggy in parts in wet weather; use insect repellent in hot weather if you're susceptible to being bitten; and you've probably gathered that this is not pushchair friendly!

The Assheton Arms (see page 100) is in the beautiful village of nearby Downham and is a great pub for lunch – well worth a visit.

Tourist Information: Discover Pendle Tel: 01282 856186
Pendle Sculpture Trail in Aitken Wood. Park at Car Park off Barley New Road, Barley, Pendle, Lancashire visitpendle.com

Rivington Pike

Rivington Pike is a hill summit on Winter Hill, part of the West Pennine Moors. This prominent local landmark complete with tower on top is a great place for families to go walking. There are several walks on the flat but for an achievable hill climb, which we have done with both a baby in a backpack and a five-year-old, park at the upper barn (Rivington Hall Barn) and walk straight up to the Pike following the red post route. This takes you on an exploration through the ruins of the terraced gardens and home of William Lever, which was burned down in 1913. With its little bridges, Japanese ornamental pool, pathways and archways, and even a pigeon tower remaining, it is good territory for kids to explore.

At the summit there were lots of families propped up against the tower taking shelter from the wind, drinking soup from flasks and eating butties. The 360-degree view spans the Reebok stadium in Horwich, the North West Coast, Rivington and the moors. Back down at the bottom, housed in The Great House Barn (a ten minute walk from the upper barn) is a cosy and bustling tea room and gift shop. Open daily, it is also where you will find another car park and toilets.

The Great House Barn, Summer 10am-8pm, Winter 10am-4.30pm.
Rivington Lane, Rivington, Bolton BL6 7SB
rivingtonhallbarn.co.uk about-rivington.co.uk

Tatton Park

Tatton Park is one of Britain's great country house estates, a fine neoclassical mansion set in 50 acres of beautiful gardens with vast surrounding parkland that is home to deer, cattle and sheep. See page 76 for full review.

Tegg's Nose Country Park

Tegg's Nose Country Park, well signposted off Buxton Old Road in Macclesfield, offers a variety of energetic family walks. When we arrived on a bright cold Sunday morning in December the visitor centre was closed, but a notice board indicated the two and a half mile walk that we were intent upon, and also several longer routes. Some walks through the park take in sections of The Gritstone Trail, a 35-mile footpath stretching from Disley to Kidsgrove.

We had been to Tegg's Nose before, in thick snow, for a magical day sledging with our children; so we were keen to return to this rugged landscape for a country walk. Directions on the website (Walk 1) kept us on track as there were sometimes several turnings to choose from, and the route itself was not particularly well signposted. There is much scrambling and climbing on offer on this walk, and some very steep paths, so it is definitely one that will appeal to adventurous little ones. It is not suitable for pushchairs. En route there is a display of quarry equipment where our children loved playing as an interlude to the walk, together with interesting information on the history of mining in this area. Another highlight is the incredible views on a clear day. At the summit of Tegg's Nose there is a map of the Cheshire plain, indicating landmarks for you to look for in the expansive scene beneath you; and there are other amazing views over the two reservoirs before you scramble down the path towards them.

Remember to pack your own drinks and snacks though, this is hungry and thirsty work and there's no café. Although, you could head to nearby **Sutton Hall** to eat (see page 105). This is a fantastic place for families who love big walks in the great outdoors!

Pay and display car park, visitor centre and toilets.
Tegg's Nose Country Park, Buxton Old Road, Macclesfield SK11 0AP
Tel: 01625 374833 teggsnose.co.uk

Yorkshire Sculpture Park

Although it is a bit out of the way, this marvellous free art gallery set in the open air in 500 acres of parkland is worth a drive for a special day outdoors. Greeting you at the entrance is an attractive gallery and visitor centre, which houses two eateries with terraces overlooking the parkland and Henry Moore sculptures, a gift shop and indoor exhibits.

On arrival, first head inside to find out what is on and pick up a map so that you can choose your route dependent on the ages and stamina of your children. There are so many things to see that you are unlikely to cover it all in one hit. I would recommend fitting in the Ha-Ha bridge, the deer shelter, underground gallery and the wonderful 'Playground' by the collective Greyworld, which as its name suggests is a sculpture to climb on and play by. Also try and get down to part of the lake. A big walk to the Longside Gallery at the far reaches of the park can be made, but taking your time, stopping to investigate the sculptures, and taking in the views is what it is really all about here. If you feel the urge to get to Longside Gallery without the walk, there is a shuttle bus with booster seats. Prams can access many places in the park.

Daily 10am-5pm. Gates locked 6pm.
Yorkshire Sculpture Park, West Bretton, Wakefield WF4 4LG
Tel: 01924 832631 ysp.co.uk

The Assheton Arms in Downham, one of the most beautiful villages in Lancashire.

Country Pubs

"There is nothing which has yet been contrived by man by which so much happiness is produced as by a good inn" – **Samuel Johnson**.

The Assheton Arms

The village of Downham is often quoted as being the most beautiful in Lancashire – lovely grey stone mullion windowed cottages and, uncommonly now, no yellow lines on the road, no television aerials, no overhead wires spoiling the countryside views.

Downham was my Grandpa's favourite place to visit, especially the pub at its heart – The Assheton Arms. After a walk with friends in nearby **Pendle** (see page 97), we chose here for lunch. We were seated at a large farmhouse table next to the bar, which though not quite as charming as the main dining area, with three boisterous seven year olds in tow, it was probably the best place to put us.

The pub is renowned for its fish, which inevitably dominates the menu, but there are meat choices too. My friend and I ordered goats cheese crumpets with rosemary honey, then fish and chips (one of the cheapest mains on the menu at £10.50). Both were good. The children's menu ranges from £3.50 to £5 and includes choices such as fishbites, cheese omelette and mild chicken curry with rice. The

Assheton Arms is a special pub that serves excellent food – it's well worth a visit.
Food: Mon-Thurs 12-9pm, Fri-Sat 12-10pm, Sun 12-8pm
The Assheton Arms, Downham, Clitheroe,
Lancashire BB7 4BJ
Tel: 01200 441227 asshetonarms.com

The Bells of Peover

After a lovely autumn walk round the Peover countryside we headed to this beautiful white-washed inn just outside Knutsford, located down a little cobbled road. In spite of muddy boots we were warmly welcomed, both by staff and the open fire burning in the bar area!

This is a country pub that prides itself on serving locally sourced, seasonal produce. It has a simple junior menu with mains from £5. Our children plumped for the homemade burger and hand-cut fries, beautifully presented on a wooden board. The Bells of Peover offers several menu choices. Prices started at £6.50 for sandwiches but we went for something more substantial. I chose the asparagus risotto that looked and tasted fabulous whilst hubby chose the Hot Dog served with chilli and cheese. This is clearly a popular establishment so I would suggest booking, especially at weekends.

Food: Mon-Fri 12-2.30pm & 6-9.30pm, Sat 12-9.30pm, Sun 12-8pm

The Bells of Peover, The Cobbles, Lower Peover, Knutsford WA16 9PZ

Tel: 01565 722269 thebellsofpeover.com

The Black Swan

Too often in the modern age of the gastro pub, style rules over content, but this homely pub nestling in beautiful Cheshire countryside delivers both in an extremely accomplished way. First impressions were promising as we pulled up. The Black Swan is very pretty and the finger-post pointing one way to the boules area and another to the outside wood-burning pizza oven indicated a pub that stands out from the crowd. It's not overly surprising, as it hales from excellent pedigree – it's the "little brother" of The Swan in Newby Bridge up in The Lakes, which has received high accolades.

The Black Swan in Lower Withington has design elements that are fun and quirky but also retains a traditional quality, with welcoming open fires and flagstone floors. Our children feasted well off a varied menu ranging from scampi to chargrilled chicken breast (£6.50) and even jam sandwiches (£3.50). My partner and I ate french onion soup and lamb tagine, both reasonably priced. Our food was superb.

With a warm and friendly atmosphere, The Black Swan is a definite new fave!

Food: Daily 10am-9pm

The Black Swan, Lower Withington, Cheshire SK11 9EQ

Tel: 01477 571770 blackswancheshire.com

The Clog & Billycock

Eating at The Clog & Billycock is such a lovely treat – I only wish that there was one a bit closer to me in Didsbury! Meeting up with an old school friend and her two-year-old son Jack, we hit this Ribble Valley Inn after a good romp round the playground delights of nearby **Witton Park** (see page 89). The Clog & Billycock is an award-winning gastro-pub with a delicious line-up of dishes from celebrity chef, Nigel Haworth.

It is a joy that there's not a nugget in sight – the kids' menu is simply a scaled down and tailored version of the adults', with the same pick of perfectly sourced local foods. Jack, our ready-made junior taste tester tucked into a burger with real chips (£5.50) and had no problem clearing his plate. Not only is the food terrific, but set in an attractive conversion, the pub itself has a pleasant atmosphere. 10 out of 10!

Food: Lunch Mon-Sat 12-2pm, Sun 12-8pm;

The Black Swan is a country pub with ooodles of unique style.

Afternoon bites Mon-Fri 2-5.30pm; Dinner Mon-Thurs 5.30-8.30pm, Fri-Sat 5.30-9pm, Sun 12-8.30pm

The Clog & Billycock, Billinge End Road, Pleasington, Blackburn BB2 6QB

Tel: 01254 201163 theclogandbillycock.com

The Crown

Well placed for a trip to **Jodrell Bank** (see page 16) or a country walk, The Crown at Goostrey is a traditional 18th century pub serving delicious food in a cosy atmosphere.

There was so much on the menu to tempt us, from nibbles and sharing platters to substantial main courses. The children's menu was small and simple, but the food was of excellent quality and portion sizes were generous. The homemade chicken and ham pie and the fish and chips, both £6.50, were absolutely delicious. We are definitely going to return soon for the highly recommended Sunday roast (child portions available)… after a walk to build up our appetites! Child and dog friendly!

Food: Mon-Sat 12-9pm, Sun 12-8pm

The Crown, 111 Main Road, Goostrey, Cheshire CW4 8PE

Tel: 01477 532 128 thecrowngoostrey.co.uk

The Dysart Arms

If a good pub is one of your criteria when considering a move to the countryside, the beautiful village of Bunbury in Cheshire may be the place for you, as it has two! **The Yew Tree Inn** (see page 107) and The Dysart Arms.

The Dysart Arms is next to the village church, with a gorgeous outlook. A couple of swings are tucked away at the bottom of its garden for young ones.

Despite being a mild October day, there were two fires roaring which always gives a great first impression. We split a fish and chips children's meal (£8.25) between two three-year-olds and it was perfect as portion sizes are generous. Other children's choices included ham, egg and chips for £6.95 and sausage and mash for £7.95. The food is very good and

COUNTRY PUBS

Picture perfect – The Dysart Arms in Bunbury.

service was extremely helpful.

The Dysart doesn't encourage prams in the pub, but it does have baby changing facilities and welcomes well-behaved children. As I fished Ted out once again from under the table, we decided not to hang around for dessert!

Food: Mon-Sat 12-9.30pm, Sun 12-9pm
The Dysart Arms, Bowes Gate Road,
Bunbury, Near Tarporley, Cheshire CW6 9PH
Tel: 01829 260183 dysartarms-bunbury.co.uk

The Hearth of the Ram

This pub and restaurant, nestling in Ramsbottom, has scooped up awards and accolades since opening in April

2012, deservedly so, as the food and setting is fabulous. Owned by a couple with two young children themselves, Euan and Dena greet you with open arms as you request their kids' menu and a highchair. We visited in winter with grandparents and were delighted to be seated on a large table next to a roaring fire.

Ollie (with his adult-sized appetite) and Grandpa both wanted starters, but the rest of us opted to go straight to main courses to ensure we had room for dessert. Our mouths were watering though, as Ollie cut into his scotch egg, served imaginatively in an egg box and Grandpa munched through a bowl of whitebait. My main was worth waiting for: seared Goosnargh Duck with an orange and ginger sauce, potato fondant, buttered kale and carrots. The others all had their hearts set on roast beef, including my seven-year-old who was provided with a smaller, still good-sized portion. For dessert, my children saw only the trio of chocolate, complete with a fondant! Granny chose a cool tangy trio of lemon, while I plumped for traditional treacle tart served with Earl Grey ice cream and lemon sorbet. All well received.

In the warmer months bi-folding doors onto the terrace provide the opportunity to dine alfresco, making this a year round choice. With the **East Lancs Railway** across the road (see page 27), great shops to potter round, and pleasant walks nearby (see **Holcombe Hill** page 94), you can make a day of it.

The Hearth of the Ram has scooped lots of awards and was a definite winner for the Redmond family too!

Next to the superb Inn at Whitewell, you'll discover the stepping stones to cross the river.

As this is a popular restaurant we recommend booking ahead.

Food: Daily 12pm till late
Hearth of the Ram, Restaurant and Bar, 13 Peel Brow, Ramsbottom, Bury BL0 0AA
Tel: 01706 828681 thehearthoftheram.com

The Inn at Whitewell

Friends visiting from London? Want to show off Lancashire? A walk in the stunning Forest of Bowland, followed by lunch at The Inn at Whitewell, fits the bill perfectly. We went to the lovely **Beacon Fell** (see page 90), a very easy walk and only half an hour away.

You're also moments away from the geographical centre of Great Britain! The lovely tiny village of Dunsop Bridge, minutes away from Whitewell, is the nearest village to the aforementioned centre, with a telephone box, BT's 100,000th, marking the spot! Dunsop Bridge is also home to an extraordinary number of ducks that love being fed by eager children (the village shop opposite the river sells duck feed). But back to *our* stomachs!

The Inn at Whitewell serves amazing, award-winning food in a beautiful, unpretentious environment. You can't book for lunch so turn up in good time. Our children ate smaller versions of offerings on the adult lunch menu – fish and chips, fish pie and a roast chicken dinner. Everyone enjoyed themselves enormously. Quite simply fabulous – everything a country pub ought to be!

Food: Daily 12-2pm & 7.30-9.30pm
The Inn at Whitewell, nr Clitheroe, Lancashire BB7 3AT
Tel: 01200 448222 innatwhitewell.com

The Plough and Flail

In a pretty setting with a big outside seating area plus a children's play frame across the car park, The Plough and Flail is especially lovely to drop into on a hot summer's day. That said, the last time we visited was autumn time and there were twelve of us wanting a Sunday dinner following a visit to nearby **Quarry Bank and Styal Estate** see page 73.

We called ahead to check The P&F could accomodate so many of us, which happily they could! Adults and kids alike feasted on tasty roast dinners with the odd burger thrown in for good measure. The food was great and the staff were incredibly patient with our noisy rabble.

We all agreed that The Plough and Flail had served us well – a friendly and relaxed atmosphere together with top-notch food.

Food: Mon-Thurs 12-9pm, Fri-Sat 12-10pm, Sun 12-8pm
The Plough and Flail, Paddock Hill Lane, Mobberley, Cheshire WA16 7DB
Tel: 01565 873537 theploughandflail.co.uk

The Ram's Head

Its proximity to **Lyme Park** (see page 73) makes The Ram's Head a perfect destination for tasty home-cooked food after a family excursion. We dropped by in winter when the blazing log fire and aroma of mulled cider made for a cosy welcome.

It has several different areas, with a few large tables tailor-made for families. The staff were very accommodating, handing out puzzles to our high-spirited bunch, which thankfully kept them amused for a while. The children's menu at £4.95 had plenty to choose from. There were the usual suspects but also a few great additions such as pigs in blanket, with mash and gravy, or chicken with crispy sweet cured bacon salad. The adult selection almost falls into the gourmet pub category; our Sunday roast beef was delicious. A grassy beer garden at the rear has plenty of room for running around. If you're

The outside play area at The Plough and Flail will keep the kids happy.

Martha and Dan battle it out over a game of chess at Sutton Hall.

Marple Bridge way, it may be worth checking out its sister pub The Midland.

Food: Mon-Sat 12-10pm, Sun 12-9.30pm
The Ram's Head, Buxton Road West, Disley, Stockport SK12 2AE
***Tel: 01663 767909** theramsheaddisley.co.uk*

The Roebuck Inn

Situated high up in Strinesdale, near Oldham, you can't fail to be impressed by the fabulous views at The Roebuck Inn. Inside, the décor is a little dated but it's homely and the proprietors take care of the restaurant and customers. On our visit the boys thoroughly enjoyed the mini roast dinners. I had a simple melon starter, then fillet of pork. There is a children's menu including pizzas and chicken at £3.75 and all dishes come with a lucky bag; half portions of any meal from the main menu can also be served. With a small play area at the back over-looking farmers' fields and plenty of country walks nearby, this is a good choice if you want to escape the city with kids.

Food: Mon-Thur 12-2pm & 5-9pm, Fri 12-9pm, Sat 12-9.30pm, Sun 12-8.15pm
The Roebuck Inn, Strinesdale, Oldham OL4 3RB
***Tel: 0161 624819** the-roebuck-inn.co.uk*

The Rope & Anchor Pub

The Rope & Anchor is exactly what you would expect from a gastro pub – it's spacious, modern and well-designed. The outside area is large, with lots of seating. I really liked the glass-walled barn with outdoor heaters – excellent for a cold, sunny day.

We visited on a warm afternoon after working up an appetite at nearby **Dunham Massey** (see page 72). We sat outside, which was perfect as it's in striking distance of the children's play area. There is a great play frame with slides and a swing. My boys enjoyed kicking a football around the grassed area, which is quite close to the car park, so not ideal, but I kept a beady eye on them.

Children's meals cost £6.50 with a selection from fish and chips, beef burger, sausage with mash or spaghetti meatballs. The food and service were pretty good and the portion size was about right for my six-year-old. The adult menu is extensive, from sandwiches to smaller bites and larger mains, including 10oz ribeye steaks. You will definitely find something that appeals.

Food: Mon-Fri 12-9pm, Sat 12-9.30pm, Sun 12-8pm
The Rope & Anchor, Paddock Lane, Dunham Massey, Altrincham WA14 5RP
***Tel: 0161 927 7901** theropeandanchor.co.uk*

The Shoulder of Mutton

On a Sunday, The Shoulder is packed with walkers, kids and dogs. There is no play area here but a walk up **Holcombe Hill** (see page 94) is on offer instead, so once you have worn out your little ones bring them in all red-cheeked and settle down for a pint and some hot chocolate.

We booked ahead when we went to eat and were given a cosy table by the fire. Due to how busy it was, my friend left her pram outside and brought in a car seat instead for her six-month-old. The seasonal menu offered tasty wholesome dishes with special touches, such as corned beef hash with a quail egg, Blacksticks twice-baked soufflé and orange-scented rice pudding as well as the usual sandwiches. On the children's menu were the ubiquitous fish and chips, burger and bangers and mash, all well received by our mob.

Food: Mon- Fri 12-2pm & 5-9pm, Sat 12-3pm, 5-9pm, Sun 12-8pm

The Shoulder of Mutton, Holcombe Village, Ramsbottom, Bury BL8 4LZ

Tel: 01706 822001 theshoulderofmutton.net

Sutton Hall

A 480-year-old manor house, once the family home of the Earls of Lucan, and a former convent – that's what I call a bit of a "wow" pub! Located just south of Macclesfield, bordering the Peak District, we enjoyed a drive through stunning countryside to get here. Less than five minutes away is **Teggs Nose Country Park** (see page 99) which would make a great detour. The pub is big – lots of nooks and crannies and seven dining areas, with open fires adding to the atmosphere. With a couple of three-year-olds in tow, Jo and I tucked ourselves away in a little snug area. We ordered one children's sized fish and chips for Eleanor and Ted to share (£7.95) and opted ourselves for a small burger with chips (£6.95) and a chicken wrap (£5.95). Service was smiley and helpful.

While we waited for the food, we took the children for a run round the garden, a sit on a static tractor, which they loved, and time on the swings. Considering the pub was pretty busy, the food arrived swiftly. The children demolished their shared meal then enjoyed playing on a couple of the pub's Etch-a-Sketches, which was a nice touch. In fact, Sutton Hall had lots of nice touches, which is why it's certainly worth a visit.

Food: Mon-Sat 12-10pm, Sun 12-9.30pm

NB: Sutton Hall welcomes children but suggests visiting in the day rather than at night!

Sutton Hall, Bullocks Lane, Sutton, Macclesfield SK11 0HE

Tel: 01260 253211 suttonhall.co.uk

Traditional, characterful and hearty food at The Swan with Two Nicks.

The Swan with Two Nicks

Enthusiastically recommended to us by friends, The Swan with Two Nicks in Little Bollington deserved their good praise. We dropped in recently, after a walk round National Trust's **Dunham Massey** (see page 72). Now, if you're in the know, it's actually quite easy to walk across the Dunham Massey estate to get to this pub. If, like us, you're not; you might get back into your car, key the postcode into SatNav (the pub's website clearly states not to do this, but I hadn't read that bit!), and then drive aimlessly round Dunham village for 15 minutes (having a row!) before arriving at a mill on the wrong side of the river! So check the website for directions if you're in any doubt!

My husband loved this pub from the moment we walked in. It's traditional, characterful and totally devoid of any gastro-pub, glossy makeover that he hates, often stripping the heart out of these old inns. With its wooden beams, roaring log fire and dogs aplenty (it's very canine-friendly), the ambience is cosy and welcoming. It was busy and we were lucky to get a table (next time I would definitely book).

The menu is good hearty fare. Hubby went for Gamekeepers Pie (£12.95). I couldn't resist old-fashioned pub fave, scampi and chips (£10.95), and the kids chose from the under-10's menu, pasta carbonara and a burger with chips (£5 each). The food was excellent. The Swan with Two Nicks is just how a country pub should be, a great tradition!

Afternoon Tea and cakes served Mon-Fri 2.30-5.30pm

Food served daily Mon-Sat 12-9pm and Sun 12-8pm

Swan with Two Nicks, Park Lane, Little Bollington, Altrincham, Cheshire WA14 4TJ

Tel: 0161 928 2914 swanwithtwonicks.co.uk

Heidi and Ellie enjoy a girly chinwag and their dinners at The Wizard in Alderley Edge.

The Three Fishes

We have always enjoyed a Sunday trip to The Three Fishes which, for us, involves a long lunch and a nice countryside ramble. However this year, as both the kids have been inspired by hobbits, elves and a very well rubbed ring, we decided to extend our normal walk and work up an appetite by trying out the five-and-a-half-mile Tolkien Trail (we downloaded the map from www.forestofbowland. com) which started in Hurst Green at the Shireburn Arms Hotel. Though not a pushchair-friendly walk, it takes in some beautiful scenery and, if you are familiar with *The Lord of the Rings* trilogy, does give clues as to where Tolkien got his ideas from. Feeling thoroughly deserving, we then jumped in the car for the five-minute drive to The Three Fishes.

The pub has maintained its lovely atmosphere, with welcoming staff and burning log fires. Food was up to its usual standard with seasonal ingredients offered both to adults and children. The children's menu is especially good. We all enjoyed a three course meal, with the kids loving the milkshakes, chipolata sausage, chicken breast with mash and vegetables, and pancakes for pudding.

The quality and choice at The Three Fishes ensures that you can enjoy a family meal in a restaurant devoted to excellent local food.

Food: Lunch Mon-Sat 12-2pm, Sun 12-8pm; Afternoon bites Mon-Fri 2-5.30pm; Dinner Mon-Thurs 5.30-8.30pm,

Fri-Sat 5.30-9pm, Sun 12-8.30pm
The Three Fishes, Mitton Road, Mitton,
Near Whalley, Lancashire BB7 9PQ
Tel: 01254 826888 thethreefishes.com

The Travellers Rest

The location here is fab – on the eastern slopes of Frodsham Hill looking eastwards, with wide vistas over the Cheshire Plain towards Manchester, The Pennines and The Peaks. The Travellers Rest seemed initially more restaurant than pub and we were all starving and looking forward to some good grub; we were not disappointed.

The choice of three menus ranged from sandwiches, to pub favourites and a beautiful sounding A La Carte option offering in-season exotic dishes such as pan-fried sea bass with wild mushroom risotto scented with white truffle oil! Our family played it safe. The kids settled on sandwiches – grilled cajun chicken and classic BLT – which came with a small portion of fries. We chose fish and chips plus steak and ale pie, both homemade, ample and bursting with flavour.

The restaurant was busy, friendly and accommodating. The service was a little slow for our liking, but that would not put us off going again. It's clearly very popular, and would be an ideal choice following a visit to nearby **Manley Mere** (see page 58) or **Delamere Forest** (see page 91).

Food: Mon-Sat 12-2.30pm & 6-9pm, Sun 12-6pm
The Travellers Rest, Kingsley Road, Frodsham,
Cheshire WA6 6SL
Tel: 01928 735125
travellersrestfrodsham.com

The Wizard

This superb ancient coaching inn, bordering the forests of mystical **Alderley Edge** (see page 90), is a firm favourite with us. Our last visit was for an early tea – there were three families with eight kids between us – I did phone ahead first to book!

Inside this old pub, you'll find a maze of dining rooms, tastefully designed with rather nice antique furniture. The owner took us through to a large room towards the back where other families were dining. We were made to feel really welcome, there's no doubt that this is a very child-friendly place to come. Children can order almost anything from the adult menu, in smaller portion sizes. Our brood chose fish and chips, sausage and chips, and sticky ribs. Clean plates all round, the food is excellent here!

The Wizard also has a charming back garden, perfect for lunch on a summer's day while the little ones run around (though it's too close to a main road to let them wander off). We had picked a late afternoon in winter, making the most of the cosy inn. Handing over Top Trumps and colouring books from my handbag ensured we grown ups could enjoy our meals too; everyone was happy!

It's a simple winning formula really. Run your kids ragged through the woods, fill their heads with tales of wizards and dragons, and then settle in for a hearty lunch at The Wizard!

Food Mon-Fri 12-2pm & 6.30-9pm, Sat 12-9.30pm, Sun 12-7pm. Booking advisable.
The Wizard, Macclesfield Road, Nether Alderley, Cheshire SK10 4UB
Tel: 01625 584000 ainscoughs.co.uk

The Yew Tree Inn

We set off for a late lunch to The Yew Tree Inn in Bunbury – our second pub review in this gorgeous Cheshire village! (See page 101 for **The Dysart Arms** review.) It was a perfect day for this type of pub –

cold, a bit rainy and definitely worthy of an open fire. It didn't disappoint.

Built in the 19th century by The Earl of Crewe, the inn has been lovingly refurbished, with lots of nooks and crannies in which to find a bolt-hole for your family.

The staff were friendly, helpful and seemingly happy to see a family with three young boys. An excellent selection of children's meals was available, starting with one course for £5, two for £6.50 and three for £8. Starters included soup, garlic bread or cheese fingers on toast. We just had a main each and the boys tried the chicken strips, sausage with mash and fish pie, which all went down well. On Sunday it also offers children's portions of the roast dinner. For dessert it's ice cream, or an old favourite – rice pudding! All food is freshly made and supplied locally by the Foster family on Bunbury Heath. The menu changes every eight weeks, plus there are lots of daily specials.

There is seating outside but no outdoor play area. The Yew Tree's website says it welcomes well-behaved children; they have got colouring pens and books but perhaps take more entertainment if you think you might need it.

Food: Mon-Thurs 12-2.30pm & 6-9.30pm, Fri 12-2.30pm & 6-10pm, Sat 12-10pm, Sun 12-8pm
The Yew Tree Inn, Long Lane, Spurstow, Bunbury, Cheshire CW6 9RD
Tel: 01829 260 274 theyewtreebunbury.com

The Yew Tree has lots of nooks and crannies in which to find a bolt-hole for lunch!

Places to eat

Dining out with the kids is no longer a headache due to the terrific amount of child-friendly restaurants out there. If you're in need of a reviving cuppa, a bite to eat or maybe something stronger! – here are some of our favourites to wheel your buggy into.

CAFÉS AND RESTAURANTS IN THE CITY CENTRE

The Albert Square Chophouse

If like me you've been desperate for lunch at Mr Thomas's Chophouse, but blanched at the prospect of squeezing your pushchair or indeed your children through its famously long and slim ever-bustling bar, you'll be delighted to discover the owners have opened a child-friendly restaurant within the stunning Memorial Hall on Albert Square. The building has been fabulously restored and includes a downstairs à la carte restaurant, bar area, function rooms and a boutique hotel.

We decided to eat in the bar area, although staff assured us that children are very welcome in the restaurant. The children's menu was simple, aimed at a variety of different ages, and well-priced. It included: soup £3; scrambled eggs on toast £2; mini corned beef hash; grilled haddock, mash and carrots; or chicken strips for £5.50. Sam chose a roast and had definitely made the correct choice – his yorkshire pudding was almost the size of the plate! Adult starters ranged from goat's cheese tart to duck terrine with main courses including Chophouse favourites such as steak & kidney pudding and homity pie. It's a slightly different adults' menu in the restaurant, but the prices were similar. All in, we had a lovely relaxed meal in an impressive setting.

Food Mon-Fri 12-3pm and 5-9.45pm,
Sat 12-9.45pm, Sun 12-8.30pm
The Albert Square Chophouse, Memorial
Hall, Albert Square, Manchester M2 5PF
Tel: 0161 834 1866
albertsquarechophouse.com

Café Rylands

This is one of our favourite city centre cafes. Tucked into the modern glass extension of the gorgeous John Rylands Library on Deansgate, this place manages to be welcoming and cosy, whilst still beautiful and serene. It's a great place to eat local, traditional food whilst watching the world go by or reading the paper.

Whilst we waited for our food I took Ellie on a little tour of the fabulous gothic reading room – trying to spot the dragons that are synonymous with this building. Another highlight was the wonderful wooden automaton in the shop depicting Mrs Ryland taking tea with a dragon – our kids were fascinated by it!

Mon-Fri 8.30am-4.30pm, Sat 9am-4.30pm,
Sun 11am-4.30pm; Last food orders 3.45pm
Café Rylands, The John Rylands Library,
150 Deansgate, Manchester M3 3EH
Tel: 0161 275 3764 library.manchester.ac.uk

City Babies LOVE & Kids in

El Rincon De Rafa

Hidden away off Deansgate, located in a cavernous cellar down a fair few steep steps, you'll find El Rincon, a Spanish tapas restaurant that I would describe as a Manchester institution. It's been around for years and is frequented by many a different type of person. It's got a tremendous atmosphere; the decor, ambience and sangria all serve to make you feel like you're hanging out just off Las Ramblas. And the food? Well opinions do vary, and in all honesty I've had great meals there in my time, and less than great meals. But I do think it's one of those places you've got to give a whirl, and make your own mind up about. And taking the kids? You've got to be a bit gutsy – it's not the most child-friendly of places. The aforementioned steps at the entrance are troublesome with a buggy, and the menu makes no concession to kids; but last time we went there our two and five year olds tucked happily into garlic bread, calamari, meatballs and manchego. El Rincon always seems to be busy, particularly at the weekends. If you're going with kids, I suggest you get there at teatime in order to stand a chance of getting a table, and that all-important fix of chorizo.

With the same great food as Tom's Chophouse, The Albert Square Chophouse is a bit more child-friendly.

Daily 12-10.30pm
El Rincon, off St John's Street, 244 Deansgate,
Manchester M3 4BQ Tel: 0161 839 8819

The Great Hall Café

In the most splendid setting, this is where you get your coffee and cake if you are watching a performance at the Royal Exchange Theatre. It doesn't have to be limited to theatregoers however, as this pleasant café is a lovely spot to stop with kids or a baby at any time.

Firstly there's bags of space, so if you have a pram or scooters, coats and kid's stuff, you can plonk them all down easily. Also there is plenty to look at in the hall – barefooted actors milling around, odd bits of scenery being wheeled into the theatre, high-domed ceilings, and the fabulous architecture of the building itself together with the modern theatre within. It's all light food – sandwiches, scones and cakes. Mine enjoyed brownies and cartons of orange, as well as helping themselves to a small jug of milk each from the condiments area as I collected cutlery. As the café is adjacent to the box office, make sure you buy some tickets for the next production!

Mon-Sat 9.30am-6pm, Sun 11am-5pm
You might also want to check out The Round Restaurant which serves meals into the evening and has a dedicated children's menu.
The Great Hall Café, Royal Exchange, St Ann's Square, Manchester M2 7DH
Tel: 0161 833 9833 royalexchange.co.uk

House of Fraser Kendals Restaurant on the 6th Floor

Probably one of the country's oldest department stores, House of Fraser or Kendals as it's locally known, is an imposing city landmark and I enjoy shopping there whenever possible! It's a useful place to consider if you have got the children and are after an easy, stress-free lunch in the city centre.

Situated on the same floor as children's clothing, this well-sized restaurant offers a wide range of hot and cold food for children, all priced at £3.95, including a dessert and drink. The lunch boxes looked super and you can also buy the items separately. The big bonus though is the Kids Zone – a little area of the restaurant given over to a few toys, chalkboard and a television, which was playing Peppa Pig to a happy bunch of three year olds when I was last in.

Mon-Fri 9.30am-7pm, Sat 9am-7pm, Sun 11am-5pm
House of Fraser, Deansgate, Manchester M60 3AU
Tel: 0161 833 0025 houseoffraser.co.uk

Jamie's Italian

Jamie Oliver has rolled out his eponymous Italian restaurants all over the UK and finally in 2012 Manchester got one. Installed within the fabulous former Midland Bank building on King Street, this is a pretty spectacular place to dine. We were greeted at the door by very sparkly, groomed staff (who made me feel like I need to go for an eyebrow shape or makeover) and taken to a table on the upstairs mezzanine.

109

Most Haunted star Yvette Fielding's new tearoom Proper Tea is gorgeous.

The view over the bar (which was festooned with hams) restaurant and kitchen was fab. The boys were given a red viewfinder each, which contained pictures of the children's menu and they spent the next ten minutes happily flicking through the choices over and over again. Felix ordered the chicken lollipops (surely not nuggets?!) and a shake-me salad, but Ollie wanted spaghetti with clams off the main menu. They both washed it down with an organic cordial, and had a 50p scoop of ice cream.

Surprisingly a toilet visit ended up being the highlight of my children's lunch, when they discovered they are housed within the former bank vaults in the basement. Our lunch for four cost £76 with soft drinks, coffee and no adult desserts; so Jamie's Italian is one to visit for a treat, rather than simply a shopping stop.

Mon-Sat 12-11pm, Sun 12-10.30pm
Jamie's Italian, 100 King Street, Manchester M2 4WU
Tel: 0161 241 3901 jamieoliver.com

Moose Coffee

Tucked behind Piccadilly Gardens, on the corner of Fountain Street, this New York style diner is a real find. It's reasonably priced, extremely popular and the food portions are huge!

We had a ten minute wait on a busy Saturday lunchtime, but the staff were very patient with our three rowdy boys whose football session had been cancelled and thus were on pretty hyper form!

The two older boys were wowed by the adult menu. Harry opted for New York Moose (Eggs Benedict on a bagel, with parma ham, and the hollandaise on the side!) while Sam had his favourite breakfast of all time (waffles with smoked bacon and maple syrup). Ted chose from the kids' menu, which was perfect for him – promptly demolishing a full cooked breakfast. Ed and I decided to share a Mighty Moose, wrongly assuming that we'd also be able to tuck into the kids' meals! (Two free range over easy eggs, with bacon and homemade potato hash, delicious!) The cafe also offers sandwiches, salads and burgers, but you really have to try their breakfasts. The coffee was good and the atmosphere fantastic – Moose is definitely my kids' favourite place in town.

Mon-Fri 8am-4pm, Sat 9am-5pm, Sun 10am-4pm
Moose Coffee, 20 York Street, Manchester M2 3BB
Tel: 0161 228 7994 moosecoffee.co.uk

Proper Tea

This modern tearoom with a traditional twist is bang on trend and already extremely popular. Owned by *Most Haunted* presenter Yvette Fielding, along with Teacup proprietor Gary McLarnan, it is housed in a fabulous Victorian building opposite the Cathedral.

The decor is gorgeous with beautiful black and white floor tiles, and the whole place has an airy feel. A multitude of loose-leaf teas are lined up on the shelves; I ordered the Cream Tea at £4.90, a

All year round, Spinningfields' events are a must for families... From open-air cinema, the annual duck race, fun-fairs and an ice-rink – there's more here than just smart shopping!

Carluccio's

Nestled in the centre of Spinningfields and surrounded by a large square, there is opportunity to scooter here or perhaps watch the big screen close-by which shows films and sport during the warmer months.

For £6.50 my boys chose from the children's menu: a bit of Grissini and juice to start, followed by their chosen dish Milanese de Pollo, and topped off with a tub of ice cream. The menu came on an attractive colouring and activity sheet. As the restaurant is mainly frequented by suits on their lunch break, service is quick – a bonus when dining with kids!

If it is too cold to eat outside, there is plenty of room for buggies, bags and toddlers inside the colourful restaurant.

Screenfields on the green in summer.

Mon-Fri 8am-11pm, Sat 9am-11pm, Sun 9am-10.30pm

Carluccio's, 3 Hardman Square, Spinningfields, Manchester M3 3EB
Tel: 0161 839 0623 carluccios.com
Also at Piccadilly Station and the Trafford Centre

Giraffe

It's interesting when revisiting restaurants, particularly national chains, to see if standards remain high. I'm pleased to report back that our recent trip to Giraffe was a wholly happy experience! Giraffe is a restaurant that prides itself on being friendly and welcoming, and the Spinningfields branch we visited could not have been more so. The staff were marvellous from start to end – entertaining the kids (and indeed us!) and providing slick service.

The kids' meal deals, which cost £4.95 including a drink, offered a good choice ranging from sausage & mash to fish fingers and chips. To conclude – the much-loved neon Giraffe stirrers are still to be found in their drinks!

Mon-Weds 8am-9.30pm, Thurs-Fri 8am-10pm, Sat 9am-10pm, Sun 10am-9pm

Giraffe, Hardman Square, Spinningfields, Manchester M3 3AB
Tel: 0161 839 0009 giraffe.net
Also at the Trafford Centre

Wagamama

We went along to the Spinningfields' branch of Wagamama to give it a whirl and we were not disappointed! First of all, the welcome was lovely. We were taken immediately to a spot near the floor-to-ceiling windows and the waiter swiftly armed Eleanor and Will with their "Hoshi" noodle doodle activity sheets, enabling us to browse the menu peacefully! Highchairs clip directly onto the long wooden tables, so there's no problem sitting wherever you like.

I was taken aback (in a good way!) with the amount of choice on offer for the kids, and how reasonably priced it was. With advice from our waiter, Eleanor and Will chose mini cha han (chicken, vegetables and stir-fried rice) and grilled fish noodles. Service was perfectly efficient – their meals arrived promptly with our grown-up sides of chilli squid and ribs. The children tucked in and absolutely loved their food. I tried it too and was equally impressed – flavour-some, fresh and healthy.

In Japanese, rather delightfully, Wagamama means "naughty child" – wilful and determined. Thankfully ours were on best behaviour, but I'm sure the friendly staff would have remained unfazed if they'd not been!

Mon-Sat 11.30am-11pm, Sun 11.30am-10pm

Wagamama, 1 Spinningfields Square, Hardman Street, Manchester M3 3AP
Tel: 0161 833 9883 wagamama.com
Also at The Printworks, Manchester and MediaCity, Salford

Also in Spinningfields you'll find Gourmet Burger Kitchen and Zizzi.

Eleanor goes Japanese-style at Wagamama.

THE NORTHERN QUARTER

The bohemian Northern Quarter is a thriving part of Manchester's City Centre – full of great independent cafés, restaurants and shops, it's got a whole lot of soul.

Home Sweet Home

Aptly named, this homely café is the latest of the Northern Quarter's independent establishments. We had brunch which was a good mix of generous British fare, American-style pancakes and some healthy options too. Service was friendly (they were completely unfazed by a smashed glass, courtesy of our three-year-old), coffee was plentiful and milkshakes luxurious. We were able to get a table no problem – Home Sweet Home is bigger inside than it appears, though it was getting busy as we left at lunchtime.
Mon-Thurs 9am-10pm, Fri-Sat 9am-11pm, Sun 9am-9pm
Home Sweet Home, 49-51 Edge Street, Manchester M41 1HW
Tel: 0161 244 9424 cheeseburgertoastie.co.uk

Drop in to the tranquil Oak St. Café in the Craft Centre.

Oak St. Café at Manchester Craft & Design Centre

If you've never visited the Manchester Craft & Design Centre, you really must. With eighteen studios, it's a terrific place to find handmade jewellery, sculpture, furniture and original artwork amongst many other unique things. My particular fave is the lady selling cacti pincushions!

The Craft Centre is tucked away in Manchester's Northern Quarter area, which is only a five minute walk up past the Arndale. As well as being a source of fabulously original gifts for friends or yourself, the pretty Oak St. Café at the heart of it is a tranquil place to drop in and have lunch. The menu was diverse and included soups, frittatas, stews and chillis as well as some beautiful homemade cakes. There are no children's options as such, but ours happily tucked into flatbread and houmous together with some hot choco-late. The café's situated in the open space of the centre's ground floor, so there's plenty of room for buggies. Though we didn't need them at all, a nice touch is the supply of red blankets to keep you warm from draughts!
Mon-Sat 10am-5.30pm
Manchester Craft & Design Centre, 17 Oak Street,
Northern Quarter, Manchester M4 5JD
Tel: 0161 832 4274 craftanddesign.com

Oklahoma

Three-year-old Ellie and I went for a girly lunch here one Saturday. We ambled for as long as little legs would allow through the bohemian Northern Quarter and fell happily into vegetarian café-cum-gift shop – Oklahoma. It's a bit crazy, and a lot retro, with a hippy vibe. We like it a lot. Managed to get a seat fairly easily, which was a relief. People do seem to come and go quite quickly; so if it was full, hopefully you wouldn't have to wait long. Off the kids' menu Ellie chose baked beans on toast with a chocolate milkshake. I opted for a toasted goats cheese with chorizo sandwich and a cappuccino. All very good and service was swift. We couldn't leave without a wander round the shop of course, and subsequently Ellie left wearing a pair of super kitsch palm tree and pina colada sunglasses. Cool.
Mon-Fri 10am-6pm, Sat 8am-6pm, Sun 10am-6pm.
Oklahoma, 74-76 High Street, Manchester M4 1ES
Tel: 0161 834 1136 oklahomacafe.co.uk

Teacup Kitchen

Does the soft play centre leave you jaded? Are you tired of your regular haunts? Then this hip café should prove the perfect antidote. Sit and soak up the atmosphere as the in-crowd stroll by and watch your little ones happily munching their way through multi-coloured rainbow cakes or a plate of home-baked madeleines.

This is a sizeable café with plenty of space to manoeuvre a pram. Kids, young and old, will be delighted by the tantalising display of cookies and cakes. The menu ranges from 'All Day Eggs' (any style) and sourdough toast with a delicious selection of spreads; to more substantial soups, pies and pastries. There are over twenty types of tea to pick from. I was very tempted to try the Red Lychee £4.20, but played it safe with Teacup's NQ Brew at £3.50!
Sun- Weds 10am-6pm, Thurs- Sat 10am-8pm
Teacup Kitchen, 53-55 Thomas Street, Manchester M4 1NA
Tel: 0161 832 3233 teacupandcakes.com

A catch up over coffee and cake in Teacup Kitchen.

For a spectacular display, you can't beat Sapporo Teppanyaki – watch your eyebrows though!

gigantic homemade scone with clotted cream, along with Sunshine Earl Grey tea. On its arrival I was handed a very cute egg timer, and instructions by my waiter on how to brew the tea properly. I have to admit, despite my scepticism, it was lovely and definitely 'enlivened my senses' as the tea menu had promised!

I was visiting with my nine-year-old and his friend and, although there is no children's menu, the boys chose a couple of Fentiman's ginger beers and a toasted sandwich, happily rounding it all off with chocolate brownies! Proper Tea is best suited to families with older children or mums with young babies... I just hope none of Yvette's spooky friends come to check it out!

Mon-Sat 10am-6.30pm, Sun 10am-5pm
Manchester Cathedral, Visitors Centre, 10 Cateaton Street, Manchester M3 1SQ
Tel: 0161 832 3220 properteadeveloper.com

San Carlo Cicchetti

When award-winning Italian San Carlo opened its chic, all day dining restaurant "Cicchetti" on the ground floor of Kendals, there wasn't a hotter table to be had in city centre Manchester. The concept, a menu that offers a multitude of Venetian tapas-style dishes, has had appreciative diners flocking. I've been a few times now for lunch with girlfriends and

not failed to be impressed by the attentive, warm service and first class food.

I dropped by most recently with mum, sister and eight-month-old niece. Interestingly there were several mothers in with their babies and the staff were lovely with all bambini, cooing appreciatively and putting mums at ease. The idea is to order several of the small dishes and share them amongst each other – perfect for someone like me who loves tasting lots of different things! We ordered lamb cutlets, spaghetti carbonara, beef carpaccio and a piadina, which was plenty between three of us. Atmosphere is buzzing and unpretentious – it does always seem busy and you can't book in the daytime, so probably best to get there early for lunch. A sterling restaurant that I think deserves its reputation. I hear they do a mean old breakfast too!

Mon-Fri 8am-11pm,Sat & Sun 9am-11pm
Cicchetti Manchester, House of Fraser Ground Floor (separate entrance on King Street West) M3 2QG
Tel: 0161 839 2233 sancarlocicchetti.co.uk

Sapporo Teppanyaki

If you are looking for somewhere a little bit different, Sapporo Teppanyaki in Manchester's Castlefield district is a great bet. We tried it with our three children aged 13, 10 and 7 early on a Saturday evening; lots of other families had had the same

113

PLACES TO EAT – CITY CENTRE

idea. We were seated on a horseshoe-shaped table overlooking a large metal grill, along with two other families, so don't come here if you only like private dining! The kids' menu is really good value – for £6.95 they can choose a main meal and a drink (pudding is an extra £2 but our kids couldn't eat another thing!) The kids' menu yakisoba noodles (chicken or vegetable) and the salmon teriyaki are both cooked on the grill in front of you, and so they are the most exciting options to go for. The show was almost ready to start!

First of all our Teppanyaki chef set fire to oil on the grill. The flames leapt a spectacular three feet high. The kids loved it! I over-protectively stopped them from leaning in for a closer look as I'm sure they would have regretted the singed eyebrow look! Then the chef cooked sauté potatoes. Your first three chips are served to you via the air. Yes, you are expected to catch a flying chip in your mouth. In front of your family and other strangers. This was actually not as daunting as it might sound, in fact it was very funny and everyone completely got into the swing of it. Just for the record, I managed it on my second go!

The food is really fresh, and is cooked on the grill in front of you – stir-fried vegetables, noodles, meat or fish with a variety of sauces. Our meals were absolutely delicious. And it was great fun too. Our verdict: it's an inspired place to go for a celebratory meal. We will definitely be looking for a reason to go again.

Mon-Sat 12-11pm, Sun 12-10.30pm
Sapporo Teppanyaki Manchester, 91-93 Liverpool Road, Manchester M3 4JN
Tel: 0161 979 0575 sapporo.co.uk

Tai Pan

Often we go here when we are celebrating a birthday or have lots of family visiting. It's fun and we can always get a big enough table, whether we've booked or not.

My kids love the 'Lazy Susan' – twirling round the little cups of green tea to ninety-year-old Grandpa seems to them like a children's tea party. Usually we order masses of dim sum and starters, and there is plenty here that goes down well with little ones. A favourite is the crispy duck, as they love the spectacle and the ceremony of preparing their own rolled pancakes. Often with young children we want a meal to be over and done with quickly, before they either start flicking peas, crying or running wild; at Tai Pan though, our children are interested enough in what's going on around them to easily tolerate a couple of hours.

This restaurant is usually buzzing with families and it certainly attracts the Manchester Chinese

Little ones love the easy-to-use chop sticks at Tampopo.

community, bearing testament to the high quality food. Complete your visit with a trip to the wonderful Chinese supermarket below.
Mon-Sat 12-11.30pm, Sun 11.30am-9.30pm
Tai Pan Restaurant, Brunswick House,
97 Upper Brook Street, Longsight, Manchester M13 9TX
Tel: 0161 273 2798 taipanmanchester.co.uk

Tampopo

This is our fourth book and yet Tampopo remains one of my favourite child-friendly restaurants. It's quick, reasonably priced and consistently good. We tend to meet my in-laws from Bolton two or three times a year here; we all like the menu, which is healthy and has a fine choice of Asian dishes. The little ones love the easy-to-use chop sticks and the placemats conveniently double up as activity colouring sheets.

Harry, who's now eight, still likes their Junior Explorer menu – noodles with chicken, broccoli and sweet soy sauce. Sam always has the Mini Explorer – chicken satay, vegetable tempura, carrot and cucumber sticks with a plum sauce. Both dishes are £3.95. For £4.50 you can progress to the Mini Adventurer, which is a small portion of any of the adult main dishes.

NB: Tampopo Albert Square is accessed by a steep staircase on the way in, which can be a struggle with the pushchair; and there are no baby-changing facilities. Tampopo at The Corn Exchange has easier access and does have baby changing.
Mon-Sat 12-11pm, Sun 12-10pm
Tampopo, 16 Albert Square, Manchester M2 5PF
Tel: 0161 819 1966 tampopo.co.uk
Also at The Corn Exchange and The Trafford Centre

Also in Manchester you'll find Albert's Shed, Barburitto, Croma, Dimitris, GBK, Mud Crab at Grinch, Piccolino, Pizza Express, Prezzo, Yo Sushi and Zizzi.

Bean & Brush is a great independent café and as family-friendly as you can get.

ALTRINCHAM, HALE AND SALE

Bean & Brush

Based in an old mail sorting house, Bean & Brush has been beautifully converted, with a mezzanine at the back where all the arts and crafts take place. Downstairs feels both grown up and child-friendly, with a selection of toys for little ones. The menu is appealing with locally-sourced, homemade dishes at a reasonable cost. Children's food included jacket potatoes from £2.25, pasta bowls from £2.75 and a small portion of homemade stew just £2.95.

Food and service were really good. We made it upstairs to paint some pots and found a great range, both in price and variety from Dr. Who's Tardis to Christmas Baubles. Decopatch is available too, and is ace if your child is not that artistic, as whatever happens, the end results all look amazing! Overall we thought Bean & Brush was fab – a brilliant place to meet mummy friends, or hook up with other families for a weekend brunch. 10 out of 10!

NB: The M&S car park is a maximum stay of one hour for 50p and a very efficient attendant is on patrol. The Tesco one opposite is better.

Mon-Fri 8am-7pm, Sat 8.30am-7pm, Sun 9.30am-6pm
Bean & Brush Family Art Café, The Old Sorting Office,
12 Hayfield Street, Sale M33 7XW
Tel: 0161 973 2140 beanandbrush.co.uk

Café Ark

During a walk or cycle ride in **Chorlton Ees** or **Sale Water Park** (see page 78), Ark is a great spot to stop for a hot chocolate, juice and cake, or some homemade vegetarian fare. Housed in part of the triangular Mersey Valley Visitor Centre, step through the double doors below the neon café sign and you'll find polka dot cloths covering six little tables, cute artworks hanging from the ceiling, books, mags and colouring pencils for kids. Outside, if you get the weather, there are plenty of tables too. Choose for yourself from the chalkboard – a selection of soup and sarnies, lasagne and halloumi pittas; all the food looked delicious.

Following a good walk from Chorlton Ees, a relaxing coffee outside Café Ark is just the ticket.

115

Danilo's is a traditional pizzeria with lots of character.

Weds-Sun 11am-4pm. Baby change and toilets in the adjacent public visitor centre.
Café Ark, Mersey Valley Visitor Centre, Sale Water Park (at Rifle Road), Sale M33 2LX
Tel: 0161 969 6775

Danilo's Pizzeria

This long-established pizzeria is an institution in Hale. The restaurant doesn't have great curb-appeal, and inside the decor is very traditional, but it has a super atmosphere and was busy with a mixture of groups and families. We shared three pizzas between a family of five, priced from £6.95 to £9.95, and all were delicious. The pasta looked extremely appetizing and smaller portions are available for £5.95; the restaurant is happy to downsize pretty much any of the main dishes. We were keeping it light so decided to forego the ice cream but, much to the children's delight, staff brought over a bumper jar of lollies.

At times service was a bit slow, but it was more of a relaxed 'laissez-faire' slow. The waiters were extremely friendly and happy to chat, plus the food was excellent. A great recommendation, and miles better than your average pizza chain.
Mon-Sat 12-2pm, 6.30-10.30pm, Sun 2-8pm
Danilo's Pizzeria, 151 Ashley Road, Hale, Altrincham WA14 2UW
Tel: 0161 928 0453   danilos.co.uk

Gastronomy

Upstairs at Gastronomy, the sumptuous deli on Hale village's main drag, you'll find a lovely café serving breakfasts, lunches, and traditional afternoon teas on antique china; with a glass of bubbly should you fancy! There's also a children's platter priced at £4.95, which consists of a sandwich, hummus, cucumber and a few chips. Gastronomy are clearly used to serving younger diners as there were several children's books scattered about and baby changing is available. The stairs could be a problem if you bring a pram though; you'd probably have to collapse it and carry it up with you, as there's no room to leave it in the shop downstairs.

We popped in on a weekday lunch-time and, tempted by Gastronomy's freshly-baked bread and imaginatively-named sandwiches, plumped for "The Flamenco Fowl" and "The Big Bad Wolf". A gastronomic delight!
Mon-Sat 8am-5pm, Sun 10am-4pm
Gastronomy, 191 Ashley Road, Hale WA15 9SQ
Tel: 0161 928 7870 gastronomydeli.co.uk

The Lavender Barn

This family-run business on the Dunham estate is a very pretty stopping-off point if you've been walking in and around the area. There's a garden to sit in, with wrought iron furniture, and you're surrounded by fields and a few animals. The previously unfenced duck pond has now been fenced off, more tables have been added, and there are some wooden Wendy houses for children to play make-believe. Inside, The Lavender Barn has expanded into space next door, so there's more seating room plus a cute play area for little ones. The food remains the same, with staples such as soup, sandwiches and jackets, and a healthy selection of cakes.
Tues-Sun 10am-4pm. Cash or cheque only.
The Lavender Barn, Dog Farm, School Lane, Dunham, Altrincham WA14 4TR
Tel: 0161 941 2153 lavenderbarn.net

Urmston Bookshop

This is a small bookshop which packs a huge punch! It's bustling with energy; organising a wide variety of events such as beginners' crochet workshops, books and buggy sessions for new mums and babies, together with interactive story-telling amongst others.

Urmston Books is bigger than it first appears.

Gastronomy is a lovely deli with a café upstairs.

Books and gifts sit at the front whilst towards the back there's a little seating area, forming part of the café. With gorgeous cakes and coffees on offer, our needs were well catered for. There's a few toys and games to keep toddlers entertained too. We were warmly welcomed. It's terrific to see a local shop with such marvellous ambitions thriving.

Tues -Sat 9am-5.30pm
Urmston Bookshop, 72 Flixton Road, Urmston M41 5AB
Tel: 0161 747 7442 urmston-bookshop.co.uk

Y... McGregor

After a morning spent in nearby **John Leigh Park** (see page 86) I took Sam and Ted to Y...McGregor's in Altrincham. The café prides itself on locally-sourced, homemade fare and no processed foods. They specialise in smoothies, juices and frozen yoghurts; very appealing and healthy for kids.

My regret was that I was only popping in for a snack, as the all-day breakfasts looked divine. Most dishes are available in children's portions, just ask, or there's a lunch box at £3.90. It was clean, appealing and very friendly; and was also getting pretty busy as we were leaving! You'll find a selection of books for little ones tucked in a box around a corner.

Daily 8am-4pm
Y...McGregor, 29 Stamford New Road,
Altrincham WA14 1EB
Tel: 0161 928 1487 ymcgregor.com

Also in this area, you will find Pizza Express and Piccolino (both in Hale).

Ted and Ellie play games in the Design Museum Café.

ALDERLEY EDGE, KNUTSFORD AND WILMSLOW

The Botanist

After a diligent week at school, a treat for the children is going out for tea. This particular Friday we decided upon The Botanist in Alderley Edge. Displayed in cabinets within the restaurant there's lots of gardening paraphernalia, a nice nod to the restaurant's moniker. There is now a dedicated children's menu, priced at £5.95 including an ice-cream and choices such as mini-burgers, scampi & chips and bangers & mash. We actually plumped for rotisserie chicken and fries, which was £9.75 to share. I had a "hanging kebab" of halloumi and veg (£9.95), which was very tasty. It came with a small bowl of couscous under the suspended kebab. We all enjoyed our food and found The Botanist very friendly.

Mon-Sat 12-11pm, Sun 12-10pm
The Botanist, 15 London Road, Alderley Edge SK9 7JT
Tel: 01625 865637 thebotanist.uk.com

The Design Museum Café

On a clear day, a scenic drive over Snake Pass to the David Mellor shop and café always boosts my spirits! It's worth popping in if you're heading over to the pool at **Hathersage** (see page 54) or perhaps just on a day trip to the Peak District. The country shop is a delight for all foodie parents and there's a small cutlery factory to stick your nose into (set in the architecturally award-winning Round Building).

The café serves up wonderful wholesome food and I can vouch for the sandwiches; I had the bacon and brie with onion marmalade, which was gorgeous. For children there are smaller versions, including ham, simple cheddar or salmon, all priced from £3.60. The café is within a tiny museum showcasing some of Mellor's achievements – everything from cutlery and a cathedral candelabra through to post-boxes, litter bins and benches. But for the kids, the star of the show has to be the set of full-sized traffic lights flashing away alongside the tables.

Mon-Sat 10am-5pm, Sun 11am-5pm
Cutlery Factory: Mon-Fri 10am- 5pm
The Design Museum Café, Hathersage, Sheffield S32 1BA
Tel: 01433 650 220 davidmellordesign.co.uk

Real Penny Farthings provide a wonderfully unusual backdrop to lunch at The Courtyard Coffee House.

Chilli Banana

This hugely popular family-run restaurant has just moved up the road in Wilmslow to stylish new premises on the corner of Water Lane. It's two-storey now, with plans for an open-air decked terrace in the future! Right now though, a new feature is their daily 'Street Food' menu (noon-3pm) with delicious sounding dishes like hot & sour soup, Thai beef salad and king prawn skewers.

Our visit however was an early tea with the children – Chilli Banana absolutely welcomes youngsters (though there isn't a separate menu for them) and staff are delighted to help choose dishes for little ones. There is plenty of choice for vegetarians, and a mouth watering selection of seafood dishes, as well as the simple Thai dishes that our children favour.

Spare ribs, chicken satay and miniature spring rolls were all presented beautifully, delicious, and devoured in minutes – our youngest even had a go at the decorative carrot garnish! Stir fried soft noodles with chicken and vegetables and steamed rice which our two boys shared were also polished off with gusto. The prices aren't cheap, but the food was all freshly cooked and really tasty. It was all the more satisfying that our children were choosing different foods from the usual sausages and fish

fingers – on our way home they announced that their new favourite food was Thai!

Tues-Sat 12-3pm & 5.30-10.30pm, Sun 12-9pm (buffet 12-3pm)
The Chilli Banana Thai Restaurant, 71 Water Lane, Wilmslow SK9 5BQ
Tel: 01625 539100 chillibanana.co.uk
Also at Macclesfield

Cook & Baker

With its white tiled counter, exposed red brick and industrial pendant lighting; this newest addition on the Wilmslow block has a cool New York design feel about it, and a very warm welcome. Located opposite Hoopers, and with several tables and chairs at the front for warm weather dining, Cook & Baker excels at offering a huge array of delicious-looking cakes to deliberate over. It's a perfect place to meet friends for coffee, but there's also a couple of sandwich options, salads, quiche and soup to choose from if you wanted to extend into lunch. It's nice and spacious too, if you've got a little one in a pram, and I'd certainly recommend it as a place to try out.
Mon-Sat 9am-5.30pm
Cook & Baker, 12 Alderley Road, Wilmslow SK9 1JX
Tel: 01625 522155

The Courtyard Coffee House

…AKA the café in Knutsford with the Penny Farthings in it! Quite a remarkable collection of over 30 Penny Farthing bicycles (the largest collection in the world) are on display here. And that's not all! A miniature railway circles the room at five minute intervals, on a ledge beneath the ceiling, tooting its horn. English eccentricity at its very best!

Lunch options are substantial and varied; ranging from welsh rarebit (£6.15) and smoked haddock (£9.45) to pasta carbonara (£7.75). There's no children's menu so I ended up sharing a soup and a scone with my three-year-old. I would definitely consider making a special visit here for breakfast, it all sounded delicious! I brought my mum to the Courtyard for lunch and she really enjoyed it. Service is friendly and quite traditional. It's clearly a very popular spot with the locals though, so make sure you get here early for lunch or you might struggle for a seat. In better weather, the eponymous courtyard at the front has several tables, making it a good choice if you've got small children who like to run around.

The Courtyard definitely gets my vote for most unique cafe in the area – indeed probably the whole country!

Mon-Fri 9am-4.30pm, Sat & Sun 9am-5pm (though not open Sun during winter season.)

Cook & Baker has a cool NY design feel and delicious cakes.

The Courtyard Coffee House and Restaurant, The rear of 92 King Street, Knutsford WA16 6ED
Tel: 01565 653974 thecourtyardknutsford.co.uk

Hoopers Restaurant

Located on the 2nd floor of Hoopers, the lovely old department store in the centre of Wilmslow, this restaurant is extremely popular with local mums and babies; judging by how many were there for morning coffee the last time I visited! And I can really understand why. I've popped in a couple of times now, with my mum and little one, and have

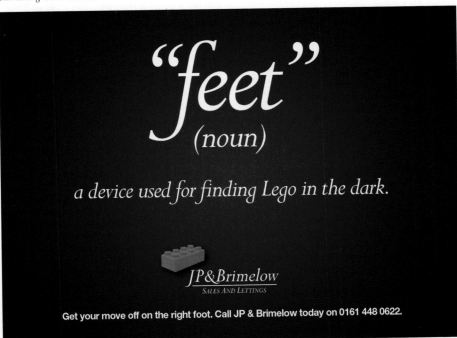

Great food, great juices, great events – great vibe at The Yard.

always found the service to be extremely friendly and welcoming. The food is consistently excellent quality, and the menu extensive. There is a good range of children's meals available, from pasta with meatballs to chinese chicken and rice (£5); or a lunch box for £4.75. For me personally, shopping at Hoopers is a much more pleasurable experience than battling the crowds at the Trafford Centre so, combining that with a lovely lunch, makes for a nice trip out from Didsbury.

Mon-Sat 9am-5pm (Weds 9.30am-5pm). Pay and display parking at rear of store.
Hoopers, 35 Alderley Road, Wilmslow SK9 1PB
Tel: 01625 525381 hoopersstores.com

Strada

A good alternative to Pizza Express, I've been a fan of Strada for a while now (and in particular its stone-baked Proscuitto pizza!) It offers a good kids menu priced at £6.75 – they can choose a starter (grissini or dip), main course (chicken breast, meatballs, pizza, various pastas), dessert (ice cream or lolly), and a drink (milk, juice or water). So even the most fussy of children should be able to find something to suit them here!

On our most recent visit to the Wilmslow branch, service was lovely as ever. We were happy to be tucked away in a squishy banquette booth. The children coloured in their activity packs while Tony and I demolished the rosemary and garlic flatbread (surely the best around?!!) in record time. Our pizzas all arrived promptly and needless to say our eyes were greedier than our stomachs, but to Will's delight, the waitress boxed all leftovers up for us to take home. As always, we left full and happy!

Mon-Fri 11.30am-11pm, Sat 10.30am-11pm,
Sun 10.30am-10.30pm
Strada, 22-24 Water Lane, Wilmslow SK9 5AA
Tel: 01625 418698 strada.co.uk

The Yard

The Yard is a café, creative venue, food store and juice bar, all rolled into one exceptionally stylish package. Located just off the high street in Alderley Edge village, (turn down next to Barclays Bank, and then left) The Yard is the perfect place to drop into at any time of day. Last time we visited for breakfast with the kids and enjoyed delicious pancakes and eggy bread with really good coffee. The juices (to go or eat in), lovingly created by owner Sadie, are exceptional. Juiced freshly to order, they have garnered a large and loyal fan base. Sadie also co-ordinates various events at the Yard, from session nights with Chris Jagger (brother of Mick!) to Breakfast with PR Guru (and Ab Fab inspiration) Lynne Franks – visit their Facebook page so you don't miss out!

Mon-Sat 8.30am-5pm, Sun 10am-2pm
The Yard, 32 South Street, Alderley Edge SK9 7ES
Tel: 01625 586962

Also in this area you will find Gusto (Alderley Edge and Knutsford), Fosters Fish & Chips (Alderley Edge), Pizza Express (Knutsford and Wilmslow) and Piccolino (Knutsford).

BOLTON

Curley's Dining Rooms

A recommendation by one of our readers led us to try out Curley's Fisheries overlooking the reservoir on the edge of Rivington Country Park. Then, when I mentioned this wonderful new discovery to my mother-in-law who lives in Bolton, of course she claimed to know all about it and had been coming here for years!

It's recently undergone a major development. (It used to be a simple shed serving a hot cup of tea to my mother-in-law and her best friend as they waited for a friendly fisherman to catch their supper!) Now a series of fabulous stone buildings, with a large dining room and decked patio area overlook the reservoir – the views are tremendous and the atmosphere idyllic.

The menu consists mainly of fish, with Curley's Fish & Chips a speciality, but there are also sandwiches, snacks and a selection of specials. The junior fisherman can choose from sausages, fresh fish bites or chicken, with chips, mushy peas and a drink (£3.95). This is a great place to come for a well-earned meal after a hike up **Rivington Pike** (see page 98). And, if you fancy trying your hand at fishing, they offer tuition and equipment hire next door in the tackle shop.

Mon-Fri 10am-8pm, Weekends 9.30am-8pm

Superb fish & chips at Curley's overlooking the reservoir on the edge of Rivington Country Park.

Curley's Dining Rooms, Walsuches, Off Chorley Old
Road, Horwich, Bolton BL6 6PP
Tel: 01204 691783 curleysdiningrooms.co.uk

Luciano's

If, like my husband, you're a fan of the
Wanderers, then this Bolton cafe will be
right up your street as most of the large
glass windows overlook the Reebok Stadium at
Middlebrook.

Luciano's, a family-run Italian cafe, is good;
really, really good. The menu is simple: sandwiches
and paninis in the daytime, with a slightly extended
choice for the evening. We were there at lunchtime
and felt they've got it just right. It's bright and clean,
and very inviting with some lovely comfy sofas to
relax on. Order at the counter and they'll bring your
food and drink to your table. There isn't a separate
kids menu, but Sam and I shared a shredded duck
panini with a honey and teriyaki sauce (£4.95)
which was excellent. If I'd had more time I would
definitely have indulged in one of their yummy
cakes. There's also a selection of specials if you want
something a bit more substantial.

Luciano's has a lovely atmosphere, knocking
the spots off other chain restaurants based at the

If you're a fan of The Wanderers, the views from Luciano's will bring a smile to your face.

shopping centre. It's well used by mums and tots in Bolton, often busy midweek after local toddler groups. It also has an extensive cocktail list, I think I might have to go back to try out a couple…in fact I can see another book idea already!

Sun-Tues & Thurs 8am-10pm, Wed, Fri & Sat 8am-midnight
Luciano's, The Band Stand, The Linkway, Middlebrook,
Bolton BL6 6JA
Tel: 01204 691111 lucianosatthemillstone.com

Pizza Express

In our opinion Pizza Express still does what it does very well indeed. The Piccolo children's menu has evolved over the past couple of years into a nicely-varied menu.

The ever-popular 'baked dough balls' thankfully remain firmly in place as a starter. Then you can choose from four different types of pizza, four different types of pasta, and three different desserts; plus you still get the Bambinoccino, a diddy cup of frothy milk with chocolate sprinkles. Within these choices there are uncomplicated dishes like 'simple pasta with garlic butter' or margherita pizza, so if you've got a less adventurous child (or like me, one that point blank refuses mince) then it's an easy menu to negotiate.

So top marks for choice. And the quality is unwaveringly good. Top marks there too. Less good is the price – the Piccolo menu will now set you back

£6.50, not including a drink. With a kid's apple juice at £2.55... suddenly you're not far off £10 per child. And has anyone else noticed that they've shrunk the kids' pizzas?!

Daily 11.30am-11pm
Pizza Express, 8-12 Wood Street, Bolton BL1 1DY
Tel: 01204 528776 pizzaexpress.com

Suzanna's at Little Scotland

After a bracing walk round **Haigh Country Park** (see page 81), my sister suggested we try nearby Suzanna's restaurant and pub for lunch with the three children. In its previous incarnation, this rather inauspicious building was locally well known as Gallaghers. Owner, Suzanna Young, has transformed it both inside and out. The premises is split into an eighty cover restaurant and a separate pub area, but a single menu covers both.

Only the pub is open during the day. It does not in any way feel like a traditional "pub"! It's quite small, just one room, and I'd say has more of a night-club/bar feel about it. Although the decor wasn't quite to my taste, the whole place was spotless. The waitress looking after us that lunchtime was one of the friendliest and nicest people you could ever hope to have taking care of you. The menu was extensive and I was initially sceptical as to whether the kitchen could pull it off; but I was wrong, the food was excellent. I chose a goats cheese and beetroot salad with slivers of fresh orange, which was beautiful dressed and presented. My sister had a fish finger sandwich which looked and tasted fab. The kids opted for fish goujons and chips and a mini lamb hot pot – again absolute winners – well prepared, very fresh food. It was all very reasonably priced too, £4.95 for one children's course, with a dessert of (homemade on the premises) scrummy ice cream offered for free. Free? That doesn't happen often does it these days!

Mon 6-9pm, Tues -Weds 12-9pm, Thurs-Sat 12-10pm, Sun 12-8pm

Suzanna's Pub & Restaurant, 38 Little Scotland, Blackrod, Bolton BL6 5LW
Tel: 01942 832639 suzannas.com

BRAMHALL, CHEADLE AND GATLEY

Coffee Fix

Coffee Fix is a regular fixture for the Gatley Mums' brigade. With a laid back vibe, this cafe is a must for coffee aficionados, but there's also plenty of home-made cakes, milkshakes and fine food to tempt! It's a good space – nice and spacious, and children are welcome with an easy kids' menu, serving simple dishes like sandwiches and cheese on toast from £2.50. For adults, there was a tempting selection, from soups to club sandwiches. Definitely worth a trip if you're in the vicinity of John Lewis, and better priced too!

Mon-Sat 9am-4.30pm, Sun 10am-4.30pm

Coffee Fix, 80 Church Road, Gatley SK8 4NQ
Tel: 0161 282 0090 wearecoffeefix.com

Gusto

I popped along to my local Gusto restaurant one Sunday afternoon with just me and the two ankle-biters. This thriving Italian chain is a popular choice for families, and the atmosphere was easy and jolly.

For £5.95 the kids had the opportunity to choose, then add, their own toppings to a pizza at the table – it's then taken off and cooked for them. I noticed later that kids are meant to be given a chef's hat, but our waiter forgot ours. Though hatless the children did enjoy it and the end result was tasty. Note that there is no children's menu available after 6pm, just smaller portions of the mains. They also had an ice cream dessert within their menu. I opted for a starter-sized portion of the primavera pasta which was ok, but nothing special.

Good to know for families all the Gusto chains have dispensed with crayons at the table and moved onto high-tech iPods! A great decision as far as my kids are concerned.

Sun-Thurs 12-10pm, Fri-Sat 12-11.30pm

Gusto, Landmark House, Station Road,
Cheadle Hulme SK8 7BS
Tel: 0161 488 1180 gustorestaurants.uk.com
Also at Alderley Edge, Didsbury and Knutsford.

Piccolino

In spite of being a national chain, every branch of Piccolino in the north west has a completely different look and feel about it and consistently delivers good food to the table. Their menu offers an interesting choice of both modern and classic Italian dishes and they now have kids' choices too.

They were extremely welcoming of our lot when we popped along for an early tea. Will opted for calamari (£2.50) and then a pizza (£5) whilst little Ellie went for a kids-sized spaghetti carbonara which cost £6.50. All the food was delicious and it was a successful evening out en famille! I took along colouring pads for the children so they amused themselves for enough time for us all to eat happily. Inevitably it was not a cheap night out, but I like the fact that if you fancy quality Italian food then Piccolino is a family option.

Mon-Sat 12-11pm, Sun 12-10.30pm

207 Moss Lane, Bramhall, Stockport SK7 1BA
Tel: 0161 439 8298 individualrestaurants.com
Also at Didsbury, Clitheroe, Hale, Knutsford, Manchester and Stockton Heath

Plumcake

After a visit to nearby **Bramhall Park** (see page 78) myself and another mum, along with our little ones, headed to Plum-cake for a light lunch and a catch up.

The kids' menu is simple and charming; beans or scrambled eggs on toast £2.05, mini all-day break-fast £3.95, or afternoon tea at £5.95 (which includes a fairy cake to decorate). They brought a basket of toys plus a huge dolls house for the kids to play with while they were waiting for their lunch. The whole atmosphere was extremely relaxed and very welcoming.

Fun toys to play with at Plumcake in Bramhall.

For the first time, Ted didn't want to leave a cafe, as him and Ellie were having such a lovely time. For the sake of peace and quiet, I promised him we'd be back soon. Lucky me!

Mon-Sat 9am-4.30pm, Sun 10am-3pm
Plumcake, 11 The Village Square, Bramhall SK7 1AW
Tel: 0161 439 8147

Simply Books

This lovely bookshop in the centre of Bramhall village has a great little café. Downstairs there's a small children's table with a selection of books, but upstairs is a big communal table that can seat about ten, plus lots of comfy chairs and more activities. As well as a relaxed atmosphere, there's space to park your buggy, highchairs and a baby changing area.

Everything is homemade – the cookies are freshly baked each morning! There are juice cartons and a child-size 'Charlie & Lola' hot chocolate that comes with squirty cream and marshmallows. On Fridays and Saturdays they offer a 'Soup Kitchen' serving delicious soup with a generous chunk of baguette.

Some parking's available on the high street or you could try the Simply Books valet parking service! Run in and Andrew the owner will take your keys and park your car in their area round the back (apparently it's a bit tight!)

Tues-Sat 9.30am-5.30pm
Simply Books, 228 Moss Lane, Bramhall SK7 1BD
Tel: 0161 439 1436 simplybooks.info

Also in this area, you will find Pizza Express (Bramhall and Cheadle).

BURY, PRESTWICH AND WHITEFIELD

Aumbry

I was rather excited to be going to Aumbry for Sunday lunch, as we'd heard rave reviews about married chefs Laurence Tottingham and Mary-Ellen McTague – in fact Mary-Ellen has recently won the 'Chef of the Year' award at the 2013 Manchester Food and Drink Festival.

We visited with grandparents and had booked ahead, which is probably advisable. The restaurant is tiny, so don't arrive expecting to park a double buggy, although I'm sure they'd try and accommodate it somewhere. The boys were treated courteously from the start, and the staff asked their names, which they then referred to throughout. As a little appetiser treat, we were all presented with a small guinea fowl terrine, wrapped in prosciutto, with a cucumber pickle and a red jus. The boys looked a bit confused as it didn't look like what they had ordered! They approved!

I'd forgotten my usual bag of toys; not to worry,

Aumbry had it covered. The boys were soon armed with a pencil case each and a bumper colouring book.

Olly and Felix had been given a choice of homemade fish and chips with vegetables or a small portion from the à la carte. They both chose the former, which they loved, and followed this up with a portion of roast lamb, roast beef and potatoes, scavenged from their grandparents. Not an indication that the children's portion was too small, just testament to how mouth-watering and delicious the grown ups' food looked and tasted.

Desserts were equally successful and the total bill, including a bottle of Merlot, sparkling water and children's juices, came to £158. A lovely spot for a special family meal.

Lunch Fri-Sat 12-1.30pm, Dinner Tues-Sat 6.30-9.30pm.
Aumbry, Church Lane, Prestwich M25 1AJ
Tel: 0161 798 5841 aumbryrestaurant.co.uk

Croma

Pizzas, colouring crayons and friendly staff are guaranteed to go down well with most; this lively and welcoming local chain do them all in great surroundings and with style. There always seems to be a buzz of activity and chatter; so it doesn't matter if your child likes to shout and wriggle, or if your baby loves hurling random things on the floor – you are bound to find another family making more mess than you!

The children's menu is £4.95 and includes a drink, pizza or pasta, salad, ice cream and Cromaccino – an excellent price for all of that. My eight-year-old (who's constantly hungry!) has shifted to the adult menu now for bigger portions, still good value, with a ten inch margherita costing £5.50.

The hugely popular Croma.

Croma is a brilliant restaurant – it's easy to see why it's so popular.

Mon-Thurs 12-10pm, Fri-Sun 12-10.30pm
Croma, The Radius, Prestwich M25 1AY
Tel: 0161 798 7666 cromapizza.co.uk
Also at Manchester City Centre and Chorlton

Metro Fish Bar

If you fancy fish and chips then you will be hard pushed to find a better spot to dine than Metro Fish Bar, situated at Blackfriars between Bury and Whitefield. Offering fabulous adult and child-sized portions of meat puddings, fish, scampi; and a host of non-chippy items, such as Whitby Crab starter, you will be spoilt for choice. Although it is more expensive than a takeaway, the restaurant is a charming place to eat. It has been tastefully decorated and tiled in black and white throughout.

To the rear of the café is a large outdoor deck with tables overlooking a wooded dell. There is also a fenced area for under-threes to play in, complete with a playhouse. Stepping down from the deck, a path leads to a fenced wooden play area for older children.

Daily 11.30am-9pm
Café Metro, 825 Manchester Road, Bury BL9 9TP
Tel: 0161 796 0134

Roma

This Italian family-run deli, café and bakery has been in Whitefield for 25 years. It adjoins Morrisons supermarket and conveniently shares their car park. The café and deli are very 'glossy' with marble floors, large windows, spotlights and shiny display fridges filled with goodies. The staff here are friendly and aren't afraid of interacting with kids, helping to maintain a family-run feel. There is plenty of space, which makes it great for prams.

With the bakery on the premises making pizzas and bread, and with all their pasta and soup dishes prepared in house too, the food tastes delicious. For the grown-ups there is wine or a proper Italian espresso to accompany a lunch; and for children, Roma's award-winning homemade ice cream.

Inevitably it is hard to resist buying something from the deli on the way out!

Mon-Thurs & Sat 9am-6pm, Fri 9am-8pm, Sun closed.
Roma, 268 Bury New Road, Whitefield M45 8QS
Tel: 0161 766 2941 roma.ltd.uk

Slattery Patissier and Chocolatier

The real appeal of a trip here is not the elegant dining room of the three-storey Victorian building that houses the Slattery empire, but walking through the Willy Wonka-style shop on the ground floor!

Children cannot fail to be impressed by the rows and rows of superbly decorated cakes, gateaux,

Generous portions for the boys at Metro Fish Bar.

chocolates of every shape and size, sweets and bottles of sarsaparilla. Unfortunately there are no oompah-loompahs but the 'chocolate factory' itself can be viewed through large picture windows at the rear of the shop.

Upstairs, a children's menu is on offer. On a recent visit my boys devoured soup served with fingers of white bread and butter for £2.25. They were delighted to find their favourite dessert, often missed off modern menus, jelly and ice cream! For Mums and Dads there are, amongst other things, sandwiches starting at £5.75, and the fabulous and famous 'Slattery Rarebit' which I can't wait to go back for. Even with a full belly, it is impossible not to stop and buy in the shop on the way out.

Mon-Fri 9am-5.30pm, Sat 9am-5pm
Slattery Patissier and Chocolatier, 197 Bury New Road, Whitefield M45 6GE
Tel: 0161 767 9303 slattery.co.uk

Time for Tea

Time for Tea owner Julie believes that tea can only be enjoyed out of a china cup, so on entry to these tearooms you'll see the shelves heaving with over 50 old-fashioned and novelty china teapots. You can choose one specifically to have your tea served in too!

The café is quite small, with around ten tables, but we got our prams in fine and were warmly welcomed. The menu is simple, serving home-cooked food at reasonable prices; Welsh rarebit at £4, bagels with cream cheese for £2.50 and poached eggs on toast at £3.50, to name but a few.

We very much enjoyed tea the old-fashioned way, and tucked into some fine cakes. For those with toddlers, there is a small children's corner with a few toys, but due to the amount of china around you'd probably be advised to accompany them in here!

Mon-Tues and Thurs-Fri 11am-4pm, Sat 10am-4pm
Time for Tea, 416 Bury New Road, Prestwich Village M25 1BD
Tel: 0161 773 3612 timefortearoom.co.uk

Also in this area, you will find Pizza Express (Bury and Prestwich).

Caffeine & Co is a super addition to Longford Park in Stretford.

CHORLTON AND DIDSBURY

Aladdin

Fairly unassuming from the front, you'd be forgiven for thinking of passing by Aladdin. Once inside, you get that first whiff of the charcoal grill. Begin eating the divine authentic Arabic and Middle Eastern cuisine and you'll realise that you've found a Manchester gem.

We first took the children for a family birthday recently. We're used to finding the restaurant extremely busy, so were surprised to find it much quieter when we went along at teatime mid-week. To start we ordered lots of small dishes to share and, with the less developed palates of little ones in mind, we included hommus, pitta and salad. Pleasingly the children sampled lots of what we ordered, some of which they enjoyed, some of which they didn't. Moving onto mains, the charcoal-grilled chicken kebab and the kafteh were both big hits. The meal came to a happy conclusion with ice cream and complimentary sweets.

There are no colouring sheets or gimmicks here but the children were made to feel very welcome. Nothing was a problem for the staff.

There is little room for a pram downstairs and awkward to carry one upstairs so take a car seat if you want baby to sleep. Daily 1-11pm No baby changing facilities.
Aladdin, 529 Wilmslow Road, Withington M20 4BA Tel: 0161 434 8588 aladdin.org.uk

Battery Park Juice Bar

Although compact, and a tad awkward with a pram, you'll find mums congregating here with their offspring at all times of the day. There is no children's menu but they serve the best smoothies and juices in town; plus there are plenty of bagels and sandwiches which can be made up to suit kids' tastes.

The atmosphere is relaxed, so feel free to take along noisy toys and colouring books. The café is split level, with wooden tables and chairs as you walk in, and some comfy chairs on the mezzanine level. There is a notice-board inside which advertises kids' classes and events.

No baby changing facilities.
Mon-Fri 8am-5.30pm, Sat 10am-6pm, Sun 11am-5pm
Battery Park Juice Bar, 615a Wilbraham Road, Chorlton M21 9AN Tel: 0161 860 0754

Caffeine & Co, Longford Park

This is a destination café. Set in a renovated pavilion in the middle of Longford Park, surrounded by playgrounds, tennis courts, cycling paths, an aviary, gardens, football nets and wide open space; it is the perfect place to plan to meet a friend with kids for lunch or a coffee.

The interior has been thoughtfully and stylishly kitted out; with a large piece of oak forming the counter, industrial lighting and white brick tiles all helping to create a modern Scandinavian feel. There

The City Babies LOVE & Kids in Spit

is plenty of seating and one enormous table, perfect for a big gang of friends. Colouring pencils are on hand in vibrant pots, and scattered newspapers create a welcoming hangout. If you only came for a coffee it would be hard to resist the tempting cakes and treats or a buttered crumpet. If you want something more substantial there are wonderful breads from The Uprising Bakery, tasty filled bagels, soups, slow-cooks and breakfasts.

Outside, brightly-painted picnic tables overlook a children's play park; in winter you could warm up with a hot chocolate or freshly-brewed coffee whilst your little ones play out. The café is keen to encourage families, organising seasonal events such as pumpkin carving and biscuit decorating. Follow their Facebook page for information on events.

Mon 10.30am-5pm, Tues-Sun 10am-5pm

Caffeine & Co, Longford Park, Stretford M32 8DA
Tel: 07787 118578

Also at St James Place and Quay House, Manchester

Coriander

Coriander has been serving mouth-watering fresh Bengali and Indian cuisine to customers in Chorlton and Withington for ten years; in 2013 they opened a third restaurant in Chorlton Centre.

The new restaurant is a little glitzier and more spacious than the others but there is still a relaxed friendly atmosphere, and most importantly the food is still amazingly tasty. We've visited a few times, early evening, with other families. It's often busy but the staff are always quick to make space for little ones, shuffling tables for prams and bringing out highchairs.

The food is freshly prepared so best to get your order in pretty quickly and then you can relax, munching happily on their delicious poppadoms while you wait for your meal.

Of course most mums, dads and kids will love the fodder on offer; but I think even the most fussy little eater will find something to entice their palate. Mine chomped their way through a pile of tikka lamb chops before polishing off a shared portion of chicken Casa.

Coriander is rightly proud that their food is free of MSG and artificial colourings, and low in saturated fat. If you have children who appear to react adversely to additives, as I have, then you can let them tuck in here without worrying.

There isn't much in the way of parking immediately outside but plenty around on neighbouring side roads.

Mon-Fri 5pm till late, Sat&Sun 4pm till late.

Coriander, Chorlton Central, 485 Barlow Moor Road, Chorlton M21 8AG
Tel: 0161 881 0340 corianderrestaurant.co.uk

Scooter into stylish Didsbury Lounge for lunch.

Didsbury Lounge

I really like this place! Relatively new, it's nicely stylish with giant silver candelabras, lime green and grey banquette seating, and book-lined library-style wallpaper. With the windows thrown back on a summer's day, it has a lovely airy feel. I visited for lunch with a friend and my four-year-old daughter. Unsure what to expect, as Didsbury Lounge is usually where I'd choose to hang out with a mojito and friends on a Friday evening, I was really impressed by the good quality of food accompanied by lovely service. Didsbury Lounge is well-known for its Smorgasbord-style platters, but I fancied Eggs Benedict (£5.99) whilst my friend opted for a Chicken Caesar Wrap (£6.50). Iris chose Fish Goujons from the Cheeky Monkeys Menu (£5.50 for main, drink and ice cream) and it went down a treat. All told, a very enjoyable lunch!

Food daily 10am-9.30pm

Didsbury Lounge, 43 Barlow Moor Road, Didsbury M20 6TW
Tel: 0161 434 2408 didsburylounge.co.uk

Expo Lounge

Expo Lounge is a great place to meet friends, for a morning coffee or a lunchtime snack. Don't be put off by the exterior (just a bit too rusty orange for my liking) as inside the decor is quirky and interesting with random pictures on the blood-red walls, and old-fashioned lampshades artily hanging from the ceiling. It's spacious, perfect if you've got a pushchair in tow – the coffee is good and reasonably priced plus they've got loads of board games for kids. During the summer months there's an al fresco feel when the windows are all open; ideal for a spot of people watching.

There's plenty of choice for kids. 'Little Loungers

Expo is very popular with new mums in Didsbury, whatever the time of day!

Menu' (£4.95) includes basics such as sausages and macaroni cheese while a second menu, 'Little Bit Bigger Loungers' (£5.50), offers more grown-up fare of cheeseburger, falafel mezze or a cooked breakfast.

My kids love coming here for a frothy babyccino (75p) while I catch up with friends. It's well worth sticking your head in- I've seen lots of mums hanging out here after local toddler groups. Beware though, there is a webcam above the bar streaming live online, so no fibbing to your partners about where you've been all day with the children!

Mon-Fri 8am-11pm, Sat&Sun 9am-11pm
Expo Lounge, 766 Wilmslow Road, Didsbury M20 2DR
Tel: 0161 448 2141 thelounges.co.uk

Head to GBK for a pukka burger.

Fosters Fish and Chips

Voted one of the Top 10 fish & chip restaurants in the UK, Fosters certainly gets the vote with my six and three-year-olds. They absolutely love it. And so does their Dad!

The restaurant itself is fun – nicely done out with exposed brick and whitewashed walls, funky slogans, fixed benches, and a full size red telephone box (this in fact houses the kiddy seats that attach to the tables, quite a novel place to store them!) The children's meal deal costs £5.50 and includes main, side, drink and a tub of ice cream. The fish is always fresh, always fantastic.

Fosters is a brilliant place to take the kids, their friends, your friends... but if you don't have time, their take-away service is the perfect alternative.

Mon-Fri 11.30am-10pm, Sat 12-10pm, Sun 12.30-8.30pm
Fosters Fish and Chips, 812 Wilmslow Road, Didsbury M20 6UH
Tel: 0161 445 4430 fostersfishandchips.com
Also at Alderley Edge

Gourmet Burger Kitchen

We put GBK in Didsbury to the test when we arrived with six boys; and instead of the usual colouring equipment, my nutty friend produced from her handbag messy homemade salt-dough for the kids to play with! The restaurant manager was brilliant and presented each child with a drinks tray to make their creations on.

The children's menu should come as no surprise,

City Babies & Kids in the LOVE

with a choice of either beef, chicken or bean burger and a side of either salad, fries or corn on the cob. For £6.50 it includes a soft drink. Ice cream is £1 extra.

If you appreciate a pukka burger, then GBK is head and shoulders above its fast-food relations. Every burger is freshly made to order with good quality ingredients. Even the sauces are homemade that day.

Sun-Thurs 12-10pm, Fri 12-11pm, Sat 11am-11pm
GBK, 651 Wilmslow Road, Didsbury M20 6QZ
Tel: 0161 448 7167 gbk.co.uk
Also at Spinningfields and The Trafford Centre

The Laundrette

Opening in August 2013, on the former site of the Soap Opera laundrette overlooking a leafy children's park, The Laundrette gives a nod to its former life. Amusingly the menu refers to the Pre Wash (starters), Easy Care (salads), Full Loads, and offers the Half Load Menu for kids. But the machines and Bella magazines are long gone and the whole place has been cleverly transformed. An outside terrace of large comfy sofas, tables and twinkling lights allow you to eat in the sun or, on chilly evenings, enjoy a hot chocolate under a blanket warmed by a heat lamp. Inside, it's bare brick walls, low lighting and chilled soundtrack make for the coolest pizza place!

We've been a few times for drinks outside with friends whilst our older children have played in the park opposite, and recently we tried out the menu on a Saturday teatime with our kids. My youngest was delighted when he was presented with his own chef's hat and ingredients to make his own pizza. My eldest, who now eats off the Full Load Menu, acknowledged that the kids' pizza was the biggest he had seen, and would probably have been sufficient even for him. It's not all about pizzas though, we also had some great carpaccio of beef, calamari and, for Dad, a burger complete with ' Bloody Mary' ketchup. Sensational!

The Laundrette make eating out fun – they serve drinks in jam jars, make mean cocktails, source locally where possible, whilst making everything themselves, so there's every reason to give it a go. Children are made to feel very welcome. We'll certainly be popping back.

Daily 10am till 11pm
The Laundrette, 32 Beech Road, Chorlton M21 9EL
Tel: 0161 881 5777 thelaundrettechorlton.co.uk

The Lead Station

This Chorlton stalwart continues to draw in families, and keeps up to date with its menu and decor. Housed in a former police station, there is a friendly and informal atmosphere; plenty of colourful seating indoors and out, and a decent-sized bar area in which to wait for a table if it is busy.

At both lunch and dinner there are several classic kids' dishes to choose from, which always go down well with my boys. The pittas and dips (together with the activity menus) are requested the moment our children's bottoms hit their seats! If you fancy a breakfast out, then the Lead Station is the place to go – frothy hot chocolates; pancakes with bacon, bananas, cream and maple syrup; yoghurt with

The Laundrette is a cool pizza place with a gorgeous outside terrace.

Tea Hive is a popular hangout for Chorlton mums.

granola; and amazing Eggs Benedict.

There are a few steps to get in to the restaurant, but you can usually find a helpful soul to assist with lifting a buggy in. Nearby is Beech Road Park, complete with playground and The Lead Station are happy to send you off with a take-away coffee.
Daily 10am till late
The Lead Station, 99 Beech Road, Chorlton M21 9EQ
Tel: 0161 881 5559 theleadstation.co.uk

Mud Crab Café

Described as an Oz café bar with a NY easy-diner vibe, since opening in late 2012, the Mud Crab Café has become a popular hangout on Didsbury's busy high street. It's food menu is certainly eclectic – ranging from small plates of shredded duck hash with deep fried egg and crab tartlette to sea-bass tempura and burgers (their speciality).

We took Ellie along one Saturday evening for tea – we hadn't booked but luckily because it wasn't too late, we managed to get one of the last few tables. The "Little Mud Crabbers"menu offered vegetarian cottage pie, cheesy nachos, macaroni, special fried chicken and cheeseburgers but Ellie went for the stone-baked pizza margherita. Together with an ice cream for dessert, this costs £5.95 so in our books , pretty good value for money. Tony and I opted for the Middle Eastern sharing platter plus half a roast charred chicken and found the food both delicious and generous.

The staff were absolutely lovely and I do recommend you give this place a go. There's a different lunch menu that looks great; personally I can't wait to go and try the breakfasts which are served daily and offer sinful-sounding waffles and pancakes.
Mon-Thurs and Sun 9.30am-11pm, Fri-Sat 9.30am-midnight
Mud Crab Café, 747-751 Wilmslow Road, Didsbury M20 6RN
Tel: 0161 445 2055 mudcrabdiner.co.uk
Also Mud Crab at Grinch in Manchester

130

Olive & Vine Dimitri's Didsbury

I popped in for tea after school with three hungry boys, a little apprehensive about whether they'd embrace the Greek food. Dimitri's aren't just a family-friendly restaurant, they are really, really friendly! The owner loved chatting with the boys and indeed all the diners.

They have a children's menu of spaghetti bolognese, keftedes (meatballs) with fries, pitza (cheese with tomato on a greek pitta) or chicken kebab, with a drink, all for £6.95. The "kiddies" portion sizes, which they recommend for up to seven year olds, were very generous. I ordered a couple of meze at £6.95 each, keftedes and chicken souvlaki; houmous with pitta for £4.95; plus a side dish of olives. The boys wolfed it all down, leaving me the odd bit of pitta and a couple of olives. All in, nothing to be worried about, in fact a big hit.
Tues-Thurs 5-11pm, Fri-Sat 11am-midnight, Sun 11am-10pm
Olive & Vine Dimitri's Didsbury, 846 Wilmslow Road, Didsbury M20 2RN
Tel: 0161 434 5151 oliveandvine.co.uk
Also at Deansgate Manchester

Tea Hive

A popular hang-out for mums in Chorlton is the elegantly decorated but chilled Tea Hive.

There are plenty of tasty lunch and savoury options, but it is hard to resist the delicious home-made cakes on display washed down by one of the superb range of teas, served in fine bone china. If bone china sounds a bit of a worry around children please don't be put off, the staff and customers here are very easygoing. This was put to the test when my friend's baby, Henry, managed to pull over a large yucca plant, scattering soil everywhere! The staff were wonderfully gracious.

There is a choice of a children's little lunch for £2.50, a big lunch for £3.95, or a kids' cream tea for £2.50. Alternatively you could all share an afternoon tea for one, which looks very impressive. Seating inside and out and now over two floors.
Mon-Fri 8am-5pm, Sat&Sun 9am-5pm
Tea Hive, 53 Manchester Road, Chorlton M21 9PW
Tel: 0161 881 0569 teahive.co.uk

Thyme Out

This is a great little spot to go with children on a summer's day because at the side of the building is a lovely fenced herb garden complete with pebbled paths and parasols. It can also be accessed via a side gate, which is useful if you have a pram.

We have visited several times with groups of friends and their children. Taking along a few toy

Libby's in Marple is an excellent choice for breakfast, lunch or dinner.

cars, the children have enjoyed messing around in the pebbles whilst waiting for their lunch. The drinks menu has fresh smoothies (£3.25) together with a selection of herbal teas, coffees and milkshakes. Food-wise the deli offers some tasty choices from a Full English breakfast to a Tuna Nicoise salad. There are some good dishes for sharing with the kids on the menu – pizza (£5.50), jacket potato (£5.95) or spanish churros con chocolate! The kitchen is also willing to adapt dishes for children where possible.

Daily 9am-5pm
Thyme Out Deli, 147 Nell Lane, Didsbury M20 2LG
Tel: 0161 434 8686 thymeoutdeli.co.uk

Also in this area you will find Croma (Chorlton), Gusto, Pizza Express and Piccolino (Didsbury).

Al fresco dining at Thyme Out in Didsbury.

THE HEATONS, LEVENSHULME, MARPLE AND STOCKPORT

The Ash Tea Rooms

Located in an austere Victorian building, a former pub on the busy Manchester Road in Stockport, I really wasn't expecting to find such delights inside! The tearooms had been enthusiastically recommended to me by a friend, so I tried it out for lunch with a couple of fellow mums and a baby.

Firstly, I was taken aback by the splendid cake emporium and chocolate shop, specialities that the Ash is famous for. Eventually I managed to drag myself away from this spectacle, and headed into the spacious tearooms beyond – spread out over a couple of floors. We hadn't booked (the website strongly recommends you do) but luckily were able to nab one of the last tables available.

The lunchtime menu offered a nice range of food, including bistro-style options such as filo king prawns, individual quiches, open sandwiches and salads (all around £6-£8). A children's menu is available too, and there's a lovely outside eating area, with a grassy play area for small children.

Good food, genteel ambience, and smartly-dressed waitresses…I'm not sure you'd want to let your toddlers run riot in here, but for us with a baby safely strapped into a highchair, it was perfect. Next time I'm going to take my mum for a treat – one of their famous traditional afternoon teas.

Mon-Sat 9am-5pm

131

The Ash Tea Rooms, 232 Manchester Road, Stockport SK4 1NN
Tel: 0161 217 1500 the-ash.co.uk

Hyde Bank Farm Tearooms

Hyde Bank Farm is situated along the beautiful Peak Forest Canal between Romiley and Marple. I was meeting a friend for lunch and it was a perfect halfway point for us both. The tearooms at the farm are within a stunning Grade II listed 17th century barn that has been lovingly restored by its present owners. Its traditional feel and friendly atmosphere make it a destination of choice for walkers and cyclists.

There is a wide selection on the lunch menu, including a Sunday roast at the weekend; the home-made cakes and desserts caught my eye. What sets this tearoom apart is the marvellous children's barn. Inside you'll find ride-on tractors, a go-cart and a menagerie of animals including rabbits, goats and a donkey called Freddie. Ted and Daniel loved it and played for ages interspersed with intervals of petting the animals. Our two were too young to be left unsupervised, but older children could happily wander between the café and the play area.

Tues-Sun 10.30am-4.30pm
Hyde Bank Farm, Oakwood Road, Romiley, Stockport SK6 4DZ
Tel: 0161 430 3582 hydebankfarm.co.uk

Libby's

Libby's in Marple Bridge is an outstanding bakery with a wonderful and friendly café attached. So unsurprisingly, it's very popular with the locals. Although not exactly a local myself, I'm more than happy to travel from Didsbury to enjoy breakfast, lunch or dinner here…yes, I can vouch for all three!

When my friend Laura upped sticks and moved this way, Libby's quickly became our favourite place to hook up. It's such a treat: the menu is too extensive and fast-changing to itemise, but you'll find delicious sandwiches, as well as various hot dishes, good coffee, and the exceptional cakes and pastries which have earned Libby's its excellent reputation. (My current favourite is the Manchester Tart!)

In the evenings, there's a super little tapas menu which makes it a perfect place to enjoy an easy early dinner with girlfriends. I cannot recommend Libby's enough!

Daily 7am-9.30pm
Libby's, 1-3 Town Street, Marple Bridge SK9 5AA
Tel: 0161 427 2310

Post Office Deli

Aptly named, for it is indeed housed in the former main post office for Levenshulme, POD is a well-established local deli-cum-café. It's quite compact and popular with Levy residents, so if you're intending to go with more than one child, pick your time. The menu is nicely varied; from homemade terrines and quiches to casseroles and corn beef hash. There are choices for kids, and a nice touch is the free veg puree offered to babies.

Mon-Fri 9am-11pm, Sat 9am-midnight, Sun 9am-4pm
POD, 30 Albert Road, Levenshulme M19 2FP
Tel: 0161 248 7990 pod-deli.co.uk

Trove

A truly beautifully designed independent café located opposite the Antiques Centre in Levenshulme. Though small in size, Trove is big on style – boxed origami artwork adorns the white washed walls, long suspended bulbs create interesting lighting and a large rustic oak communal table dominating the majority of the space, invites you to sit and ... stay.

We three rocked up for lunch on a Wednesday, with three noisy toddlers aged two, three and four years in tow. The menu is simple and fresh – delicious breakfast and sandwich options, combined with daily specials such as panzanella salad or beef stroganoff. We decided the best thing for our rowdy rabble was the boiled egg option which, when they arrived, were probably the best boiled eggs our children had ever tasted!

Is Trove child-friendly? Well they could not have been more lovely with us, but for those of you with boisterous toddlers you'd be wise to bring some colouring books as Trove really is too tiny to let your kids run around in. If you've got a baby – perfect – pop them into one of the café's highchairs and sit back and enjoy. We can't recommend Trove enough – a local treasure that's definitely worth discovering. Look our for their regular toddler mornings too.

Mon-Fri 8.30am-5pm, Sat 9am-10pm, Sun 10am-10pm
(weekends kitchen closes 4pm and re-opens at 6pm for pizza)
Trove, 1032 Stockport Road, Levenshulme M19 3EX
Tel: 0161 224 8588 trovefoods.co.uk

LYMM, NORTHWICH AND BEYOND

The Church Green

This award winning restaurant in Lymm is the creation of "celebrity" chef Aiden Byrne. The menu is dominated by its grill section – a huge variety of steaks, burgers and chicken. Alongside this are upmarket twists on pub classics such as pork belly, egg, chips and pineapple salsa or korma moules-frites together with amazing sounding starters like roasted scallops with blue cheese risotto.

I was aware of The Church Green's reputation but when a member of the *Babies & Kids in the City*

An Alice in Wonderland theme greets you at Davenport Tea Rooms.

website recommended it as "extremely child-friendly" we were surprised and intrigued, so off we went. And they were right! It is indeed totally welcoming to children – the attentive staff couldn't do enough for us. They brought cushions for Ellie to sit on to reach the table, handed out colouring sheets, and joked and interacted with the children throughout. They were lovely.

The "Young Person's Menu" offered starters such as cheesy garlic bread or calamari for £3, whilst mains such as salmon pasta, chicken goujons and chips or pizza were £5. Needless to say the quality of food, both for the kids and us was excellent. The evening was rounded off with warmed banana, chocolate sauce and ice cream and a delicious sticky toffee pudding – both first rate. Not the cheapest night out admittedly but a fine restaurant that's well worth the treat!

Mon-Thurs 12-9.30pm, Fri-Sat 12-10pm, Sun 12-7.45pm. Breakfast: weekends from 9am.
The Church Green, Higher Lane, Lymm WA13 0AP
Tel: 01925 752068 aidenbyrne.co.uk

Davenport Tea Rooms

After a visit to the nearby **Lewis Carroll Museum** (see page 18) I thought it would be a good idea to check out this Alice in Wonderland-themed tearoom. As well as serving breakfast and lunch, their speciality is afternoon tea. And, as they are winners of the 2013 Tea Guild's Best Afternoon Tea in Cheshire, we simply had to try it. A pretty outdoor seating area

awaited us, complete with an oversized chess set and chickens pottering around in the sunshine.

Inside there are hand-painted Alice in Wonderland murals, along with themed bone china tea sets. Afternoon tea arrived on a three tier cake stand; with delicately-cut sandwiches, enormous scones and, on the top, a beautiful cupcake iced with a smiling Cheshire cat. For the children they served plain cakes with pots of icing and various toppings so they could create their own masterpiece.

A child's afternoon tea cost £9.95 which also included a soft drink. It was a lovely opportunity to introduce my 12-year-old French niece to a very English tradition.

Before you go it is worth checking out the well-stocked farm shop, with over 50 local food and drink suppliers, plus a large range of looseleaf teas.

And if you really want to make a day of it they run Mad Hatter Tea Parties, but booking is essential!

Daily 10am-4pm (closed Tuesdays)
Davenport Tea Rooms, Bridge Farm, Warrington Road, Bartington, Northwich, Cheshire CW8 4QU
Tel: 01606 853241 davenportsfarmshop.co.uk

Great Budworth Ice Cream Farm

We visited the ice cream farm on our way back home after a walk around **Marbury Park** (see page 96), but it is also convenient for **Stockley Farm** and **Arley Hall** (see pages 42 and 70). It's a relaxing place to stop off for a cup of tea, and is a treat for the little ones to enjoy

A mouth-watering selection of cakes await you at Macaroon in Rochdale.

a play and an ice cream. You may also be tempted by a walk down the picturesque country lanes to Great Budworth village, an incredibly pretty chocolate-box village of timbered houses, or even a walk around the lake at Pickmere.

There is a farmhouse café with indoor and outdoor seating; tables are set up within a covered patio area and also in the garden. It was a tough decision choosing which of the delicious ice cream flavours to go for and, after wolfing their cones down, the boys went off to investigate the table-top toys and model farm. There was also a bouncy castle on the front lawn.

A visit to a farm wouldn't be complete without a few animals to watch – there are goats and comical rare breed chickens (as well as cows!) and the tearoom sells feed for them.

We enjoyed a pot of tea and a large slice of home-made cake, but there were also light lunches on offer including children's lunch boxes.

Apr-Oct Daily 12-6pm, Mar/Nov/Dec Weekends 1-5pm, Jan/Feb closed. There is a Maize trail open during summer months into autumn.
New Westage Farm, Great Budworth, Northwich, Cheshire CW9 6ND
Tel: 01606 891211 icecreamfarm.co.uk

The Hollies Farm Shop and Café

This lovely farm shop is bursting with local produce, artisan foods and gifts. Set back from the road in Cheshire countryside, you know you have found a gem as soon as you drive into the car park. The café sells gourmet sandwiches and salads (from £8.95) at lunchtime, and delicious bacon and sausage sandwiches for breakfast from their own award-winning butchery. There's no children's menu but staff offered simple sandwiches, and the chef obligingly made a small portion of sausage and mash from the adult menu.

I was tempted by much of the homemade produce in the shop, and of course I had to buy something...the onion marmalade was delicious!
Mon-Sat 8am-7pm, Sun 8am-6pm
The Hollies Farm Shop, Forest Road, Little Budworth, Tarporley CW6 9ES
Tel: 01829 760884 theholliesfarmshop.co.uk
Also at Lower Stretton

Also in this area, you will find Piccolino and Pizza Express (Stockton Heath).

OLDHAM AND ROCHDALE

The Dinnerstone

Situated in the village of Uppermill and adjacent to Saddleworth Moor, it's a lovely drive out to The Dinnerstone. Parking is limited on the high street but the restaurant has a car park at the back. On the waiter's recommendation, I opted for Ham Hock Tagliatelle, which was absolutely gorgeous. The choice of children's meals was good and included breaded haddock fingers, sausages, linguine and pizza. My five-year-old went for the 'make your own pizza' option.

The Dinnerstone is a nice place for a treat with friendly service and a warm atmosphere.

Tues-Sat 11am-10pm, Sun 11am-9pm.

The Dinnerstone, 99-101 High Street, Uppermill, Saddleworth, Oldham OL3 6BD

Tel: 01457 872 566 dinnerstone.co.uk

Macaroon

Former head chef at Manchester's Harvey Nichols, Alison Seagrave is now head chef of her own patisserie-cum-café, Macaroon, on the Bury Road in Rochdale. With this fab reference, I grabbed the opportunity to visit for lunch with my little one. Her trademark speciality is, of course, macaroons: you will find a fabulous mouth-watering selection of the multi-coloured delights here, as well as a tantalising array of other desserts and cakes. The café also offers afternoon teas (for kids too!), light lunches of soup and sandwiches, plus a lovely children's menu ranging from mini sandwiches to beans on toast. Prices start from £1.

Luckily we got there early as Macaroon isn't large and, with its sterling reputation, it gets busy pretty quickly. With all products baked freshly on site, it was no surprise that our lunch was delicious – even the jam is homemade!

Before heading back to pick up from school I chose a lovely selection of cakes to take back for the older kids as a treat – they were demolished! Alison also offers a reasonably-priced mail order service for her wonderful macaroons and I can definitely vouch for them – I ordered some for Mothers Day and my mum declared they were amazing!

Tues-Sat 9am-5pm

Macaroon, 569 Bury Road, Bamford, Rochdale OL11 4DQ

Tel: 01706 558565 macaroonbyalisonseagrave.co.uk

Salt Cellar

Nestling in the shadows of Oldham Parish Church, this large daytime restaurant started as an initiative among local Methodists in Oldham. The red brick building, with high ceilings and large arches, is beautiful, but the decor of gold chandeliers and tied-back drapes is a little dated. It was busy when we went, but there was plenty of seating on the upstairs mezzanine. There's a small play area up there too, with some books and toys; enough to keep your children happy while you enjoy a fairtrade coffee or finish your lunch.

The menu varies from breakfasts and salads, to sandwiches and afternoon teas and is very reasonably priced. Everything on the children's menu is priced at £1.50; from filled jacket potatoes or

sandwiches, to animal spaghetti on toast. Centrally located, Salt Cellar is run by volunteers and has a loyal following from shoppers and families alike, grabbing a good-value bite to eat. One warning though, it is cash only.

Worth noting is **Gallery Oldham** which is a stones throw away, perfect for a quick visit (see page 16).

Mon-Sat 10am-3.30pm

Salt Cellar Restaurant, 11a Church Lane, Oldham OL1 3AN

Tel: 0161 628 2426 saltcellar.org.uk

SALFORD, WORSLEY AND BEYOND

Albert's Restaurant & Bar

Albert's in Didsbury has been going for around two years now and is as popular as ever – testimony to its consistently excellent food and unpretentious service plus it's got a brilliant vibe. It's the sort of place you want to go and spend the evening because you know you'll definitely have a good time! In Didsbury, it's almost unbeatable in terms of position because the huge front terrace makes it a fab spot to dine alfresco and the outside heaters ensure that this is possible all year round. But in summer in particular, it's fab and where everyone wants to be. What's also great about Albert's is that it endeavours to be child-friendly too and I think it pulls this off no problem.

I decided to go and check out the brand new Albert's Worsley that has recently opened on the East Lancs road. The restaurant is a carbon copy of the Didsbury one – a sharp, modern (very blue!) space. Proportionally it feels the same with plenty of tables to go round. There's an identical front seating area too (though the East Lancs is certainly a much busier and noisier road to sit next to than its Didsbury counterpart....) It was just me and the kids one day after school and as it was winter, we were definitely going to be indoors.

The children's menu offers a "Little Ones"

Summer dining on the terrace at Albert's.

You'll be spoilt for choice at Bents.

(£5 including cordial) or a "Bigger Ones" (£7 including cordial) option. I thought the range of meals on offer to the kids was definitely one of the perkier that we've come across. Finally a few more interesting choices than just the ubiquitous pizza and fish fingers (though rest-assured these safety-net choices are still here as well!) So for example, there was also steak-frites, chicken and pea risotto, mini pie and mash, basil linguini and fishcakes to try. My youngest went for the (safe!) fish fingers, whilst the oldest who's just turned eight-years-old tried steak for the first time. Portions weren't enormous so I'd imagine older children might need to order off the adult menu, but for my two it was fine, the food was a huge hit and dinner was subsequently polished off very quickly. It got the kids' vote and it continues to get mine.

Food Mon-Fri 12-10.30pm, Sat 10am-10.30pm,
Sun 10am-9.30pm
Albert's Worsley, East Lancashire Road, Manchester
M27 0AA (parking accessed via Kildare road)
Tel: 0161 794 1234 albertsworsley.com

Fresh Approach, Bents

The name of the self-service restaurant at Bents Garden and Home references its ethos – to provide freshly prepared quality food straight from the kitchen, and sourced locally.

The seating area is extensive, so there is usually no need to worry about finding a table before choosing your food. My boys ordered a simple pasta with tomato sauce, however there was plenty more to choose from including 'Design your own Pizza,' chicken curry and bangers & mash. Alternatively a children's lunch box including a drink, a sandwich and three treats was on offer. The meals cost £4.95 and were a hearty size. For heating up baby food or milk, there's a microwave and bottle warmer. And if you've forgotten your own, Bents offer a range of Cow and Gate jars which are free with an adult meal.

Grown ups are simply spoilt for choice from sandwiches, a Deli bar to hot meals and soups. And then there are the cakes and pastries…magnificent! And generous portions too! We sat indoors in the splendid glasshouse overlooking the lake – there were a lot of families in the restaurant on our visit, so we didn't feel in the least bit self-conscious about our children being too noisy. If it had been warmer, we would have headed to the large outside seating area next to the super children's play area (see page 149). Also out here, you'll find new addition – Caffe Lago, offering a selection of specially prepared homebakes and scones as well as children's lunch bags and cold drinks. Eating out at Bents was fab and easy with the kids – it's probably the best quality restaurant you'll find at a garden centre!
Mon-Sat 8.30am-5.30pm, Sun 8.30am-5pm
Bents Garden and Home, Warrington Road,
Glazebury, Cheshire WA3 5NT
Tel: 01942 266300 bents.co.uk

Prezzo

Awash with trendy TV folk in the week, MediaCity quietens to a more chilled pace at weekends; with modern boulevards and tranquil gardens it ain't a bad place to head with kids, to scooter or stroll around.

After enjoying a **CBBC Tour** one weekend (see page 49) we found Prezzo, a glass-fronted spangling chain restaurant only a stone's throw from The Blue Peter Garden. Arriving with kids, you might think you've made a mistake as the decor's all a bit neutral, somewhat grown up. But once you've settled in, and you're perusing the children's menu, we think you'll change your mind.

For one thing, there's a great terrace to the front, perfect for relaxing on a warm day...or a good spot for the kids to play when they've tired of your scintillating conversation. Secondly the staff are very welcoming and happy to make room (there is bags of it) for pushchairs and parent detritus. Most importantly though, the kids' menu is well thought out: there are dishes for tiny tots; mini portions of classics from the adult menu; and even a few refreshing changes from the usual kids' fare. The grilled chicken salad served with cucumber and cherry tomatoes, and the calzone both sounded delicious... although, of course, mine still plumped for safe margherita pizzas!
Mon-Sat 12-11pm, Sun 12-10.30pm
Prezzo, MediaCity UK, Manchester M50 2HF
Tel: 0161 713 3742 prezzorestaurants.co.uk
Also at The Printworks, Manchester

Also in this area, you will find Wagamama and Pizza Express (MediaCity).

Barburrito

My boys love the vibrancy, taste and ease of this colourful yet simple restaurant. Ollie knew exactly what he wanted; chicken, salsa, sour cream and cheese sauce on a wrap, and his younger brother copied. I took a little longer to work my way through their three mex-steps, of choosing a dish, a filling and accompaniments. Should I have spicy beans or mild chicken or steak? Rice or avocado? On nachos or in a tortilla? Yes my dithering really annoyed the man behind me in the queue, but the staff took it in their stride! The burritos were wrapped in foil and served in a basket. The boys selected a high bar-style table, but there were plenty of cosy booths with space to park a pram too. Our three burritos plus two soft drinks and a tap water cost £15.15. Check out the website for offers as they often run "Kids Eat Free".

Mon-Thurs & Sat 11am-10pm, Fri 11am-10.30pm, Sun 12-9pm
Barburrito, 134 The Orient, The Trafford Centre M17 8EH
Tel: 0161 747 6165 barburrito.co.uk
Also at Deansgate and Piccadilly Manchester

YO! Sushi

"My kids will never eat it!" I exclaimed to my sister when she suggested YO! Sushi for lunch. However we were all starving, stuck in the middle of the Trafford Centre and the thought of walking anywhere else with three hungry children in tow seemed as attractive as pulling out my own hair. So we sat in a booth and I wearily glanced at the menu, hoping to find something vaguely acceptable to my fussy children.

Something strange then happened...my nine year old son picked something off the moving conveyor belt next to our table and... it was fruit! My daughter lifted off some edamame beans and once shown what to do by an initiated auntie, continued to pop the sweet beans out of their pods with her teeth.

A little more relaxed now, I started to recognise kid-friendly things on the menu. We ordered chicken katsu (strips of breaded chicken) and chicken yakasobi (pan fried noodles with veg). The kids were having a great

The Orient at the intu Trafford Centre.

Zizzi's dough sticks are a hit with our boys.

time, looking at everything going round on the belt. I think the genius of YO! Sushi is that we were all tempted to try different things, as the portion sizes were small but inviting. We even tried the avocado maki, which is basically four small avocado pieces encased in rice then wrapped in a small seaweed sheet. We could also help ourselves to water from the little tap on our table which was fun for the kids too. The meal ended with a helping of dorayaki – small pancake quarters filled with custard and raspberry sauce. Very fast, fun and enjoyable.

Mon-Fri 11.30am-10pm, Sat 11.30am-9pm, Sun 11.30am-5.30pm
YO! Sushi at Selfridges, The Dome, Trafford Centre, Trafford Park, Manchester M17 8DA
Tel: 0161 747 7689 yosushi.com
Also at Manchester Arndale and Piccadilly Station

Zizzi

Will loves Zizzi, 100% won over by their "Dough Sticks" brushed with garlicky butter and rosemary". We can't drive past a Zizzi without Will shouting out a demand to go back there. Will is six years old and clearly a pushover when it comes to a good dough stick. That said, I thought they were rather delicious too. Dough sticks, pasta or pizza, and a dessert for £6.50 (no drink); another national chain that's pushed its Bambini prices up, but at least the pizzas were a generous size. Adult wise, I find the pizza and pasta served at Zizzi's enjoyable enough; however I once tried their cichetti (little dishes) range and was sorely disappointed. Perhaps I was unlucky, but I'll stick to my usual chicken strozzapreti from now on!

Mon-Sat 12-11pm, Sun 12-10.30pm
Zizzi, 120-122 The Orient, The Trafford Centre M17 5EH
Tel: 0161 749 7992 zizzi.co.uk
Also at Didsbury, Corn Exchange Manchester, Spinningfields Manchester

Also at The Trafford Centre, you'll find Carluccio's, Gourmet Burger Kitchen, Giraffe, Pizza Express and Tampopo

Classes and Activities

There are all kinds of activities imaginable on offer for children. We've listed a few ideas here, so there's no excuse not to get out stretching, gluing or kicking a ball with your little one!

ART AND CRAFT

Colour You Happy

Every month, Colour You Happy has a Saturday Special art workshop suitable for children from 18 months to 7 years.

Sessions are once a month and cost £5 per child, paid on the day, email to book. 10.30-11.30am.

St Clements Church, Chorlton M21 9JF
colouryouhappy.co.uk
email:colouryouhappy@yahoo.co.uk

Happy Makers Art Class

Tel: 07775 884275
happymakers.co.uk

Kidz Kreationz

Tel: 07989 205435
kidzkreationzcraftclub.com

Little Art Bugs @ Sale Waterside Arts Centre

Messy art play sessions for children aged 18 months upwards. Each Friday this group adopts a theme, which can be anything from dinosaurs to space exploration; and the children make, paint or mould something to take home, as well as working on a big messy piece together. The ethos is to have fun and explore art materials, so old clothes are encouraged. The group stop for a biscuit, juice and a story during each session.

10-10.45am every Friday in termtime. Sessions cost £4.50 per child, £2.50 per sibling

Little Art Bugs

Didsbury Theatre School

Sale Waterside Arts Centre,
1 Waterside, Sale M33 7ZF
Tel: 0161 912 5616 littleartbugs.co.uk

Parsley Pie Art Club

Tel: 0161 904 9444 parsleypie.com

Art Baby at Whitworth Art Gallery

Art Baby – Creative sensory, discovery and play sessions for babies and their grown ups. During renovations to Whitworth Art Gallery this has a temporary home at The Bridgewater Hall in Manchester until Autumn 2014.

Every Wednesday 10.15-11.15am and 11.15am-12.30pm.
Tel: 0161 275 7450
manchester.ac.uk/whitworth

BABY MASSAGE & YOGA

The Baby Massage Company

Tel: 07866 468245
thebabymassagecompany.co.uk

Sandra Stenhouse

Children's Yoga Teacher
Tel: 0161 904 0305

Treetots Yoga

Tel: 07707 297316 treetotsyoga.com

YogaBelliesKidz

YogaBelliesKidz for blissed out babies, tantrum free toddlers and kool kidz! YogaBelliesKidz encourages freedom of movement and our motto is "the room is your yoga mat!"

Yogabellies offers Baby Massage sessions in a block of 5 at £50 (suitable from birth to mobile) and Toddler Yoga classes in a block of 6 at £36 (suitable from 10 to 36 months).

Yoga classes for three to nine-year-olds coming soon and chilled Kidz Party packages also available!

Altrincham (Monday mornings at Jubilee Centre Bowdon), Sale (Tuesday mornings at The Hope Centre) and Timperley (Wednesday mornings at Antz in your Pantz).
Tel: Angela Dobric on 07940 476 953
yogabellies.co.uk
angela@yogabellies.co.uk

COOKERY

Kiddy Cook

Kiddy Cook classes and parties are designed to encourage children to learn about "good food" and to explore new flavours in an educational and fun way.
Tel: 07411 560 011 kiddycook.co.uk

DANCE AND DRAMA

Babyballet

Tel: 0161 280 3686 babyballet.co.uk

Dancing Days

Tel: 07903 857709 dancingdays.co.uk

Diddi Dance

Diddi Dance offer funky dance classes for girls and boys aged two to four. They're the only class incorporating 14 different dance styles, everything from hip hop to disco, Bollywood to salsa and everything in between! All the music used is totally original and "pop-esque" and a variety of props are used in the lesson plans, which the children love.

Lessons are really entertaining and easy-going but designed to support a wide variety of skills including listening, memory, socialisation, co-ordination and confidence building. Above all it's about the little ones having fun and burning off some energy!
Lisa Lawson Tel: 07966 542985
diddidance.com

Didsbury Theatre School

Didsbury Theatre School has been established for over 25 years and offers classes in Ballet, Tap, Jazz, Drama, Street Dance, Singing and Musical Theatre for children aged 18 months – 18 years. Children perform at prestigious London and Manchester Theatres and the school has links with CBeebies and CBBC. Children can take dance and drama exams progressing to teaching qualifications; many have appeared on TV and in professional theatre productions. The school's mission is to nurture a life-long love of performing arts, provide expert teaching and have a lot of fun!
Didsbury Theatre School, Christ Church Hall, Darley Avenue, West Didsbury, Manchester M20 2ZD
Tel: 07841 117754
didsburytheatreschool.co.uk

FIRST AID
Bumps and Bashes

First Aid Classes specifically for parents of babies and children, in the relaxed environment of your own home.
Tel: 0800 9179525
bumpsandbashes.com

First Aid Training Stockport

They offer a 6-hour Intermediate Paediatric First Aid Course - ideal for youth workers, teachers and parents for £49
Tel: 0844 6863999
firstaidtrainingstockport.co.uk

St Johns Ambulance

Find a paediatric course covering everything from seizures to poisoning near you by simply entering your postcode on their website.
Tel: 0844 7704800 sja.org.uk

FOREST SCHOOLS AND ADVENTURE
Forest Explorers

Forest Explorers run fun environmental education sessions, events and birthday parties in Delamere Forest, Cheshire.
Tel: 07808 506308
forest-explorers.co.uk

Paupers Wood Forest School

Paupers Wood Forest School has a drop-in woodland playgroup. Stroll round the wood kicking the leaves. Sit on a log and sing a welcome song to everyone and hear the qualified forest teacher read some autumnal poems from a book.

Every week has a different theme, for example animals that hibernate & reasons why they hibernate. You'll get to make something, perhaps out of dough, sticks and leaves before sitting round the fire with a snack, perhaps some forest made popcorn, and helping in turns to carefully stoke the fire. Simple but delightful fun. There are no formal toilet facilities but a 'wee-tree'.
1pm on Wednesdays which costs £4.50.
Paupers Wood, Nell Lane, Didsbury M20
Tel: 0161 445 3520/ 07790 368117

We Are Adventurers

Encouraging a love of outdoor from babes in the wood to adults.
Tel: 07809 382 023
weareadventurers.co.uk

GARDENING
Hulme Community Garden Centre's Parent and Toddler Gardening Club

Come rain or shine, Hulme Community Garden Centre run a craft or gardening session aimed at under 5s every Thursday.

Set in one acre of beautiful gardens, it is a hidden gem in the city less than a mile from Manchester centre. The site includes a woodland area, a pond full of frogs (and the occasional newt!), a fruit corner with berries, apples and plums, a sandpit and

Paupers Wood Forest School.

tons and tons of flowers and herbs. On rainy days sessions takes place sitting on straw bales in the garden tunnel.

The activities are dependent on the season, and range from planting potatoes to painting pots. 'Creations' can be taken home afterwards. All materials are natural and found, picked and plucked from the gardens.
Thursdays 11am-12noon, £2.50 per child, includes materials, refreshments and giggles.
Hulme Community Garden Centre, 28 Old Birley Street, Hulme, Manchester M15 5RG
Tel: 0161 227 8198
hulmegardencentre.org.uk

LANGUAGE & COMMUNICATION
Sing & Sign Baby Signing Classes
Tel: 0161 408 2432 singandsign.co.uk

Talking Tots
Talking Tots classes are bursting with fun, interactive activities designed to help pre-school children communicate with confidence. Whether your child is just learning their first words or is already a fully fledged chatterbox, Talking Tots has something to offer.

The three year programme has been carefully designed

Talking Tots

to follow the natural stages of early language development and provide just the right combination of fun, excitement and learning. Children love the brightly coloured props and vibrant picture cards.

With its unique mix of games, songs, rhymes and structured activities, Talking Tots gently boosts children's language and social skills giving them a head start in the classroom.
Classes are suitable for children aged 12 months to 4 years. New customers are offered a 2 week trial for £5. Classes cost £5.50 per session payable in half term blocks. There is a £10 membership fee and all children receive a free Talking Tots t-shirt. Classes are held at venues across South Manchester and the Stockport area.
Tel: 07794 433179 talkingtots.info

Baby Sensory

MUSIC & ENTERTAINMENT
Baby Sensory
Parents and their babies (birth to 13 months) can enjoy award winning Baby Sensory classes in the Greater Manchester area thanks to their dedicated team of Baby Sensory Class Leaders. Baby Sensory, written by Dr. Lin Day (PhD Dip. Ed. BSc. PGCE. M. Phil), has been specifically designed for babies and the activities incorporate every sensory experience including sign language, fibre optic light shows, bouncy light balls, rainbows, bubbles, bells, holistic massage and much more. Baby Sensory is designed to encourage early development.

Their local class leaders are confident you'll love Baby Sensory and they offer the first fun session as a no obligation trial.

A parent from one of their Baby Sensory classes says: "Baby Sensory has been a fantastic bonding opportunity... the classes are always lively and lots of fun and I use many of the ideas at home... this is the best class we have been to".
To register please contact one of the Baby Sensory Class Leaders listed below or visit www.babysensory.com for details of your nearest class. Ring first to check availability and book your place.
Lindsay: 07590 916004 Cheadle, Heaton Moor, Offerton.
Becky: 07503 547083 Woodford, Macclesfield, Romiley, Wilmslow.
Kerry: 07841 126945 Sale, Bowdon, Didsbury.
Sarah: 07768 898093 Ashton-under-Lyne, Denton, Mottram, Dukinfield.
Emma: 07545 161358 Trafford Park.

Babywinks
Babywinks – a fun, fast-paced and jam-packed 30-minute class that incorporates movement, dance, singing and instruments for those aged 4-18 months. It involves baby signing, sensory, bells, a huge parachute to play with and the ever popular bubbles.

£3.75 per session paid in half or full term blocks; £10 registration fee.
Bowdon, Chorlton, Didsbury, Sale and Swinton
Tel: 0161 432 3624
kiddiewinksonline.com

JAMusic
Tel: 07815 049187
jamusicservices.co.uk
Jittabugs Baby Move & Groove
Tel: 07765 080350 jittabugs.com

Jo Jingles Pre School Music and Movement Classes
Jo Jingles is a music and movement provider for babies and children aged between 3 months and 5 years. Jo Jingles is throughout Manchester, Cheshire and Lancashire. To join the fun at your local class and for full details of introductory offers visit their website.
jojingles.com

Kiddiewinks
Kiddiwinks – a one hour class for walking pre-school kids that does not stop from the moment you arrive until you sing the final song. Every five minutes a new activity begins so there is no time to stop and think, let alone get bored! Each week has a different theme that also incorporates the pre-school curriculum.
Classes are £5.25 per session payable per half or full term. This includes juice and biscuits at the end. There is a £10 registration fee and all children receive a free gift.
Chorlton, Cheadle, Timperley, Didsbury, Sale and Swinton
Tel: 0161 432 3624
kiddiewinksonline.com

Kidsrock
Tel: 07855 733308
kidsrockwithchris.com

Rhythm and Rhyme
This was the first class that I enrolled in with my baby and we loved it... it involves singing, instruments, banging of the big drum, playing with a large 'parachute,' dancing and, at the end, everyone's favourite – blowing bubbles! Our teacher was lovely and really enthusiastic. While everyone's having a good time there's lots of learning going on too. The classes help memory and language development, and motor and social skills. Rhythm and Rhyme was founded by Mel Horton in 2002 and continues to be a popular choice by parents. Five months to pre-school.
Manchester, Trafford, Stockport.
Tel: 0161 860 0911 or 07584 344315
rhythmandrhyme.co.uk

Rhythm and Rhyme

READING & STORYTELLING
Bents Garden & Home Storytime
Children's Storytime held every Tuesday 9.30-10.30am in The Fresh Approach Restaurant Area. Giving you a chance to enjoy a coffee and a mooch round the lovely garden centre afterwards.
Tel: 01942 266 300 bents.co.uk

Mother Hen Storytelling
Winner of NetMums' 2013 Children's Party Award.
Tel: 07587 191394
motherhencreative.com

SPORT
Aqua Babies
Aqua Babies have now been running structured, fun, safe, baby-swim courses for 15 years! From wetting baby's head in your first lesson to underwater swims and safety skills, Aqua Babies builds on both baby's

Aqua Babies

and parent's confidence as you progress through each level.
Classes in Altrincham, Bowden, Bramhall, Didsbury, Swinton, Manchester City Centre and Oldham, Cheshire and Chester.
Tel: 0161 973 1931 aquababies.co.uk

Elite Swim School
Elite Swim School run children's swim courses for all abilities from the age of three. The teachers are in the water, increasing the childrens' enjoyment and rate of learning. Prices are £5.25 per 30 minute lesson plus the first two lessons are free! Courses run in 10 week blocks.
Elite Swim School, Manchester High School for Girls. Tel: 07977 235856 eliteswimschool.co.uk

Enjoy-a-Ball
Enjoy-a-Ball South Manchester runs weekly classes for children aged 3-9 years and is taught in a caring and positive environment. It covers 10 different ball sports and helps build confidence, coordination and concentration. Enjoy-a-Ball also run holiday camps and fun-filled birthday parties.
One parent says: "My daughter goes to Enjoy-a-Ball and absolutely loves it. When she's there the hour flies by, as it's filled with many sport-related games and activities – I didn't know there were as many ways to play with balls, beanbags, hula hoops, as well as more exotic equipment. I'd recommend Enjoy-a-Ball to any parent!"

Enjoy-a-Ball

Enjoy-a-Ball has a sister programme called Physi-Ball for younger children, which starts from 18 months – this helps develops core stability, balance, hand-eye coordination and good foundation gross motor skills.
Classes in Chorlton and Didsbury
Tel: Sam 07973 886 783
enjoy-a-ball.com
southmanchester@enjoy-a-ball.com

Kyndergym
Tel: 0161 491 0415
southmanchestergymnastics.org

Little Kickers
'Sowing the Seeds for Grass Roots Football' is the Little Kickers motto. Little Kickers is a positive, fun-filled football programme executed in a friendly, pressure-free environment. The real goal of Little Kickers worldwide, is to use football as a fun forum to instil their growing squad with a little extra confidence, co-ordination, control and sense of camaraderie; which they feel will stand them in very good stead for the future. Guided by the likes of FA qualified coaches, nursery school teachers, child health specialists

and pro-active parents, the Little Kickers programme is an ever-evolving quest to teach fundamental football techniques & elementary life skills in a vibrant, group-play environment.
They run local weekend venues for children from 18 months to 7 years in West Didsbury, Burnage, Sale, Altrincham, Urmston, Bowdon, Lymm, Cheadle & Bramhall, Knutsford, Alderley Edge. Put your postcode into their website to find the nearest venue. Children can start at anytime providing there's a space.
Tel: 0161 442 5713 *littlekickers.co.uk*
Email: *aleete@littlekickers.co.uk*

Little Superstars
Little Superstars Sports Club runs active multi-sport sessions for children aged from two upwards; introducing each child to different sports such as basketball, volleyball, lacrosse, cricket, rugby, obstacle courses and so much more. Children are given the opportunity to develop their skills including numeracy and shape recognition. Little Superstars aim for each child to develop their hand, foot and eye coordination, balance, flexibility and endurance; whilst, most importantly having fun at the same time. Everyone comes away with a sticker at the end of each session. These sessions

Little Superstars

are run through community classes, children centres, play-centres. For children aged five and over they run Sports and Dance Holiday Clubs.
Classes in Cheshire, West and South Manchester
Tel: 07904 311552
littlesuperstars.co.uk

Manchester City Football Club Academy
Babyblues: A physical play programme for children aged 18 months to four years. Aimed at improving balance, co-ordination, movement and social skills.
Every Tues at Platt Fields £2 per child: 18 months-4 yrs 5-6pm.
Play the Game: Coaching sessions focused on developing ball technique, new skills, keeping healthy and social development.
Open to boys and girls of all abilities 5-14 years. Every Tues & Thurs at Platt Fields 5-6pm. £2 per player.
Tel: 0161 256 6652
citysoccerschools@mcfc.co.uk

Play Gym at CMIG
Tel: 0161 223 5705 *cmig.net*

Puddle Ducks
What's lovely to see when you go to a Puddle Ducks lesson, is a personal touch. The teachers are picked for their dedication and passion – they are highly trained and able to adapt every activity to suit each individual child. It's a baby-led swimming approach that ensures the child's needs are expertly fulfilled – never forcing development, but rather nurturing it to ensure a positive experience and love of swimming.

The lessons are friendly, fun and full of rhyme, music and movement. The small groups of babies progress through six different stages depending on their age, right up until they start school. They can then join Puddle Ducks Swim Academy to continue developing into graceful

Puddle Ducks

young swimmers. Another great benefit is that you can start at any point during the term.

Handforth, Warrington, Macclesfield, Northwich, Runcorn, Delamere Forest.
Tel: 01477 410080
Manchester, Stockport, Oldham.
Tel: 0161 883 0222
Crewe, Nantwich, Stoke on Trent & Knypersley near Congleton.
Tel: 07429 892774 or 07916 319525
Radcliffe, Swinton, Clitheroe, Rochdale, Bolton, Bury, Burnley & Blackburn
Tel: 01257 262622
puddleducks.com

Rugbytots
Tel: 0845 313 3242 *rugbytots.co.uk*

Rossendale Ski Club
The Ski Rossendale Kids Club on Saturday mornings is aimed at children of all ages and abilities from 3 years upwards. At Kids Club, get a taster of

Ski Rossendale

skiing, progress, learn new skills and perhaps get ready for. Ski Rossendale is a place where your children will experience the skiing in the outdoors in all kinds of weather, surrounded by the hills of Rossendale.

Kids Club meets every Saturday of the year; Ski sessions at 9.30am and 11.30am and Snowboarding at 9:15am and 11.15am. Each session is £8.80 and they can be booked in blocks of 6 or 10. Kindergarten 3yrs to 4yrs (learning through play) at 9.45am and 11.45am. Each session is £8 and they can be booked in blocks of 6 or 10.

Ski Rossendale, Haslingden Old Road, Rawtenstall, Lancashire BB4 8RR
Tel: 01706 226457 skirossendale.co.uk

Bents

WORKSHOPS & EVENTS
Bents Garden & Home
Bents believe that giving a child a healthy interest in the great outdoors can really improve their lifestyle, which is why they have a special programme of events and attractions aimed just at the young ones. Face painting, treasure hunts and Bents 'Inspiring Children To Do' workshops take place throughout all school holidays, along with seasonal events such as the Summer Family Fun and Festive Family Fun weekends which have become firm favourites in the

calendar The popular Tea Parties which take place over Halloween and Christmas holidays, are loved by children and their families. The Bents website includes details of all events taking place at the award-winning Centre, including dates and times.

Bents Garden & Home, Warrington Road, Glazebury, Warrington WA3 5NT
Tel: 01942 266 300 bents.co.uk

Experitots at MOSI
Experiment with a different topic each month. Fun, creative activities, puppets and storytelling help toddlers get the most out of this hands-on science gallery.
Once a month Fri 10-11.30am £3 for one adult and one child, booking essential
Tel: 0161 833 0027 mosi.org.uk

Woodwork with B&Q Kids Can Do It
Brilliant woodwork workshops for children aged 7-11 accompanied by a parent are held at larger branches of B&Q. Get to drill, hammer, screw and saw under supervision. At each workshop there is a different project, you make something from scratch and then take the finished piece home. My son made an apple feeder which looks brilliant in our garden. Book online.
Trafford Park, Stockport, Ashton-under-Lyne, Bolton, Warrington
diy.com/kidsclasses

B&Q

Soft Play Centres

Indoor play centres are a life-saver on a rainy day. There are some brilliant venues – just turn up and play!

BOLTON

Cheeky Monkey's Play & Party
Kem Mill Lane, Chorley PR6 7EA
Tel: 01257 234287
cheekymonkeysfun.co.uk

Clown Around
Grove Park, Eccleston PR7 5TZ
Tel: 01257 451600
clownaroundeccleston.co.uk

Curly Whirleez
Boundary Industrial Estate,
Millfield Road, Bolton BL2 6QY
Tel: 01204 523620
curlywhirleez.co.uk

Fidgets Play Centre
Dunscar Business Park, Blackburn
Road, Dunscar, Bolton BL7 9PQ
Tel: 01204 309998 fidgets.biz

Party and Play Funhouse
Party and Play Funhouse moved in summer 2013, adding lots of new facilities to its already extensive range of soft-play equipment. Housed in a large warehouse with a central seating area, you can see your child playing almost anywhere in the room.

There are all the usual climbing structures you'd expect to find plus a four-lane wavy-slide, a curly tree-slide and tunnels to crawl through. New play equipment includes four enclosed trampolines, Princess Tower, drop slide, large enclosed football court plus pay-to-go go-karts.

There's a large Toddler Area which has the bonus of Little Tikes Cars and an enclosed ball-pool and sports court. Facilities for babies include high-chairs, baby-bouncers, baby-walkers, baby-changing and food-warming facilities. There is also good access and facilities for disabled visitors.

The café serves a wide range of hot and cold drinks, snacks and meals all freshly cooked to order, as well as real dairy ice-cream, while the Party Shop stocks every-

Party and Play Funhouse

thing for kids' parties and loads of fancy-dress costumes.Party and Play also have a state-of-the-art Sensory Studio available for private-hire.
Mon-Thur, Sat & Sun: 9.30am-6pm;
Fri: 9.30am-7pm
Weekdays: under 6 months free, 6-12 months £1.50, 1-12 years £4.99
Weekends & Bank Holidays: under 6 months free, 6-12 months £1.50, 1-12 years £5.50
Party and Play Funhouse,
Unit 12 Barrs Fold Close, Wingates
Industrial Park, Westhoughton,
Bolton BL5 3XA Tel: 01942 818195
partyandplayfunhouse.co.uk

Playmates Children's Play Centre
Mill Lane, Coppull, Chorley PR7 5BW
Tel: 01257 470288
playmatesplaycentre.co.uk

BURY

Boomerang
Woodhill Street BL8 1AT
Tel: 0161 764 4842
boomerangcentre.co.uk

Funtastic
Kenyon Street, Radcliffe M26 1NF
Tel: 0161 425 8248 funtastic.org.uk

Go Wild
No 5 Crompton Street BL9 0AD
Tel: 0161 764 8268 gowildbury.co.uk

Jungle Mayhem
Next to Castlecroft Camping, Eton
Hill Road, Radcliffe M26 2XT
Tel: 0161 724 7402
junglemayhem.co.uk

MANCHESTER

Anchors Away Play
Simonsway, by Jn4 M56, M23 2XQ
Tel: 0161 437 0665
anchorsawayplay.com

Head over Heels Chorlton
This was one of the first soft play centres I went to, and it still remains a firm favourite. The Deli Restaurant is comfy and grown-up with leather benches. A windowed wall looks onto the main play area which, at three storeys high with a three-lane astro slide, keeps the children suitably busy. There is also an exclusively under-threes soft play section – well equipped with

Party and Play Funhouse

Head over Heels Chorlton

favourites like a ball pool with air fountain, slide, Perspex tunnel, soft play roundabout and animals, and play panels. A small climb up from this area is a sensory room with bubble tubes, lights, and illuminated ball pit. Worth a special mention is the disco room, with a fabulous Saturday Night Fever, 70's style dance floor. Get on down!

Daily 9.30am-6.30pm
Babes in arms free, 6-12 months £2.20,
1-2yrs £4.40, 3-11yrs £5.20,
Adults £1.20
Kwirky Club Mornings (Mon-Fri)
Under 3's £3.95
Two and a half hours play time, any
meal from the children's menu and a
carton of Aqua Juice all for £8.50 during
peak times, £7.99 off peak.
Parties start at £12.99 per child
Head over Heels, Unit 1a, Albany
Trading Estate, Albany Road,
Chorlton, Manchester M21 0AZ
Tel: 0161 881 4433
headoverheelsplay.co.uk

Little Rascals & Cheeky Monkeys
28-30 Partington Street, Failsworth
M35 9RD Tel: 0161 657 6205
littlerascals-cheekymonkeys.co.uk

OLDHAM
Cheeky Chimps
Acorn Street, Lees OL4 3PD
Tel: 0161 626 2552
cheekychimpsplaycentre.co.uk

Play! Oldham
Laurel Trading Estate OL2 6LH
Tel: 0161 627 3000 playoldham.com

ROCHDALE
Mischief Makers
No. 1 The Pavilions OL11 5BX
Tel: 01706 653656
mischiefmakersltd.co.uk
Planet Play
2 Bradshaw St OL10 1PJ
Tel: 01706 627627 planetplay.net
Snakes and Slides
Rule Business Park, Grimshaw
Lane, Middleton M24 2AE
Tel: 0161 653 1221
snakesandslides.co.uk

SALFORD
The Funhouse
Little Moss Lane, Swinton M27 6HA
Tel: 0161 727 8222 the-funhouse.co.uk

STOCKPORT
Anchors Away Play
Houldsworth Mill, Houldsworth
Street, Reddish SK5 6DA
Tel: 0161 432 4020
anchorsaway.org.uk

Head over Heels Wilmslow North Arena
This stylish indoor play venue is exciting for all ages. The climbing frame is vast and the toddler area is both large and beautifully-designed with a soft play section, ball pit and book corner; and a fantastic home-play area with cooker, prams, dolls, highchairs and shop. There are lots of lovely wooden wheelie bugs too which my two year old adored. As well as all this, Head over Heels boasts a bungee trampoline, electric car track, disco room, sensory room and mini-cinema. There are state of the art party booths with iPod docks and an adult party zone for those attending kids' parties. There is a large café and seating area for adults too.

Open daily 9.30am-6.30pm
Babes in arms free, 6-12 months £2.75,
1-2yrs £5.20, 3-11yrs £6.20,
Adults £1.20
Kwirky Klub Morning(Mon-Fri) Babes
in arms free, 6-12 months £2.50, 1yrs
and over £4.50, Adults £1
Two and a half hours play time, any
meal from the children's menu and a
carton of Aqua Juice all for £9.99 during
peak times, £8.20 off peak.

Head over Heels Wilmslow North Arena

Parties start at £12.99 per child
Head over Heels, Unit D1,
Commercial Avenue, Stanley Green,
Cheadle SK8 6QH
Tel: 0161 485 2200
headoverheelsplay.co.uk

Jump Space

For children with special needs this is a great place to check out. They offer a sensory room, a hoist if required in the play area, rebound therapy as well as lots of fun. Trampolining and toddle fit also available. Worth calling ahead to see if your child's needs are met and to book.
Chestergate, Stockport SK3 0BJ
Tel: 0161 637 2800 jumpspace.org.uk

Rough 'n' Tumble

Goyt Mill, Marple SK6 7HX
Tel: 0161 427 0007
roughntumble.co.uk

Run of the Mill

Pear Mill Industrial Estate,
Bredbury SK6 2BP
Tel: 0161 494 7137
runofthemill.co.uk

Wild Things

Headlands Road SK7 3AN
Tel: 0161 440 9040
wildthingssoftplay.co.uk

Zoom Play Centre

Run by Didsbury mums Antonia and Patricia, Zoom is just minutes off the M60. It serves yummy cakes and very good coffee, plus a range of snacks and meals for children and adults.

There's a dedicated toddler area with manageable climbing frame, ball pit and Little Tikes cars to ride in. There's also a large playroom off the café area which has been filled with toys and dressing-up clothes that is another great diversion.

Zoom holds daily 11 am toddler sessions during term time, with a sing-along followed by a craft/games session. These are held at no extra charge.

For the older children there is a large play frame with a huge ball pool and football area. There is also a vertical drop slide for the daring ones!

Party prices start at a very reasonable £6.95 per child and the centre is available for private hire seven days a week between 5-7pm.
Daily 9.45am-6pm
Under 7mths free, 7-11mths £1, 1-3 years on Mon-Fri 9.45-3pm in Term Time £2.99, all other times 1-3years £3.75, 4's and over £4.20
Zoom, Mentor House, Stockport,
Cheshire SK3 0DY
Tel: 0161 477 2225
zoomplaycentre.co.uk

TAMESIDE

Bizzy Bouncers

Berkeley Business Park,
Ashton-under-Lyne OL6 8LB
Tel: 0161 339 6284
bizzybouncers.com

The Fun Depot

Albion Trading Estate, Mossley Road, Ashton-under-Lyne OL6 6NQ
Tel: 0161 343 5507 thefundepot.co.uk

Slide & Seek

SK14 Industrial Park, Broadway, Hyde SK14 4QF
Tel: 0161 366 8080
slideandseek.co.uk

TRAFFORD

Antz in Your Pantz

Crown Ind Est, Canal Road, Timperley WA14 1TF
Tel: 0161 962 2266
antzinyourpantz.co.uk

Land of Play

Astra Business Park, Trafford Park M17 1SU
Tel: 0161 872 9434 landofplay.co.uk

Play Factore

Play Factore, Trafford Quays Leisure Village, Trafford Park M41 7JA
Tel: 0844 824 6030 playfactore.com

WIGAN

Gioco Play and Party Centre

Unit 1 Lockflight Buildings, Wheatlea Industrial Estate, Wheatlea Road, Wigan WN3 6XP
Tel: 01942 248222
giocoplaycentre@gmail.com

MACCLESFIELD

fun4all

Queens Avenue, Hurdsfield Industrial Estate, Macclesfield, Cheshire SK10 2DG
Tel: 01625 440044 fun4all.co.uk

Pirate's Paradise

Holmes Chapel Business Park, Holmes Chapel CW4 8AF
Tel: 01477 549008
piratesplaycentre.co.uk

WARRINGTON

Fun2B

Portland Place WA2 7NS
Tel: 01925 659888 fun2b.co.uk

Giddy Kidz

Priestly Street, Warrington WA5 1TF
Tel: 01925 232 600 giddykidz.co.uk

Zoom Play Centre

The Jungle

The Jungle, Warrington & Skelmersdale

The Jungle's award winning play centres are exceptionally clean and safe and both are highly recommended by local parents as two of the best in the North West. Multi-level themed play areas are packed with opportunities for adventure and highlights include numerous slides, ball pool, aerial runway, bouncing boulders and enclosed trampolines as well as separate areas for under threes with mini-roundabouts, ball juggler and slide.

The Jungle Express Café offers comfortable seating on two levels and serves great cappuccinos as well as a full range of snacks, light meals, pizzas and ice cream.

Additional activities are always available courtesy of The Jungle's dedicated Activity Co-ordinators. Jungle Tots toddler sessions which are held from 10am-3pm Mon-Fri during term time include arts and crafts, music, story time and funky fitness and a complimentary tea or coffee biscuit and juice. Bumps and Baby mornings are held every Thursday from 10.30am when entry is free for pregnant and new mums and includes a complimentary tea or coffee. Twins/multiples get a special deal every Monday and Thursday, when entry is just £5.50! Every Friday from 4-6pm is Disco Night, when the lights are turned down and the music is

turned up. Check out the website for themed holiday fun too!

Members of the Jungle Explorer Club can enjoy lots of benefits including discounted entry, free play after 3.30pm every Wednesday, discounts on parties and meal deals. It's free to become a member of the Jungle Explorer Club online so why not join up before your first visit!

Open daily 10am-6pm
Members Entry Prices: Toddler Time Mon-Fri (term time 10am-3.30pm) £4 for your 1st child/£3.50 for additional children. Includes free tea/coffee, juice and biscuit. Under 1s free at all times. Peak times entry is £4.50. Non-members £1 extra at all times.
The Jungle, 12 Chetham Court, Calver Road, Winwick Quay, Warrington WA2 8RF
48 Westgate, Skelmersdale WN8 8AZ
Tel: 0844 324 9995 thejungle.uk.net

Play Central
The Bridge Shopping Centre, Knutsford Road, Latchford WA4 1JR
Tel: 01925 638313 playcentral.co.uk
Prendoolys
25 Queen Street, Earlestown, Newton-le-Willows WA12 9AH
Tel: 01925 299599 prendoolys.co.uk

ROSSENDALE
Runamok Play & Party Centre
10 Commerce Street, Haslingden, Rossendale BB4 5JT
Tel: 01706 213213
widebeech.co.uk/runamok

Cinema
"Nobody puts Baby in the corner!" **Dirty Dancing**

Baby Screenings
If you fancy a trip out to see a film, we've found a cinema chain that offers parent and baby screenings: Newbies at the Odeon, currently running once a week. There is no choice of film, but it is usually one of the most recent releases. Legally it has to be a 12A rating or below, as children are in the audience. You pay only for the adult, at normal cinema entrance price.
Odeon at The Trafford Centre and Rochdale
Tel: 0871 22 44 007
odeon.co.uk

Kids Cinema
Every weekend (and sometimes during the school holidays) most cinemas host cheap screenings for children – ideal if you haven't been to the cinema with them before and aren't sure if they're going to like it. They are not always the latest releases, but the majority of under-fives don't seem to care what they're watching. This is a great rainy-day activity and, if you don't get too caught up in buying popcorn and drinks, it doesn't cost the earth.
Kids AM Weekends at Vue Cinemas £2 per person.
Tel: 08712 240 240 myvue.com
Movies for Juniors Sat and/or Sun morning at Cineworld, £1 per person
Tel: 0871 200 2000 cineworld.co.uk
Kids Club Weekends and school holiday mornings at the Odeon, £2.50 per child, Free Adult per child.
Tel: 0871 22 44 007
odeon.co.uk

Paint-a-pot and cafés with studios are a great place to visit with kids.

Craft Cafés

If the weather's off or you fancy letting your child's artistic temperament bloom, then check out these crafty cafés!

Bean & Brush Art Café
Mon-Fri 8am-7pm, Sat 8.30am-7pm, Sun 9am-6pm
The Old Sorting Office, 12 Hayfield Street, Sale M33 7XW
Tel: 0161 973 2140
beanandbrush.co.uk

Brooklyn Ceramics
Weds-Sat, 10am-5pm, Sun 11am-4pm
104 Shaw Heath, Stockport, Cheshire SK2 6QS
Tel: 0161 480 5139
brooklynpottery.co.uk

Brookside Pottery
Next to miniature railway – see page 24. Weekends 11am-4pm (can open any day so please call).
Brookside Garden Centre, Macclesfield Road, Poynton, Cheshire SK12 1BY
Tel: Liz 07946 637 499
brooksidepottery.com

Cheshire Candle Workshops
Daily 10am-4.30pm
Cheshire Workshops, Barracks Lane, Higher Burwardsley, Tattenhall, Cheshire CH3 9PF
Tel: 01829 770401
cheshireworkshops.co.uk

Craftelicious
Tues Group and Party Bookings only, Weds-Sat 10am-5pm (Thurs 7pm), Sun 12noon-4pm
127 Oswald Road, Chorlton, Manchester M21 9GE
Tel: 0161 860 4814
crafteliciousuk.com

Create It Cheadle
Mon-Sat 10am-5pm
37 Wilmslow Rd, Cheadle SK8 1DR
Tel: 0161 222 3445
createitcheadle.co.uk

The Ladybird Lounge
Tues-Sat 10am-5pm, Sun 10.30am-4.30pm
The Farmers Market & Craft Centre Heskin Hall, Wood Lane, Heskin, Nr Chorley, Lancs PR7 5PA
Tel: 07511 517 631
theladybirdlounge.co.uk

Minikin Emporium
Mon-Sat 10am-5.30pm
11 Northenden Road, Sale M33 2DH
Tel: 0161 973 6822
minikindesigns.com

Pik a Pot n Paint
Tue-Sun 10.30am-3pm
351 Wellington Road North, Heaton Chapel, Stockport SK4 4QG
Tel: 0161 222 7679
pikapotnpaint.co.uk

Pottery Corner
Tues-Sat 10am-6pm (8pm Thurs), Sun 11am-5pm.
34 Beech Road, Chorlton, Manchester M21 9EL
Tel: 0161 882 0010
potsareforpainting.co.uk

The Potty Sheep
Fri-Sun 12-5pm
Blaze Farm, Wildboarclough, Macclesfield, Cheshire SK11 0BL
Tel: 01260 227229 pottysheep.co.uk

The Star Tree Studio
Closed Tues and Sun.
42 Victoria Street, Littleborough, OL15 9DB
Tel: 07778 543233
thestartreestudio.com

Tiny Tots and Teapots
Tues-Sat 10am-5pm
318 Palatine Road, Northenden, Manchester
Tel: 0161 945 1080

Garden Centres

Gardening is lots of fun with little ones, so combine it with a visit to an extra special garden centre.

Altrincham Garden Centre

What sets this garden centre apart is the indoor softplay climbing frame, set right in the middle of the café. It is an enclosed glass box were kids can safely play, and be seen. Meanwhile you can finish your lunch in peace, or catch up with friends over a coffee. With children's picnic boxes, pasta or fish and chips, this is a garden centre that clearly wants the family market.

Mon-Sat 9am-5pm, Sun 10.30am-4.30pm

Altrincham Garden Centre, Green Lane, Timperley, Altrincham, Cheshire WA15 8QP
Tel: 0161 980 6036 thegardencentregroup.co.uk

Bents is a fabulous destination garden centre.

Ashton Park Garden Centre

With a children's play area and a locally renowned restaurant serving homebakes, it's worth a trip and can be combined with a visit to nearby IKEA.

Mon- Sat 9am-6pm, Sun 10.30am-4.30pm
Ashton Park Garden Centre, Lord Sheldon Way, Ashton-under-Lyne, Manchester OL6 7UB

Bents Garden and Home

This family-run, award-winning garden centre began life in the front garden of a terraced house on the very same road in the 1930's. Two generations on and it is still expanding. It has become the Harrods of garden centres. If visiting with children there's plenty to keep them amused; story times, fish, flowers, fountains, little wooden garden houses and a toy shop, and more importantly a brilliant outdoor and well-fenced play area. Overlooked by the restaurant's terrace it's perfect for a summer's day. If you fancy a stroll there is a three mile walk in the woods suitable for prams, and also Wild Wings, birds of prey are now at the Centre, Tues-Sun, making this a must destination with little ones.

Mon-Sat 8.30am-5.30pm, Sun 8.30am-5pm
Bents Garden and Home, Warrington Road, Glazebury, Cheshire WA3 5NT
Tel: 01942 266300 bents.co.uk

Marple Garden Centre

Part of the same chain as Altrincham Garden Centre above, you'll also find a colourful soft play area and a family friendly restaurant. Look out for the Farmer's Market on the fourth Sunday of the month.

Mon-Sat 9am-5pm, Sun 10.30am-4.30pm
Marple Garden Centre, Dooley Lane, Otterspool, Stockport, Cheshire SK6 7HE

Ned Yates Garden Centre

A lovely garden centre in Wilmslow that wants its little visitors to have a good time. Outside you will find a great enclosed wooden play area with swings and a slide, right next to outdoor seating. Inside they have a small room with toys for under-fives, and a colouring table.

Winter: Mon-Fri 9am-4.30pm, Sat & Sun 9.30am-4.30pm, Summer Daily 9am-5.30pm
Ned Yates Garden Centre, Moor Lane, Wilmslow, Cheshire SK9 6DN
Tel: 01625 522128 nedyates.com

Summerseat Garden Centre

Set in a pretty hollow in picturesque Summerseat, this well-stocked garden centre is a great spot for lunch and a bit of shopping. There is no play area but, as it is pleasant for a stroll here, just over the river on Waterside Road you'll find a large playing field, together with swings and slides.

Mon-Sat 9am-6pm (5pm Jan & Feb) Sun 9am-5pm
Café: Mon-Sat 9.30am-4.30pm, Sun 9.30am-4pm
Summerseat Garden Centre, Railway Street, Summerseat, Bury BL9 5QD
Tel: 01204 883048 summerseatgardencentre.co.uk

Retail Therapy

Some of our favourite independent places to shop for children's gifts, books and clothes.

ALTRINCHAM & HALE

Baby Bumkins
16 The Downs, Altrincham WA14 2PU
babybumkins.co.uk

Pixie Childrenswear
A gorgeous designer childrens-wear boutique which also sells toys & gifts from White Rabbit night lights, to traditional wooden toys and crafts. There are Burts Bees products for mum and baby too.
Century House, Ashley Road, Hale WA15 9SF Tel: 0161 927 9259
pixiechildrenswear.com

Village Toy Company
74 Stamford New Road, Altrincham WA14 1BS Tel: 0161 941 4123
villagetoycompany.co.uk

BOLTON & BURY

Bear Feet
Stocking a wonderful range of children's shoes, you'll get a personal and professional service.
484a Bury Old Road, Prestwich, Manchester M25 1NL
Tel: 0161 772 0600 bearfeet.co.uk

Bossy Boots
Designer clothes for kids.
364 Chorley Old Road, Bolton BL1 6AG
Tel: 01204 494974 bossybootskidz.com

Jeanne Toys
Alan and Jean have been trading here for 32 years, selling beautiful wooden toys and brands. They specialise in personalised gifts such as wooden stools and hand-painted names in watercolour by Jean.

Cedar Farm in Mawdesley is well worth the drive out. It's gorgeous!

A personal service from a lovely little shop in a parade where it's easy to park.
544 Chorley Old Road, Heaton, Bolton BL1 6AB Tel: 01204 495583

Little Wanderers
A family run children's shoe shop specialising in continental shoes.
144-146 Tonge Moor Road, Bolton, BL2 2DP Tel: 01204 522 533
littlewanderers.co.uk

Spruced Goose
A gorgeous boutique selling funky kids clothes.
1 Moss Lane, Whitefield M45 6QE, Tel: 0161 796 8096 spruced goose.com

Whittakers the Shoemakers
Whittakers has been selling shoes to families in Bolton for generations. Stocking the largest collection of shoes in the north west, experienced and knowledgeable staff provide an expert fitting service. The children's department downstairs is nice and big and also has lots of toys for the children to play with. Well worth a special trip.
108-110 Deansgate, Bolton BL1 1BD
Tel: 01204 533931

CHESHIRE

Blakemere Village
A whole host of family activities and shopping are on offer here. For Mum and Dad there's Cheshire Segway, antiques, and artisan shops. For the kids the list is endless; Cheshire Falconry centre, a miniature railway, bank holiday circus workshops, a children's outdoor adventure play park for ages two to ten years, Barnaby's Play Barn, Wzu toyshop, and Cheshire Craft Workshop where you can make a candle or paint or create a pot on the potters wheel!
Blakemere Village, Chester Road, Sandiway, Northwich CW8 2EB
Tel: 01606 883261
blakemerevillage.com

Curiosity Bookshop
52 High Street, Runcorn WA7 1AW
Tel: 01928 575956
curiositybookshop.co.uk

Forget-Me-Not, Culcheth

Owners Naomi and Victoria are mums themselves and they have created a place for families to visit and relax in. It is a well stocked toy and bookshop with a café. They host regular family events such as story telling and dance performances.
The Old Telephone Exchange, Common Lane, Culcheth, Warrington WA3 4HA
Tel: 01925 765187
toysandbooks.co.uk

Nantwich Bookshop

46 High Street, Nantwich CW5 5AS
Tel: 01270 611665
nantwichbookshop.co.uk

Nino Kids

Sells lovely designer kids clothes.
35 Millfield Lane, Tarporley CW6 OBA
Tel: 01829 733 317 ninokids.co.uk

Giddy Goats in Didsbury has a huge selection of toys for all ages.

CHORLTON & DIDSBURY

Belly Button

In a great parade of independent shops and cafes, this is a one-stop shop for beautiful personalised cards and a huge selection of unique gifts for all ages. Rachel sells fabulous gift brands including Orla Kiely, Jellycat, Caroline Gardner, Art Slice by Terramundi, Nature's Purest and Really Good.
240 Burton Road, West Didsbury M20 2LW Tel: 0161 434 4236
155 Heaton Moor Road, Stockport SK4 4HY Tel: 0161 442 2022
bellybuttondesigns.com

Chorlton Bookshop

A little stool in the children's section encourages kids to sit and leaf through the colourful books.
506 Wilbraham Road, Chorlton M21 9AW Tel: 0161 881 6374
chorltonbookshop.co.uk

EJ Morten (Booksellers)

6 Warburton Street, Didsbury M20 6WA Tel: 0161 445 7629

Giddy Goat Toys

A pleasure to shop in – Amanda is always ready to help steer you in the direction of the perfect present. Giddy Goat Toys stocks a really brilliant range of toys for babies and up to 15 years. The shop is laid out into small departments: something for baby; beads and crafts; science kits; books; Lego and Playmobil. With lots of leading brands you won't struggle to find what you are looking for.
2 Albert Hill Street, Didsbury M20 6RF Tel: 0161 445 1097
giddygoattoys.co.uk

Go Great Toys

12 Lane End Road, Burnage M19 1TU Tel: 0161 637 2257 gogreattoys.co.uk

Milly Mog

Quality funky clothing and footwear for 0-10 year olds.
238 Burton Road, West Didsbury M20 2LW
Tel: 0161 438 0300 millymog.com

No.68

Great for new baby gifts and unusual toys, this Aladdin's cave is full of delights. Jo and the girls sell lovely little shoes, bookends and clothes, as well as loads of treats for Mums and Dads!
Beech Road, Chorlton M21 9EG Tel: 0161 860 6847

KNUTSFORD

Beau Bebe

4 Minshull St, Knutsford WA16 6HG Tel: 01565 220027
mybeaubebe.com

Hal Whittaker's Toyshop

5 Princess Street, Knutsford WA16 6DA Tel: 01565 632003
toyshopscheshire.co.uk

JoJo Maman Bebe

Maternity clothes, baby clothes and nursery products.
Royal George Centre, 15 Regent Street, Knutsford WA16 6GR
Tel: 01565 621821
jojomamanbebe.co.uk

LANCASHIRE

Carousel (Childrenswear)

98-100 Gisburn Road, Barrowford Lancashire Tel: 01282 692352
carouselchildrenswear.wordpress.com

Cedar Farm

We couldn't resist telling you about this great place in Ormskirk, Lancashire. Its not only got great artisan shops, art studios, gallery, cafe, design centre and a 'Pig Barn' hosting craft courses and beauty treatments but also a whole host of farm animals for little ones to coo over.

A new addition here is the playground complete with wooden tractors and wicker teepees where children can play to their hearts content. There are art courses on offer for children, and for parents there is a Farmers Market on the first Saturday of the month and a vintage fair on the second Sunday. A perfect opportunity to combine retail therapy with a fun outing for the kids.
Admission and parking free.
Cedar Farm, Back Lane, Mawdsley, Lancashire L40 3SY
TEL: 01704822038

Colne Bookshop
4 Market Street, Colne BB8 0HR
Tel: 01282 871 440
bookshopcolne.co.uk

Cowgills Toys and Gifts
4-6 Market Place, Clitheroe BB7 2DA
Tel: 01200 423587
cowgillsofclitheroe.co.uk

Little Feet
1 Nora Street, Barrowford BB7 8NS
Tel: 01282 698111
littlefeetbarrowford.co.uk

Pam's Bookend
67 Queen Street, Great Harwood, BB6 7QP Tel: 01254 882477
pamsbookend.com

Tots to Teens
A selection of children's clothing, gifts, toys and accessories.
31 Castle Street, Clitheroe BB7 2BT
Tel: 01200 423677
totstoteensclitheroe.co.uk

MANCHESTER

Oklahoma
A colourful gift shop full of unusual nik-naks. Primarily aimed at adults, there's lots for little ones including wind-up donkeys, kitsch lunch boxes, Whoopee cushions and Fisher Price retro toys.
74-76 High Street, Manchester M4 1ES
Tel: 0161 834 1136
oklahomacafe.co.uk

Simply Books is a brilliant, well-stocked book shop.

Waterstones
Fabulously child-friendly!
91 Deansgate, Manchester M3 2BW
Tel: 0161 837 3000 waterstones.com
Also at Manchester Arndale, Altrincham, Bolton, Bury, Knutsford, Oldham, Stockport, The Trafford Centre, Wigan and Wilmslow.

OLDHAM & ROCHDALE

Kids Stuff
Established for over 30 years their extensive showroom is full of essential baby products.
Duke Street Mill, Rochdale OL12 0LW Tel: 01706 645 267
kidsstuffrochdale.co.uk

Pitter Patter
Prides itself on selling high quality children's footwear.
1 St Thomas Parade, Lees, Oldham OL4 6DA Tel: 0161 627 1506
pitterpattershoes.co.uk

Puddleducks
Established in 1994 they offer baby and childrenswear, accessories, gifts and toys as well as beautiful christening outfits.
125 High Street, Uppermill, Oldham, OL3 6BD Tel: 01457 875 769
puddleduckskids.co.uk

STOCKPORT

Button Nose
Pop in for their wide choice of lovely childrenswear.

10 Bramhall Centre, Stockport SK7 1AW Tel: 0161 440 7667
buttonnose.co.uk

Simply Books
A well stocked bookshop for all ages, plus a super little café.
228 Moss Lane, Bramhall SK7 1BD
Tel: 0161 439 1436 simplybooks.info

Toys & Tales
A large shop stocking toys from birth and brands such as Playmobil, Sylvanian Families, Galt and Wow. Plus a great collection of books and jigsaws. There's a toy table for the children to play at.
74 Park Lane, Poynton SK12 1RE
Tel: 01625 873445 toysandtales.com

The Bookshop
70 Stockport Road, Marple SK6 6AB
Tel: 0161 427 4921

TAMESIDE

Thackeray's Books
Denton Civic Square, Denton M34 2XW Tel: 0161 320 4220
thackeraysbooks.co.uk

TRAFFORD

Urmston Bookshop
A friendly bookshop selling coffees and cakes too.
72 Flixton Road, Urmston M41 5AB
Tel: 0161 747 7442
urmston-bookshop.co.uk

Getting around Greater Manchester

If you're daunted by the idea of taking young children on buses, trains or trams then the following provided by Transport for Greater Manchester should help.

On weekdays we recommend that you start your journey after 9.30am – when it's off-peak, services are less busy and there is more space to carry a pushchair. Train and Metrolink tram tickets cost less at off-peak times which also include all day Saturday, Sunday and public holidays. Children under five travel free.

Buses

Modern buses are child-friendly with wide doors and space to store your buggy. If the bus is busy you might need to fold your buggy. On newer buses, the driver can lower the bus to pavement level to let you get on and off easily. Accessible buses are shown in bus timetables with a wheelchair symbol.

When you arrive in Manchester city centre there are two main bus stations – at Piccadilly Gardens and Shudehill Interchange.

Trains

Local trains are a great way to travel with many well-located stations in Manchester and other town centres. Trains are spacious, comfortable and most have toilets and plenty of luggage space.

There are five train stations in the centre of Manchester. Piccadilly and Victoria are the main stations and Oxford Road, Deansgate and Salford Central are served by many local routes. All main stations have baby-changing facilities.

Stations vary in their design and many have ramps for your buggy. Some still have steps plus there is usually a step up onto the train. If you don't live near a station, and have to drive, many have free parking.

When you buy a rail ticket to Manchester centre from a Greater Manchester rail station you can use it to travel free on Metrolink trams in Manchester city centre.

At off-peak times you can buy a Rail Ranger ticket that lets you travel anywhere in Greater Manchester.

Tip – if you already have a rail season ticket between two Greater Manchester rail stations you can use it to travel anywhere in Greater Manchester at weekends and public holidays!

National Rail Enquiries 08457 48 49 50 nationalrail.co.uk

Metrolink trams

Greater Manchester's Metrolink trams provide links between many towns in Greater Manchester and new lines are being added all the time. Metrolink was specially designed with easy access so there is no gap between the platform edge and the tram itself and all stops have either a ramp, lift or escalator access. Every tram has an area specifically designed for wheelchairs and prams. The sign

Ollie on the tram into Manchester.

on the platform (disabled access) will tell you where to wait to board at the correct doors. Trams run frequently, so there isn't a timetable – simply turn up and wait for the next one to arrive.

Metrolink Day Travelcards let you make as many tram journeys as you like for a whole day and are available at any time. Buy your ticket from the ticket machine at the Metrolink stop before you make your journey.

Metrolink Customer Services
Tel: 0161 205 2000 metrolink.co.uk

Getting around Manchester city centre

Metroshuttle is the name of the free bus services running around Manchester's city centre streets. There are three circular routes, covering all of the main city centre areas. Metroshuttle buses are low-floor, easy access with a frequency of about five to ten minutes. Metroshuttle links Piccadilly, Victoria, Oxford Road and Deansgate rail stations and many bus and Metrolink tram stops. So whatever the reason for your visit, you can use Metroshuttle to get around, hopping on and off as often as you wish.

Combined bus, train and tram journeys

DaySaver tickets let you make as many journeys as you wish at off-peak times using a combination of buses, trains and trams. The DaySaver ticket range lets you choose which combination of travel you want. Buy a DaySaver from the bus driver, station ticket office (or conductor on the train if closed) or tram stop ticket machine before you make your first trip.

Finding out more from TfGM

For all the information you need, complete with a journey planner, maps of the area and timetables for individual services to download, go to tfgm.com or get advice by calling Traveline 0871 200 22 33.

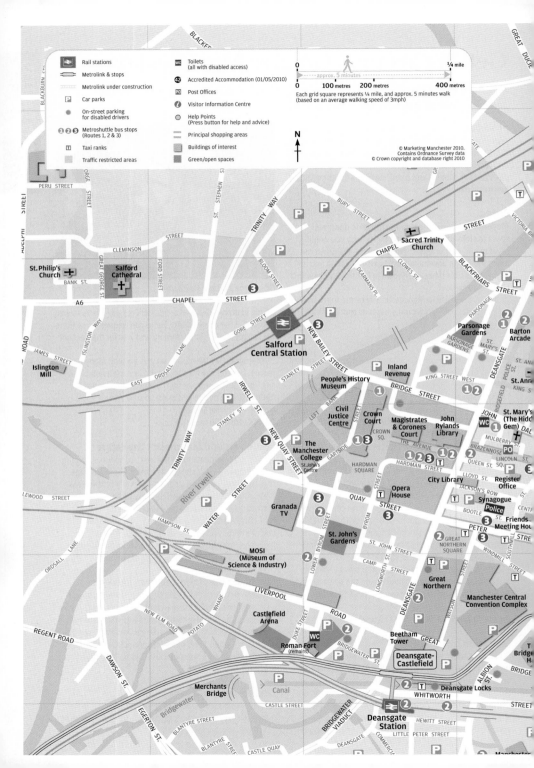

Index

*Front Cover Photos
(top left to right)*
1. *Dunham Massey*
2. *Bramhall Park*
3. *Jodrell Bank*
4. *Eureka!*
5. *Eureka!*
6. *CBBC Tour*
7. *Madame Tussauds*
8. *Airkix*
9. *Martin Mere Wetlands*

*Back Cover Photos
(top to bottom)*
1. *Apple Jacks*
2. *National Media
Museum*
3. *Ordsall Hall*
4. *Head over Heels*
5. *Stonerig Raceway*